Tobruk

Three British soldiers and a wounded officer

FORTUNES OF WAR

Tobruk

ANTHONY HECKSTALL-SMITH, DFC

CERBERUS

First published in the UK, by Anthony Blond Ltd, in 1959.

PUBLISHED IN THE UNITED KINGDOM BY;
Cerberus Publishing Limited
22A Osprey Court
Hawkfield Business Park
Bristol
BS14 0BB
UK
e-mail: cerberusbooks@aol.com
www..cerberus-publishing.com

© Anthony Heckstall-Smith, 2004

British Library Cataloguing in Publication Data.
A catalogue record for this book is available from the British Library.

ISBN 1 84145 051 0

PRINTED AND BOUND IN ENGLAND.

Contents

Dedication

To the everlasting memory of Sub-Lieutenant Leonard ('Nobby') dark, DSC, DSM, RNVR, and all those others and men who were killed on the 'Spud Run', I dedicate this story.

Author's Note

I wish to thank all those who helped me in the writing ofthit story. At the Admiralty, the Librarian, Lt-Commander Kemp, RN, Commander G A Titterton, RN, and Miss Buszard, m the Historical Section, and Mr Holly in the Records Department. In the Historical Section of the Cabinet Office, Brigadier H B Latham, CBE, DSO, MC, who put me in touch with many indispensable sources of military information.

For the true facts of the battle between the 'A' lighters and the U-boats, I am indebted to my old friend and wartime companion, Lieutenant Dennis Peters, DSC, RNVR, who dug deep into his memory and amongst his papers to help me. Also to Petty Officer W A Henley, DSM, PM, the only man left alive who knew what happened on that fatal night in October, 1941, who lent me his diary with permission to quote from it.

To both Lt Commander W R Harris, DSC, and Lieutenant Charles A Curtis of the South African Navy, I owed great thanks for sending me detailed accounts of their experiences during the last hours of the fortress. Private X, whose wish to remain anonymous I have respected with regret, is another South African to whom I am most grateful.

Amongst the hundreds of 'tobruk Rats' who have so kindly written to me from Australia, since I cannot name them all personally, I would like to thank Chaplain J C Salter, Lt-Colonel A B Millard, George Millhouse,

Waiter E Cass, Douglass Stuart, T W Pulsford, R G Appleton, and C R A Moore. The cooperation I received from these and many other Diggers enabled me to fill in many of the gaps in my story. I believe that I have replied to all their letters, but in case I may have failed to do so, I offer them here my deepest thanks.

Anthony Heckstall Smith London, SW1

CHAPTER ONE

PRELUDE

On June 2nd, 1940, the aged Marshal Pétain, as head of the French Government, signed the armistice with Germany.

General Archibald Wavell, General Officer Commanding-in-Chief Middle East, received the news of the French capitulation in a telegram handed to him on the sixteenth tee of the Gezirah Club golf course in Cairo. He read it with calm and said quietly; 'Well, I don't think I can do anything about it,' and then proceeded to do the last two holes in bogey.

The morning after the same momentous news had reached Admiral Andrew Cunningham, Commander-in-Chief, Mediterranean, Vice-Admiral Tovey came aboard the flagship Warspite in Alexandria harbour and greeted his senior officer with: 'Now I know we shall win the war, sir. We have no more allies.'

A young RAF fighter-pilot on hearing the news in the mess at Maaten Bagush, remarked: 'At least, that puts us in the bloody final.'

Italy's entry into the war and the collapse of France, following so swiftly one upon the other, changed the entire strategic picture in the Mediterranean by swinging the balance of power heavily in the enemy's favour. A few weeks later, when the fate of the French Fleet had been decided by the tragic actions at Oran and Dakar and the fortuitously peaceful demilitarisation of Vice-Admiral Godfrey's squadron at Alexandria, it appeared that the Mediterranean was in truth the Duce's *mare nostrum*. Indeed, Their Lordships viewed the situation with such growing concern that they contemplated evacuating the Eastern Mediterranean Fleet.

Shortly before the final surrender of France, the First Sea Lord, Admiral Sir Dudley Pound, actually signalled to the Commander-in-chief a tentative proposal that part of the Mediterranean Fleet should sail for Gibraltar while the remainder made its way there by way of the Cape. Mercifully, such a course was never adopted, since it was staunchly opposed by Admiral Cunningham and Churchill, then First Lord. But that it should ever have been considered proves with what gravity the Admiralty viewed our plight during those dark, months in the summer of 1940.

Neither on land nor in the air was our situation less perilous. With the Mediterranean virtually closed to our merchant ships. all the men and the paraphernalia of war so desperately needed by the Army of the Nile and the RAF had now to be transpotted by the long sea route round the Cape of Good Hope. The few fighters that could be spared from the defence of Britain also reached the Middle East after the same tortuous voyage, until the Air Ministry devised a plan whereby aircraft were shipped to Takoradi and then flown 4,000 miles across Africa, via Khartoum, to Egypt.

Numerically the enemy's forces arrayed against us in the Middle East were vastly superior. The Duce's Fleet consisted of 6 battleships, including the *Vittorio, Veneto* and *Littorio* of 3,000 tons mounting nine 15-inch guns, which were nearing completion; nineteen modern cruisers, seven of which mounted 8-inch guns and were capable of 32-35 knots; sixty-one fleet destroyers; sixty-nine escort and local defence destroyers; 115 submarines, and a considerable force of minelayers, escort vessels, and MTBs.

Opposing this formidable force was Admiral Cunningham's Eastern Mediterranean Fleet, comprising four old battleships, nine cruisers, twenty-five destroyers, twelve submarines, and a single aircraft-carrier. At Gibraltar, under Admiral Somerville's command, were three battleships, one cruiser, four destroyers, and one carrier.

'The morale of the men in our Mediterranean Fleet was wonderful,' Cunningham wrote of that time. '…We, who knew and were responsible, were troubled by much. Our ships were old, and we were short of aircraft, destroyers, and minesweepers.

We were anxious about Malta and the matter of its supply. Alexandria, also poorly defended, was a bad substitute (for Malta) as a fleet base. The questions of refits and repairs, the supplies of essential stores and ammunition, all added to our burden. There was much that had to be improvised.'

General Wavell's problems were equally grave. When Italy entered the war, Mussolini's Army in Cyrenaica and Libya numbered some 215,000 troops. After the fall of France, our intelligence reported a further force of about 30,000 moving slowly from west to east in Cyrenaica. All that stood between this great host and Egypt and the vital Suez Canal was Wavell's newly formed Western Desert Force, commanded by Major-General O'Connor, a wiry little Irishman, consisting of the 7th Armoured Division and the 4th Indian Division, neither of which were up to strength. The first lacked two of its armoured regiments while the second was short of a whole brigade of infantry, that is, a third of its strength. The entire force was short of artillery, in particular anti-aircraft guns. As well as these two ill-equipped divisions, O'Connor had under his immediate command the 22nd Guards Brigade and the 6th Infantry Brigade.

To support the Western Desert Force Air Chief Marshal Sir Arthur Longmore, the Air Officer Commanding-in-Chief Middle East, assigned No. 202 Group, under the command of Air Commodore Collishaw. This Group consisted of roughly half the 300 aircraft in the Middle East at the time. Its bomber squadrons were armed with short-range Blenheim Is, while two of the four naval cooperation squadrons were equipped with Sunderlands, and the reconnaissance squadrons had to depend entirely on defenceless Lysanders. As for the five fighter squadrons, all they possessed were obsolete Gladiator biplanes. The rest of the squadrons in the Middle East theatre were mounted on a heterogeneous collection of out-of-date machines including Wellesleys, Battles, and even a few Ju 86s belonging to the South African Air Force.

In the desert the Italians had some 280 aircraft, while many more of the 1,200 aeroplanes of the *Regia Aeronautica* were concentrated near at hand in the Dodecanese, Southern Italy, and Sicily. Of the enemy aircraft in North Africa in June, 1940, the Cr 42 fighter was evenly matched with our Gladiator, while the S79 bomber, though slower than the Blenheim I, carried a greater weight of bombs and had a longer range. Thus, while in performance our machines were equal to those of the enemy, we were out numbered by four to one. Moreover, the Italians had replacements as well as repair bases on their doorstep, a fact that gave them an overwhelming advantage during the opening rounds of the Mediterranean campaign.

We were indeed fortunate in having four such courageous and determined men as Cunningham, Wavell, Longmore, and Somerville to face the crisis in the Middle East in the summer of 1940, undaunted by the odds against them, the pathetic shortage of weapons and supplies. Of the four, Wavell possibly shouldered the most onerous task. The area under his command was vast, for it stretched south as far as Northern Rhodesia, north into the Balkans, east beyond the Persian Gulf, and west to Algeria. Within a year, General Wavell was to fight no fewer than nine campaigns; a herculean duty that no other British general had ever been called upon to undertake. And, unless we have failed dismally to learn from the mistakes of the past, it is unlikely that any man will ever again be loaded with such a fearful burden.

It has been said that as a theatre of war the Western Desert is a tactician's paradise and a quartermaster's hell. Certainly logistics were to prove perhaps the most difficult problem the opposing Commanders-in-Chief had to face. And in this respect from the outset the Italians held a tremendous advantage. For many months prior to declaring war Mussolini had poured supplies into North Africa by way of Tripoli, Benghazi, Derna, Tobruk, and Bardia. Moreover, the Italians had constructed a road in fact, the only road that ran the full length of the coasts of Cyrenaica and Libya over a distance of 935 miles to the borders of Egypt.

Nevertheless, Marshal Graziani complained bitterly to the Duce that his troops in North Africa were not ready to fight. He had assumed command of that area in July after his predecessor, Balbo, had been killed when his plane was shot down by the Italian anti-aircraft batteries at Tobruk. Collishaw dropped a wreath from the air at his funeral.

For two months Graziani continued to find excuses for postponing his offensive. 'The water supply is entirely insufficient' he told Ciano in August, adding with astonishing foresight: 'We move towards a defeat which, in the desert, must inevitably develop into a rapid and total disaster.' When Mussolini heard of these gloomy predictions he remarked: 'One should only give jobs to people who are looking for at least one promotion. Graziani's only anxiety is to remain a Marshal.'

It was not until September that the Marshal reluctantly consented to attack, and on the 14th the Italian 10th Army started its advance.

Long before that date, however, the enemy had been attacked by sea and air. Collishaw's Blenheims had bombed the airfield at El Adem within twenty-four hours of the declaration of war. And on the following night, June 12th, our bombers raided Tobruk, damaging the old Italian cruiser *San Giorgio* lying in the harbour. At the same time, Cunningham's ships were harrying the Italian convoys off Benghazi and Tobruk and shelling troop concentrations ashore.

At the end of June, Admiral Tovey's 7th Cruiser Squadron had its first brush with the enemy and sank the destroyer *Espero*.

'This in itself was a minor incident,' Admiral Cunningham wrote, 'but it brought into high relief the paucity of our reserves of ammunition at Alexandria. A tremendous expenditure of 6-inch shells had been necessary to sink this one 1,100-ton destroyer. With *Gloucester* and *Liverpool* pumping out 12-gun salvoes the ammunition just melted away. Our only reserves near at hand were 800 rounds in the Suez Canal Zone.'

Air Chief Marshal Longmore had similar worries. Early in July he was obliged to reprimand the exuberant Collishaw for allowing his fighter pilots to use low flying tactics against enemy vehicles. 'I consider such operations unjustified, having 'regard to our limited resources.' So acute had the shortage of aircraft become that by mid August Longmore was forced to ask the Army not to call for support except in the event of an enemy offensive. Collishaw, on the other hand, was inspired by this situation to resort to bluff, and in order to impress the enemy with his modern fighter strength he repeatedly shifted his only Hurricane known as 'Collie's Battleship' from airstrip to airstrip.

By September 16th, Graziani's forward troops had arrived 'at a collection of mud huts and houses grandiosely named Sidi Barrani, some sixty miles short of the Western Desert Force's main line of defence at Mersa Matruh. A few miles beyond Sidi Barrani the Marshal called a halt, unwilling to stretch his extenuated lines of communication any further in the face of growing opposition from O'Connor's front-line troops under the command of Brigadier Gott.

In October, while Graziani was still preoccupied with supplies and reinforcements, Mussolini, determined upon proving to his Axis partner his aggressiveness, attacked Greece. Since we were bound by a guarantee given by Chamberlain in April, 1939, to come to the latter's aid, Longmore, supported by Anthony Eden. the Secretary of State for War, who was in Cairo. immediately sent a squadron of Blenheim fighters and bombers to defend Athens. This action was quickly approved by the Government at home and the Chiefs-of-Staff, and shortly afterwards General Wavell was ordered to send anti-aircraft guns and the men to man them, as well as medical and other supplies.

Before it even started, the Greek campaign was a muddle. While invoking the guarantee we had given, the Greek Government politely but firmly refused our offer to send troops to their assistance and asked only for our aeroplanes. General Metaxas, the Prime Minister, was shrewd enough to appreciate that unless we could support him in overwhelming strength it was better for us to keep away than to send a token force that would give Hitler a pretext for coming to his partner's help. Thus, in addition to the RAF, it was agreed that a British garrison should be sent to Crete, together with anti-aircraft guns, to defend Suda Bay where the Royal Navy established an advanced base. But since it was never possible to provide adequate batteries or a proper boom defence, this harbour on the northern shore of the island was of little real value to us.

In *The Second World War, Volume II*, Churchill describes with complete frankness the misunderstanding which arose between his Secretary of State for War and General Wavell on the one hand, and the Prime Minister and the CIGS on the other, over the question of aid to Greece. Eden was told in the greatest secrecy that Wavell was planning to attack Graziani's Army instead of waiting for the latter to start his offensive against Mersa Matruh. According to Churchill, Wavell 'begged the Secretary of State not to send any telegram on this subject, but to tell us verbally about it when he got home. Thus for some weeks we remained without knowledge of the way their minds were working.'

As the result of this confusion, Wavell was left with the impression that the War Cabinet and the Chiefs-of-Staff were pressing him to dissipate the forces he was assembling for the Western Desert offensive in order to give aid to Greece. Eden, who was still in Cairo at that time, shared this belief, and sent the Prime Minister a long telegram in which he set forth his reasons why he was against a plan which would 'imperil our whole position in the Middle East and jeopardize plans for an offensive operation now being laid in more than one theatre.'

Churchill describes this telegram as cryptic. Yet in the light of what happened later, Eden's belief that 'the best way in which we can help

Greece is by striking at Italy, and we can do that most effecrively from areas where our strength has been developed and where our plans are laid', would appear to have been correct. In March, 1941, some; 58,000 troops with their transport, stores, and full equipment, were sent to Greece. They not only arrived too late, but their despatch drained the Western Desert Force of the strength to hold the enemy at El Agheila.

After the final débâcle when the remnants of this expeditionary force had been rescued at a terrible cost in men and ships by the Royal Navy, there were many who declared the entire campaign to have been a failure from its inception. Others argued that ethically we were bound to go to Greece's aid. While some believed that, since in the first instance the Greeks had refused such aid, we were relieved of our obligation.

However, in the autumn of 1940 when Mussolini so treacherously attacked Greece, the three Commanders-in-Chief in the Middle East viewed this new turn of events with apprehension while they continued to fight the enemy with increasing pugnacity.

On November 11th. Fleet Air Arm Swordfish attacked the Italian Fleet in Taranto harbour, crippling three battleships, including the new *Littoria*. Long range bombers from the Suez Canal airfields and Malta continued to strike at the enemy's supply ports, landing-grounds, and lines of communication.

On the ground, O'Connor's tactical reconnaissance patrols had discovered the existence of the 'Enba Gap' as it came to be known; a fifteen-mile wide stretch of practically undefended country between two of the enemy's camps. So important was this area to our impending offensive that the 7th Armoured Division was given the duty of keeping it open by attacking any Italian force attempting to set up an advanced post in the neighbourhood. Meanwhile the newly arrived brigade of 'I' tanks were undergoing intensive exercises in company with the 4th Indian Division.

On December 1st, Wavell held the first of a series of conferences in Cairo. Although it was attended by all his subordinate commanders, the Naval and Air Commanders-in-Chief, as well as Generals Wilson, Cunningham, Platt, and Blamey, no mention was made of the battle due to start in ten days' time. In general terms Wavell merely informed those present of his future plans, which included driving the Italians from Eritrea, Abyssinia, and Italian Somaliland within the next ten months.

Three days later, Wavell held an important conference attended only by

Admiral Cunningham, Air Chief Marshal Longmore, Lt-General Sir Henry Maitland Wilson and General O'Connor. On this occasion the final plans for the offensive against Sidi Barrani were discussed in detail. O'Connor explained his plan of battle, while Cunningham promised to give the Army every possible support. To this end the Inshore Squadron, under the command of Rear-Admiral Rawlings, had been formed. Rawling's only order was to give every possible help to O'Connor. The old monitor *Terror* was brought down from Suda Bay to join the three ancient gunboats from the China Station, *Ladybird*, *Gnat*, and *Aphis*, in shelling enemy transport on the coastal road and bombarding Sidi Barrani, particularly on the night before the attack was launched.

Collishaw was in command of the 'Tactical Air Force' that was to support the Army's advance. But this high sounding title deceived no one at the conference of the fact that with its commitments in Greece, the RAF could muster never more than a hundred fighters for this task.

Shortly after this conference, Cunningham carried out a further westerly sweep with his Fleet, supported by Somerville's Force 'H' from Gibraltar, which enabled another precious convoy beating troops and supplies to reach Alexandria.

Wavell went to great lengths to keep his plans secret. And in Egypt such measures were necessary. Ever since he had been 'debagged' one rowdy night in the mess at Woolwich as a youngster, while learning the ways of the British Army, King Farouk had ceased to love us, while his Queen was known to confide in her Italian hairdresser. Cairo and Alexandria were crawling with enemy agents and spies. In June, when Italy had declared war, there were some 20,000 Italians in Alexandria alone. 7,000 of whom were eventually rounded up and sent to concentration camps. But still there were any number of Axis sympathizers at large, amongst them the Japanese Consul in Alexandria. He was a fat little man with a broad backside which caused him to be known to Cunningham and his Staff as 'the blunt end of the Axis', and they all knew that it was his habit to report the movements of the Fleet to the enemy. Another menace to our security were the pretty rich women who entertained our officers so lavishly in their homes in Alexandria and Cairo. And, of course, there were the French officials of the Canal Company, many of whom were tainted with 'Vichyism'.

It was scarcely surprising, therefore, that Wavell insisted on the maximum degree of security and the minimum of written directives concerning his forthcoming battle, the success of which depended on its element of surprise. For this very reason it was not until the evening of December 8th, when the Western Desert Force had already advanced over seventy miles to the concentration area near the Enba Gap, that officers commanding regiments and battalions were told the truth. Until then they had been led to believe they were advancing to repulse an Italian attack against Mersa Matruh.

From dawn until sunset the men and their armour remained motionless, making the best they could of the stunted thorn bushes and scrub for camouflage. Throughout the interminable hours of waiting our fighters swept the forward areas, questing the enemy bombers and reconnaissance planes. But none was seen.

When night fell and the moon rose above the desert, O'Connor's little force moved forward again, the grind and clatter of its tanks and amoured cars drowned the roar of a Bombay's engines overhead. Once through the Gap, Major-General Beresford-Peise's force of heavy tanks, guns, and Indian infantry, turned north to attack the camps at Nibeiwa and East and West Tummer from the rear. Another force of armoured cars and light tanks, commanded by Major-General Creagh, swept north and west towards the coast to cut the Italian lines of communication, while a detachment was despatched to deal with the camps at Sofafi in the south-west. Meanwhile, in the coastal area to the north, a force from Mersa Matruh advanced on Makita Camp, with orders to fight its way along the coast to Sidi Barrani.

This battle plan, which was conceived by O'Connor, succeeded beyond all expectation, and resulted in the British Army's first victory of the war. The campaign, for that is what it turned out to be, was the most brilliant ever fought in the Western Desert. Inevitably, even unjustly, it was eclipsed by the blaze of publicity that attended General Montgomery's final victory in the desert, so that many have forgotten what Wavell and his commanders in the field, Generals Wilson and O'Connor, achieved.

Outnumbered by five to one, short of tanks and guns, with inadequate repair shops at base, without reserves, and supported by never more than a hundred aircraft, these remarkable soldiers drove Graziani's 10th Army out of Cyrenaica. Starting with supplies sufficient for five days' desert fighting, the Western Desert Force fought for two months and advanced more than 500 miles. At a cost of less than 2,000 casualties, 130,000 prisoners were captured, 1,000 guns, 400 tanks, and 450 aircraft. With two divisions, the

13th Corps, as the Western Desert Force was by then called, halted at El Agheila in February, 1941, having routed four Italian corps with nine divisions.

On February 9th, 1941, General Richard O'Connor signalled to his Commander-in-Chief: 'Fox killed in the open.'

The Duce summed up the situation somewhat differently in his communiqué concerning Marshal Graziani's defeat, when he wrote: 'the Tenth Army and the 5th Squadron of the *Regia Aeronautica* have been wiped out.'

CHAPTER TWO

TOBRUK CAPTURED

By the night of January 21st, 1941, the greater part of the perimeter surrounding Tobruk had been captured by the Australian troops under Major-General Mackay's command. From the escarpment could be seen the smoke and flames rising from the town, and the rumble of explosions warned the General that the Italians had already begun their work of demolition. So, during the night, he ordered a general advance on the following morning so that the town might be taken before the garrison had time to create havoc amongst the harbour installations.

Early on the morning of the 22nd, Brigadier H C H Robertson, commanding the 19th Australian Infantry Brigade, sent forward carriers in charge of Lt-Colonel E C Hennessy, of the 6th Australian Cavalry Regiment, to reconnoitre the situation within the fortress. Soon the leading carrier was met by a dapper little Italian officer who informed Hennessy that he had been detailed to lead him to the naval headquarters where the Admiral was waiting to surrender. Seating this envoy on the front of carrier 'as a guarantee of good faith', Hennessy drove to a grandiose building facing a wide courtyard where stood the Italian Admiral surrounded by his staff. Bowing, he offered his sword to Hennessy, but the Australian refused it, and sent one of his carriers back to tell his Brigadier what was happening.

Robertson was with Brigadier Leslie Morshead, the commander of the 18th Australian Brigade, who was in Tobruk simply as an observer, and together they drove into the town. At the entrance of the naval headquarters they were met by a nervous Italian commander who conducted them to the room where Admiral Massimiliano Vietina was standing with his staff. Through an interpreter, Robertson was told that the Admiral and some 2,000 officers and men wished to surrender. But before accepting Vientina's sword, the Brigadier demanded to know whether there were any booby traps or mines in the town, adding menacingly that if a single one of his troops were killed, the Italians would suffer the consequences. The interpreter answered that all the mines and traps had been sprung.

Thus the fortress of Tobruk was surrendered into the hands of two brigadiers, fewer than a dozen Australian cavalrymen, and a party of war correspondents who had followed Robertson's car into the town.

When the interview ended, an officer went out to the courtyard and fired Very lights into the clear blue sky as a signal that Tobruk had fallen. A triumphant Australian hoisted a Digger's hat to the truck of the flagstaff outside the Admiral's headquarter's.

By the end of the day, when the last strongpoints had laid down their arms, it was estimated that 27,000 prisoners had been taken, together with 208 field and medium guns, eighty-seven tanks, and some 200 vehicles. It was discovered that the demolitions had been confined for the most part to guns and ammunition, while in the harbour where the old cruiser *San Giorgio* lay beached and burning amongst other wrecks, the naval fuel plant had been destroyed and the floating crane smashed. The jetties, although damaged, were usable. But the power station, with its 4,000-tons of coal, was intact, as, too, were the refrigeration and distillation plants. There was also a complete bulk petrol storage installation, as well as 10,000-tons of stored mineral water for the garrison in order to avoid drinking the bitter brackish water from the local wells.

Within a matter of hours after the surrender, sweepers of the Royal Navy began clearing the mines in the harbour, and by the morning of January 24th the port was declared ready to receive the first supply ships.

Tobruk owes its importance to the fact that it is the only good harbour on the North African coast between Alexandria and Sfax. In the middle ages it was the hideout of the corsairs raiding the trade routes through the Mediterranean, and in 1798 Napoleon Bonaparte called there for water with units of the French Fleet on the way to his campaign in Egypt. In 1911, when the Balkan States went to war with Turkey, Italy annexed Tripoli and established a naval base at Tobruk, building a small town on the northern shore of the U-shaped bay. When Mussolini came into power, the defences and fortifications were considerably strengthened; a hotel, restaurant, and the Church of St Francis were built, as well as shops, offices, and accommodation for a permanent garrison of about 10,000. The Fascists built themselves an impressive glaringly white concrete headquarters which was destined to be known after our capture of the fortress as 'Navy House'. It stood on the high ground on the north shore of the harbour and its wide terrace commanded a splendid view across the whole bay to the distant escarpment.

In the years immediately preceding the war the Italians had constructed a series of wide defences enclosing an area round Tobruk of roughly 135 square miles. These consisted of a double ring of concrete emplacements eight or nine miles from the town and harbour covering a frontage of some thirty-five miles. The eastern and western extremities of this perimeter were well protected by steep wadis, impassable to tanks and mechanized vehicles. But for the greater part of its length the perimeter ran across a flat featureless plain protected by rusting barbed wire and an anti-tank ditch. The Italians had never bothered to complete this ditch and had also left many dangerous gaps in the wire.

The Australian Generals, Lavarack and Morshead, who were responsible for the safety of Tobruk, had no alternative but to make the best they could of these existing defences, the chief virtue of which was that they were constructed far enough away to prevent any enemy attempts to interfere with the working of the harbour except by air attack. And beyond all else it was the harbour at Tobruk that was then vitally important to the Army in the Western Desert.

This fact was made clear by Churchill in a directive of January 6th, 1941, to the CIGS for the Chiefs-of-Staffs Committee, in which he wrote:

'...With Bardia and Tobruk in our hands it should be possible to drop the land communications with Alexandria almost entirely and to rely upon sea transport for our further westward advance... The distance from Tobruk to Benghazi by the coastal road is not much above 250 miles, compared with about 370 miles from Alexandria to Tobruk. Thus, once Tobruk is established as the base, and out land communications begin from there, no greater strain should be thrown upon land transport than at present, and it should be possible to start afresh from Tobruk as if Tobruk were Alexandria, and to maintain the moderate but adequate striking force required. With the capture of Benghazi this phase of the Libyan campaign would be ended.'

Within the limits of their powers the three Commanders-in-Chief faithfully carried out their orders. Immediately after its capture, Wavell flew to Tobruk, and was delighted to find that the port had suffered less damage than he had anticipated and that the Royal Navy was working round the clock to render it serviceable.

Two days after the port had been reported open to sea traffic, Admiral Cunningham and his Chief-of-Staff, Rear-Admiral Willis, also flew to Tobruk to inspect the harbour and shore defences.

'It was an interesting visit,' the C-in-C. wrote. 'The harbour, though fouled with wrecks, had far more sheltered accommodation than I expected. There was ample room for our supply ships.'

Hard on the heels of the advancing army, Collishaw's bombers and fighters moved forward to the airfields at Benina and El Adem.

While the supplies began to flow into Tobruk by sea and the garrison was reinforced, the Army continued its rapid advance towards Benghazi, for no sooner had the assault on Tobruk opened, than the Chiefs-of-Staff told the Commanders-in-Chief that the early capture of Benghazi was of paramount importance. The latter, in view of the increasing German threat to the Balkans, was considered to be the limit of out advance in North Africa.

'I cannot look beyond Benghazi at the present time,' Churchill informed General Ismay on January 6th. Two days later Smuts in a telegram congratulating the Prime Minister on the Western Desert victories wrote;

'...Flowing tide will soon carry Wavell to Tobruk. Should he go further? Tripoli is much too far. Even Benghazi is as far beyond the frontier as the frontier is from Alexandria.' The shrewd old Boer added that while there might be sound reasons, naval or otherwise, for advancing as far as Benghazi, 'in the absence of good and special reasons Tobruk seems to me the terminus. Beyond it lies risks not necessary to entail. Leaving an adequate defence force there in a fortified position, the rest of the Army should be withdrawn to Egypt and the Middle East, where a strong army of manoeuvre will be required against possible attack through the Balkans.'

If this prophetic and sound advice had been heeded, the outcome of events in the Western Desert might indeed have been very different. But, alas, it was not. Churchill replied to Smuts that he fully agreed that no heavy price should be paid beyond Tobruk. Nevertheless, flushed with easy success, he did not attempt to call a halt when Tobruk fell like an over-ripe plum into his lap. Indeed, such was his exhilaration when Benghazi fell, that he cabled on February 15th to General Smuts; 'Joyful acceleration capture Benghazi, Cyrenaica, gives us secure flank for Egypt.'

In the exuberance of the moment, it appears that he had forgotten the arrival in Tripoli three days before of a German General called Erwin Rommel.

CHAPTER THREE

THE OTHER SIDE OF THE FENCE

On October 4th, 1940, when Hitler and Mussolini met on the Brenner Pass, the former had offered his partner mechanized troops for the campaign in Libya. The Duce had received this generosity coldly. Until such time as Marshal Graziani had taken Mersa Matruh, he needed no aid from his ally. Later, perhaps, for the triumphant advance eastward to Alexandria and the Suez Canal, it was possible that he might need dive-bombers, heavy tanks and armoured cars.

At about this time General von Thoma visited Libya and reported directly to his Führer on the state of affairs in that theatre of war. The supply problem, he said, was already vexed, and the presence of German troops would only complicate the situation. Therefore von Thoma strongly advised against the sending of German soldiers to North Africa until Graziani was in possession of Mersa Matruh. And so the matter rested. Apart from sending long-range bombers to mine the Canal, Hitler took no further interest in the North African campaign.

However, after the disastrous winter of 1940, Mussolini had occasion to remind his partner that Italy was not only short of oil and other raw materials, as well as vital weapons, but was virtually fighting the war against the British unaided. But Hitler seemed disinclined to come to his help, and on the last day of the year told the Duce that the moment was not auspicious to launch a major counter-attack against Wavell's forces. Nevertheless, having listened to the opinions of Admiral Raeder and his Naval Staff, who viewed the situation in the Mediterranean with growing apprehension. Hitler was obliged to change his tune. Graziani's defeat Raeder argued, would completely alter the balance of power in the Eastern Mediterranean, and the British would be in a position to give strong support to Greece. Moreover, so long as Admiral Cunningham's Fleet commanded that sea, there could be no possible hope of the war developing in favour of the Axis.

These views were supported by those of General von Rintelen in Rome, who expressed the opinion that Italy's unfortunate position in Libya was primarily due to lack of the proper equipment; particularly anti-tank guns and tanks. Von Rintelen reported that as the result of this the morale of the Italians was low, while the tactics of the senior officers were old-fashioned, so that even with the weapons available they were unable to fight a modern war in the desert. At the same time he made it clear that if the Germans provided the troops and the arms for which the Italians now pleaded, the former should at least be allowed some say in the conduct of the North African struggle.

But it was not until the fall of Bardia that Hitler realized that in order to prevent the total collapse of the Italians in Libya he would have to take immediate action. He could not, however, impose his will too precipitously upon the Duce, nor did he deem it possible to be an ambitious offensive against Egypt. Nevertheless, he was determined to come to Italy's aid with tanks as well as anti-tank and anti-aircraft units. Also he stepped up the number of aircraft based on Sicily whose task it would be to attack the British naval forces and the enemy's lines of communication through the Mediterranean.

Early in January, 1941, Hitler issued a directive in which he stated that the German assistance in the Mediterranean had become essential for 'strategic, political and psychological reasons'. At whatever the cost, he made it plain that Tripolitania must not be allowed to fall into the hands of the British, and in order to prevent such a disaster the German General Staff was to prepare *Sperrverbund* – a special blocking force. In the meantime the Italian General Staff had arranged to ship two divisions – the Ariete Armoured and the Trento Motorized – across to Tripoli between the middle of January and the last week of February.

Von Rintelen had received a written statement from General Guzzoni, the new Deputy Chief-of-Staff, as to the situation in Libya. It was not exactly encouraging. Tobruk was already considered lost. Thus Wavell's force possessed the advanced base it so sorely needed. Nevertheless, it was the General Staff's considered opinion that the British supply line was becoming stretched to its limit, and so Wavell would be obliged to halt, at least for a while, at either Tobruk or Benghazi. But, whatever happened, with the reinforcements being despatched to him Graziani should be in a position to lunch an attack against the British.

On January 18th, when the dictators met at Obersalzburg, the Führer seemed disinclined to mention tht Libyan situation, beyond remarking cynically that he could see no purpose in sending German soldiers to Tripoli if they were to remain kicking their heels for an unspecified time. He left it to General Jodi to tell Guzzoni what aid would be given to Italy. This, Jodi said, would consist of the 5th Light Motorized Division. strong in anti-tank units, which would be ready to embark by mid-February. He stressed that this was in no sense a reserve division, but an aggressive spearhead to be employed against the British armour, if and when the latter attacked.

At the end of January, von Rintelen sent yet another disturbing report to his Führer on the North African situation. In this he said that Guzzoni considered it improbable that any units of the 10th Army would survive to defend Tripolitania, and it seemed likely that only Tripoli itself could be held. In the light of such gloomy predictions. Hitler ordered von Rintelen to investigate the position more fully, since it would be futile to send German troops to Africa simply to defend Tripoli. Von Rintelen's inquiry revealed the alarming fact that Graziani had decided to evacuate Cyrenaica altogether, while the Italian Navy had no plans for denying the British establishing bases along the coast. Only the *Regia Aeronautica*, reinforced with bombers and fighters, appeared to have the spirit to fight.

Graziani's final disgrace took place at Beda Fomm on February 9th, when the 10th Army finally disintegrated. The battlfield was a shambles. For fifteen miles the desert was littered with abandoned tanks, guns, and trucks. Prisoners wandered about in their thousands like flocks of goats. Amongst the captured were the dying General Tellera, the 10th Army's Commander, and General Bergonzoli, Commander of the 23rd Corps, who surrendered to the Rifle Brigade. Although in this final battle the Italian medium tanks outnumbered the British by about four to one, our victory was complete. More than 100 tanks and twice that number of guns were captured or destroyed. Indeed, so successful was the cutting off of the 10th Army that scarcely a soldier or vehicle escaped from the trap.

On February 11th, the day before Rommel's arrival. Marshal Graziani left Tripoli, and on March 25th, King Victor Emmanuel accepted his resignation.

Although Graziani was the scapegoat, the blame for Italy's defeat in Libya was, in fact, Mussolini's, for it was he who forced his country into the war before it was prepared. Moreover, together with his Chief-of-Staff, Marshal Badoglio, he shared the responsibility for the conduct of the campaign. Thus the wretched Graziani was forced against his judgement to launch his offensive on the Egyptian frontier; an offensive that ended in the rout of his Army at Beda Fomm.

This débâcle caused Hitler to write to the Duce criticizing the entire conduct of the Italian campaign and at the same time expressing his views as to how it should have been conducted. The Führer went on to say that the anti-tank division he had originally intended for North Africa would no longer be sufficient to stop the rot. Therefore, provided the Italians were still prepared to fight, he was willing to embark a complete, armoured division for Tripoli. But, he insisted, the latter must be held. At the same time, Malta must be bombed day and night to prevent attacks on Axis shipping bound for Tripoli, while combined air and naval operations must be undertaken against Benghazi and Tobruk, and the British sea-lines along the coast. Only if the Duce agreed to such aggressive action, Hitler wrote, would Germany come to Italy's aid.

Mussolini agreed. General Gariboldi replaced Marshal Graziani, and on February both the German General Staff issued orders for Operation 'Sonnenblume' – the intervention of German forces in North Africa, to take place.

In these orders it was laid down that while for tactical purposes the German troops would be subordinated to the Italian *Comando Supremo*, except in extenuating circumstances, they were to function as a formation under a German commander. Should the latter be given orders which he considered might lead to failure and the discredit of his troops, he had the right to refer to the German General Staff. So far as the *Fliegerkorps* X, the German Air Force in the Mediterranean, was concerned, it was responsible only to Marshal Göring.

On February 12th, Lt-General Erwin Rommel flew to Tripoli, by which time the first of the German Expeditionary Force had already arrived. Shortly afterwards Hitler announced that his forces under General Rommel would henceforth be known as the *Deutsches Afrika Korps*.

CHAPTER FOUR

AGAINST THE TIDE

Too little – too late' might be the epitaph for the expeditionary force of British and Dominion troops which finally reached Macedonia. But the onus for what happened in that brief campaign must rest with the Greeks themselves, because of their vacillating attitude to our offers of support many weeks before the advance guard of Hitler's Army crossed the Bulgarian frontier.

On January 29th, shortly after a meeting with General Wavell, in Athens, General Metaxas died suddenly. The German radio made great propaganda of this coincidence, hinting that Metaxas' death was the result of an 'extremely agitated' meeting with the Commander-in-Chief. In retrospect, however, it is true that with Metaxas' untimely end, the tide of Wavell's fortunes began to ebb.

On February 8th, the Greek Government, now headed by M Alexander Koryzis, declared its intention of resisting the Germans, and requested to be informed as to the extent of the British forces available to aid them.

This request resulted in a lengthy directive on the British Government's Middle East policy being despatched by the War Cabinet to the Commanders-in-Chief in that area. The latter had cause for reflection.

So far as General Wavell was concerned, he now had to pursue his two offensives in East Africa, collect and equip an army for Greece, and simultaneously decide upon the strength of a 'minimum force' needed to secure his flank in Cyrenaica against attack.

Air Chief Marshal Longmore was ordered to send from his already depleted squadrons the strongest possible force to Greece. He had but recently protested vigorously against despatching precious squadrons to Turkey while the advance to Benghazi was still in progress. Then he had signalled to the Chief of Air Staff:

'Your message received. Quite frankly contents astounds me. I cannot believe you fully appreciate present situation Middle East, in which Libya drive in full career and Sudan offensive progressing satisfactorily... Arrival aircraft Middle East by all routes now hardly keeping pace with casualties... However strong political advantages may be of impressing the Turks, can you afford to lock up squadrons you propose in Turkey where they may well remain for some time inoperative? Would it not be forsaking the substance for the shadow?'

To this the Chief of Air Staff replied:

'It is not a question of trying to impress the Turks. It is a question of trying to deter Germany by fear of bombing of Romania from absorbing Bulgaria, Greece and Turkey without a shot and then dominating the Eastern Mediterranean and Aegean as she now dominates the Narrows. If we can prevent or even delay this, the squadrons in Turkey will have pulled far more weight than in helping to beat the Italians in Africa.'

This exchange of signals succinctly sums up the perplexed situation at the time as well as the overwhelming problems exercising the minds of the War Cabinet.

Admiral Cunningham, too, was concerned by this latest directive from London. He was, however, of the opinion that the Navy could move the expeditionary force to Greece in comparative safety.

'The fourth item of the War Cabinet directive,' he wrote afterwards, 'the attack on the Dodecanese, rather led me to think that the authorities at home were living in a land of optimistic dreams.'

Indeed, such suspicions were justified, for there can be no doubt but that the War Cabinet's appreciation of the situation in the Middle East was not realistic, in spite of the spate of signals that had been made by the three Commanders-in-Chief stressing their lack of the vital weapons of war.

On the evidence of the prolific telegrams he despatched, it is apparent that even Churchill had failed to grasp the truth. What, he demanded, were all those troops doing in the Middle East?

'My impression is one of enormous jumbles of ration-strength troops in the Middle East with many half-baked tactical formations.... Latest Middle East ration-strength returns shows increase of nearly 50,000 between December 31 and January 31. Does nothing emerge in the shape of fighting units from this reinforcement?' he asked of his Secretary of State on February 20th, after the latter had arrived in Cairo with General Dill, then Chief of the Imperial General Staff.

Eden was quick to appreciate the 'limitation of our resources... especially in the air', and expressed the opinion that it was 'a gamble to send forces to the mainland of Europe to fight the Germans at this time'.

The question whether or not we were stragetically right in sending troops to Greece will probably always be debated. The fact remains we were bound by treaty to do so. And while the three Commanders-in-Chief accepted the ethics of the case, they shared doubts as to the military wisdom of the undertaking. Certainly it was as a direct result of our decision to give active aid to Greece that we were unable to hold the ground gained in Cyrenaica. In our efforts to sustain the Greeks everything we had won in North Africa was sacrificed.

It is tempting to speculate as to what might have been the outcome had we abandoned the Greeks to their fate and used all the forces available to advance westward to vanquish the Italian divisions in Tripolitania. General O'Connor was, in fact prepared to move forward from Sirte by February 20th, with this object in view, when it appeared there were only ill-equipped and depleted Italian divisions opposing him. Fully supported by the Navy and the Air Force, he might have driven the enemy from North Africa, rendering it impossible for the Axis ever again to invade Egypt without attempting a major sea-borne invasion. Furthermore, the capture of Tripoli would have given us another base from which to attack Sicily, relieve Malta and make contact with the French forces in Tunisia. It is feasible that once Tripoli had been lost by the Italians, Hitler would have taken no further interest in North Africa. But then, the divisions which did, in fact, form the *Afrika*

Korps would have been free to employ in the Balkans.

However fascinating, it is futile to indulge in such speculation, for the truth is that in 1941 the German High Command, exploiting its mastery of Europe and the resulting mobility of its armies, held all the trumps. And until the fatal decision was taken to launch Operation '*Barbarossa*', against the Russians, the Germans played their hand brilliantly.

While massing troops in the Balkans, the *Luftwaffe* came south to the shores of the Mediterranean to dominate that sea, bomb Malta, close the Suez Canal, and safeguard the transport of Rommel's forces across the Narrows, while harassing our long lines of communication in Libya.

'War,' as the military historians wrote of that period, was not 'one damned thing after another', it was everything in all directions at once.'

By the time Wavell had collected together his Army for Macedonia, our forward positions in North Africa at El Agheila were held by the 9th Australian Division and what was left of the 2nd Armoured Division after one armoured brigade group had been withdrawn and refitted to go to Greece. The 9th Australian Division, commanded by Major-General Morshead had also parted with two of its brigades. Both divisions were miserably short of Bren-guns, anti-tank weapons, signal equipment, and transport. General Sir Henry Maitiand Wilson had scarcely assumed his duties as Military Governor of Cyrenaica and General Officer Commanding-in-Chief before he was hurried off to command the Army of the Nile in Greece. He was soon to be followed there by General Blamey and the headquarters of the Australian Corps. Lt-General Percy Neame, VC, arrived from Palestine, with no experience of desert fighting, to take over the Cyrenaica Command at Barce, where he found no corps headquarters to handle purely military matters. And while the 2nd Armoured Division and the 9th Australian Division both came under his command, he was lacking a trained staff or the signal equipment to control mobile operations over large expanses of desert.

But this was not all. The newly arrived *Luftwaffe* was already making its presence felt. Early in February its bombers were attacking Tobruk and mining the harbour. Benghazi, too, was being frequently bombed, as also were the ships of the Inshore Squadron running supplies into Tobruk.

It was the losses suffered by this force that caused Admiral Cunningham to remark when he was created a Knight Grand Cross of the Most Honourable Order of the Bath, that he would sooner have had three squadrons of Hurricanes. As things were, his little ships had to depend largely upon the doubtful protection of a squadron of Hurricanes of the Royal Australian Air Force, based at Benina, which lacked a mobile radar unit.

This situation caused Admiral Cunningham to express his grave misgivings to Admiral Sir Dudley Pound concerning the state of the Royal Air Force in the Middle East. He said that it was his opinion that the Chiefs-of-Staff were misinformed as to the number of fighter squadrons available.

'Longmore,' he wrote, 'is absolutely stretched to the limit, and we seem to have fewer (fighters) than are supposed at home. We are getting sat on by the Germans in Cyrenaica. The figures there are over two hundred German and Italian fighters against thirty of ours. It seems to me that if the fighter situation is not taken in hand drastically and speedily we are heading straight for trouble, not only in Greece, but if the Germans advance in Libya we have no air force to stop them, and actually little else either.'

The Admiral was right. For by the time the Army had been prepared for Greece, there remained only sixteen heavy anti-aircraft guns between Benghazi and Alexandria. The few ships which survived the vicious *Stuka* attacks while en route were immediately set upon in Benghazi harbour with such fury that they were often forced to sail before their cargoes were fully discharged.

Thus what hopes we had of using Benghazi as an advanced base were soon dissipated. Once again it was necessary to rely upon lorries for the 200-mile haul from Tobruk to the front line. And this at a time when some 8,000 vehicles, later to be abandoned to the enemy, had been consigned to Greece.

Wavell was to be criticized for much that happened in North Africa in 1941. However, it should be clear from what has been written above concerning the opinions of the men on the spot that neither Churchill nor his War Cabinet viewed the Mediterranean scene in its right perspective. This being so, the continual prodding and goading from Downing Street were the harder to bear and became increasingly irritating. However well intended, they did nothing to urge on the men who were already doing their best. Indeed, had all this energy, thought, and time been directed to ensuring that the tanks and aircraft sent to the

Middle East arrived in operational order, it would have been more usefully employed. As it was, weeks were wasted fitting the necessary filters to make their engines desertworthy *after* their arrival.

The Staff at GHQ Middle East were not above reproach. And when Churchill took them to task for ordering the 7th Armoured Division back to Egypt, condemning this manoeuvre as an 'act of improvidence', he was right.

The Division's armour, consisting of some 162 tanks, was said to be worn out. Yet these tanks trundled back under their own power more than 400 miles to the repair shops. At the time such an action was justified by the opinion held by the Staff in Cairo that no serious enemy counter-attack was to be expected until May. This, of course, was a grave miscalculation. However, even if the tanks had to refit, there was no reason why the officers and NCOs, than whom there were none more skilled in the art of desert warfare, should not have remained behind to train and advise the troops who replaced them. Instead, these experts went back to Egypt, where they kicked their heels in base camps or were set to guarding the Canal Zone.

Certainly the Staff in Cairo were slow to realize that German troops were pouring into Tripoli, and were curiously disinclined to believe the evidence reaching them from the front that German units were operating with the Italians.

On February 20th, a troop of the Dragoon Guards, commanded by Lieutenant E T Williams, later to become Brigadier Williams, CB, CBE, DSO, Warden of Rhodes House, Oxford, actually exchanged fire with German armoured cars.

Having described this encounter, the regiment's historian goes on to say:

'Whether this was accepted as accurate information by higher formations is a matter for conjecture, but at the time the Regiment certainly received the impression that its reports were treated with reserve, and that as we were "new to the job", the imagination of a few troop leaders had magnified an Italian rearguard into something altogether different. However that may be, the report that German ground forces had started to appear created none of the stir which one might have expected – no visits from Staff Officers and Commanders;... and no suggestions that our hard-won territorial gains in North Africa should be protected by anything more than one armoured car regiment armed with Boyes rifles and machine guns.'

In fact, the German officer who had led this particular patrol was taken prisoner in November, and on him was found his diary recording his encounter with the Dragoon Guards.

The following day a pilot of one of our reconnaissance aircraft reported seeing a number of eight-wheeled vehicles whose crews wore a 'bluish uniform' unlike anything he had seen before in Libya. A few days later, two troops of armoured cars of the Dragoon Guards and a troop of Australian anti-tank guns, patrolling in the environs of El Agheila, were fired on by an armoured force, including tanks. Lieutenant Rowley, leading the anti-tank troop, and two members of an armoured car which had been knocked out, were captured by the Germans, who then withdrew with their prisoners, and towing away the disabled armoured car.

But while reports of these and other incidents were sent to headquarters, calm reigned in Cairo. A happy frame of mind fostered by the fact that at the time a properly organized intelligence service, with its agents in Tripoli, did not exist, since to our cost we had relied on the French for such information. Added to this, as there were no long-range fighters to protect our reconnaissance aircraft against the growing aggression of the *Luftwaffe*, accurate knowledge of the enemy's troop concentrations was not forthcoming. Nevertheless, this lethargy at GHQ Middle East was deplorable.

In the second week in March, General Wavell took time off from his excursions to Athens and flew up to Cyrenaica with General Dill to review the position. Both were shocked by what they saw. The troops under General Neame's command were green and their tanks mostly run-down. Dill was particularly apprehensive and warned the Australians that before long they would probably get 'a bloosy nose', adding laconically, 'and that won't be the only place either!'

Having made his appreciation of the situation, Wavell ordered Neame in the event of attack to fight a delaying action 'back to Benghazi. He even authorized him to evacuate the town if necessary, but to hold on to the high ground to the eastward as long as possible. Before flying back to Cairo he warned his unfortunate commander not to expect any armoured reinforcements for two months.

CHAPTER FIVE

ENTER ROMMEL

Contary to the myth that was later to be believed as 'gospel' by the majority of our troops in the Middle East, at its inception the *Afrika Korps* was by no means highly trained or perfectly equipped for desert warfare. In fact, the Germans had no practical experience of the conditions of war existing in North Africa to guide them. What was more, the Italians were sullenly reluctant to help them in this respect.

The 3rd Panzer Division, from which units were detached to form the backbone of the new 5th Light Motorized Division, commanded by Major-General Streich, had been standing by to go to Spain, if and when Franco could be inveigled into joining the Axis. It was not until later that the reinforcements of the DAK were given strenuous training in the heat of the summer at Grafenwoehr in North Bavaria.

The organization and equipment of the 5th Light Division was thus based largely on theory and what information the German Staff officers had gleaned during their visits to Graziani's Army. Inevitably, therefore, the Germans suffered their teething troubles. Doubting that their diesel-engined vehicles were suited to the desert, they fitted a number of them with twin tyres which dug into the sand and soon wore out. Their tank engines at first lacked the proper oil and air filters, with the result that their life was short and after a thousand or so kilometers they needed a major overhaul.

Initially the troops themselves were not suitably clothed for the desert, and, while they had an over-abundance of water, they lacked the necessary fresh food and vegetables so vital to the health of men fighting in a hot climate.

Nevertheless, the 5th Light Division was a tough adversary. It comprised a 12-gun battery of field artillery a regiment of two motorized machine-gun battalions, with their own engineers, anti-tank guns, and armoured troop-carrying vehicles. There was also a strong semi-armoured reconnaissance unit, and two powerful *Panzerjager* or anti-tank battalions, equipped with 88-mm guns, which were destined to inflict fearful injuries on our tanks and their crews. The armoured regiment consisted of two Panzer battalions with about eighty medium tanks mounting 50-mm or 75-mm guns and seventy light tanks.

To this force was allotted a *Staffel*, or air reconnaissance squadron. And with typical Teutonic thoroughness it was equipped with its own mobile workshops, supply units, and administration services.

But, perhaps the DAKs greatest strength lay in the fact that its training was based upon the vast practical experience gained during the *blitzkriegs* in Poland and France. Now, all that it needed was to acclimatize itself to the conditions in North Africa.

General Rommel, who landed in Tripoli forty-eight hours ahead of the first flight of his troops, immediately made contact with the Commander-in-Chief, General Gariboldi. The Italian's orders from his *Comando Supremo* had been to make a stand at Sirti, and already the Pavia, Bologna, and Ariete, Divisions were on the move eastward to this line, where they were shortly followed by the Savona and Brescia Divisions.

Like ourselves, the Germans had their transport problems at this time. Since priority had been given to the forthcoming Operation 'Barbarossa' against the Russians, the DAK was short of vehicles. The divisional staffs were at loggerheads over administrative matters and the priority of supplies. But so far as Rommel was concerned, he remained aloof from such squabbles, demanding imperiously that the necessary supplies be delivered where and when he required them.

Indeed, from the moment of his arrival, Rommel was only concerned with assessing the strength of the forces ranged against him. And to this end he hurried forward his reconnaissance and anti-tank units as soon as they landed. By February 16th they had reached Sirti. Three days later they were at Nofilia.

To help him in this initial task, Rommel called upon the planes of the *Fliegerkorps X*, units of which had already arrived from Sicily, under the command of General Fröhlich, *Flieger führer Afrika*. This force consisted of some fifty dive-bombers and about twenty twin-engined fighters. But Fröhlich also had at his disposal a number of Ju 88s and He 111s from the airfields in Sidly. His orders were to cooperate with General Rommel and to destroy the enemy air force in Cyrenaica.

Having made up his mind that, since there were few British troops in the forward area, any large-scale operation was unlikely to be launched against him, Rommel planned to occupy the coastal strip along a line of salt marshes running south about twenty miles west of El Agheila. And by the second week in March, the German and Italian troops had established themselves in their forward positions, defended by minefields and protected from a surprise attack by air reconnaissance units.

With his front line thus secured, Rommel flew to Berlin to lay his proposed plans before the OKH, the High Command of the German Army. He was received almost coldly and left in no doubt that, apart from the 15th Panzer Division which had been allocated to him, he could expect no further reinforcements. It was also made clear to him that until such time as this Division arrived, probably in mid-May, his task was to guarantee the defence of Tripolitania while preparing to win back Cyrenaica. Only after the arrival of the 15th Panzer Division were the DAK and the Italian forces under its command to attack in the Agedabia area in order to gain a springboard for any further offensive. The result of this battle would decide whether or not an advance upon Tobruk could be made. The OKH emphasized that until the reinforcements were landed safely, caution should govern all the *Afrika Korps'* activities in North Africa. Rommel listened with but half an ear to these orders.

It is not intended to describe in detail the *Afrika Korps'* spectacular advance from Mersa Brega to the Tobruk perimeter. It was a brilliant manoeuvre carried out with a drive and dash that astonished and even alarmed the German High Command. It resulted in Rommel's name becoming a legend in North Africa. He made it in spite of vigorous opposition from General Gariboldi, who, at one stage, hurried to Rommel's headquarters late in the evening to protest against any further advance being made until permission had been granted by the *Comando Supremo*. Rommel's reply was typical of the man. He blandly refused to waste valuable time, and said that as a German general he must give orders appropriate to the position at the moment.

That day, he wrote to his wife that his superior officers in Tripoli, Rome, and even Berlin would gasp at what he had done. In the end, however, they would approve.

To sum up briefly this rapid reversal of our fortunes is not difficult, although at the time Churchill admitted he was 'for some time completely mystified about its cause'. Because of his commitments in Greece, Wavell had been forced to take a risk in Cyrenaica. In calculating that risk he underestimated not so much the enemy's strength, but rather the fighting capability of his own small Army. He was aware that the 2nd Armoured Division and the 3rd Armoured Brigade lacked experience. But he had hoped that both would have time at least to learn the rudiments of desert warfare in skirmishes with enemy patrols before any serious attack was staged.

In fairness to Wavell, such a hope was justified, for Rommel's initial attack was never planned to be more than a reconnaissance in strength. Its success surprised even Rommel.

The real tragedy was that the British Armoured Brigade in Cyrenaica opposing Rommel was only a brigade on paper. When Wavell realized this it was too late to do anything about it, for the despatch of the expeditionary force to Greece had left the cupboard bare. After that, there were no tanks or spares left in the whole of the Middle East, for the only other armoured brigade had sailed for Piraeus.

'I did not become aware till just before the German attack of the bad mechanical state of the cruiser regiment, on which we relied,' Wavell informed Churchill after the battle. Thus it was, that when Rommels reconnaissance units came snuffing forward we had no well-equipped mobile force to deliver the punch on the nose which might have deterred them from venturing further.

But the moment Rommel discovered our weakness he immediately took advantage of it. His plan to cut the British line of retreat was conventional in its conception, but the determination with which he executed it was masterful. He was everywhere at once, like a brilliantly intuitive huntsman, 'lifting' his hounds whenever they lost the scent. But when at last, his fox went to ground in Tobruk, he never succeeded in digging him out.

CHAPTER SIX

BELEAGURED FORTRESS

On April 6th, Cunningham, Wavell, and Longmore, together with Eden and Dill, sat in conference at Cairo to review the situation in the Middle East. The outlook could scarcely have been more sombre. Four theatres of war had to be considered, Greece, Cyrenaica, Abyssinia, and Eritrea. Dark clouds, too, were gathering over Syria and Iraq. But on that day their first concern was for Cyrenaica, where three columns of the *Afrika Korps* sweeping across the desert threatened to cut off an entire division of the Western Desert Force.

In the confusion of a retreat accurate information is always hard to gather. Now in Cairo the air was rife with alarming rumours. Triumphant German broadcasts were claiming that six British generals had been captured in the desert. But, as yet, those rumours were unconfirmed.

Wavell faced his companions with characteristic calm. He was a man of high courage and a crisis such as the present brought out his finest qualities.

Overnight, the entire aspect of our position in the Middle East had changed. Now the full flood had turned against us. Now our main base in Egypt was in peril. Drastic decisions must be taken and taken forthwith.

There could no longer be any question of sending a second Australian division to Greece. No matter what repercussions might result in Canberra, the 7th Australian Division waiting to join General Blamey's Corps in the Aliakhmon line must now be diverted to the Western Desert.

For the time being any operation against Rhodes or the Dodecanese Islands, which the War Cabinet was urging, must be shelved.

Since there were no reserves of armour left in the whole of the Middle East, and none would be available for many weeks, a counter-attack against the enemy could not be contemplated. Nevertheless, unless Egypt was to be lost, a stand must be made against Rommel.

Where?

At Mersa Matruh? Perhaps even at El Alamein? Or further west, at Tobruk?

The Commanders-in-Chief faced one another across the conference table tensely, while Eden and Dill listened in silence. This fateful decision could only be taken by the men controlling the forces on the spot.

Longmore, denied the use of the forward airfields by the enemy's rapid advance, declared his intention of reopening those landing-grounds east of Mersa Matruh. From them he promised to operate every available aircraft in Egypt. Furthermore, he would strip the Sudan, Aden and East Africa still further of planes, and allot his reinforcements arriving by the Takeradi route either to Greece or the desert as urgency dictated, giving priority to the safety of our bases in Egypt.

Cunningham, who viewed the enemy's approach to Alexandria with growing concern, supported the proposal to hold Tobruk. In spite of his commitments, he said, he believed his ships could keep the garrison in the fortress supplied.

It was indeed a brave decision, for without it there could have been no question of holding Tobruk. Afterwards, Admiral Cunningham wrote of it:

'Had I been gifted with second sight and been able to foresee the long tale of ships lost and damaged supplying the fortress, I very much doubt if I should have been so confident in saying that it could be done.'

Supported by the Royal Navy and the Royal Air Force, Wavell determined to make a stand at Tobruk.

He had no sooner done so when the blow fell.

At half past six the following morning he was called to the telephone to be told by Harding that he feared both O'Connor and Neame had been taken prisoner. That afternoon Harding telephoned again to confirm the report that the Commander of the Western Desert Force had been captured together with Neame and Brigadier Combe. Gambier-Parry, whose car had overturned near Derna, was also a prisoner, Harding told his Commander-in-Chief. But for Wavell the greatest tragedy was the loss of O'Connor, his finest expert in desert warfare.

Yet the capture of the fiery Irishman had been touched with comedy. Together with Neame and Combe, he had left his old headquarters at Maraua for Timimi at eight o'clock on the night of April 7th. It had been an exhausting day for everyone in the Western Desert Force, but for no one more than its Commander. With Rommel close on his heals, his little army was fighting fierce rearguard actions as it retreated eastwards. Communications had broken down badly so that for hours at a time during the day he had been out of touch with his brigade commanders. The 2nd Armoured Division had taken a hammering at Mechili. So, too, had Morshead's Australians and Vaughan's 3rd Indian Motor Brigade.

Tired and angry, O'Connor urged his driver on, swearing impatiently as the car was halted by the continual traffic jams. But at Giovanni Berta, where they left the road and took to the desert track, they made better progress, and O'Connor relaxed. There was nothing more that he could do until he reached his new headquarters at Timimi, where Harding, his senior Staff Officer, would be waiting for him. Nothing except snatch a few minutes' rest.

O'Connor was half asleep when the car jolted to a standstill and a soldier in the uniform of the *Afrika Korps* flashed a torch in his face and let out a guttural cry of astonishment.

In that split second, as the German gaped at his captives, O'Connor, Neame, Combe, and their driver might have escaped. But the German was not alone, and soon the little party were surrounded by a triumphant circle of troops from Lt-Colonel Ponath's 8th machine-gun Battalion.

Only when it was too late did O'Connor realize that while he had been dozing his driver had turned north towards Derna instead of continuing east to Timimi.

Months later the story reached Egypt of how O'Connor had been conducted to Rommel's advanced headquarters. His protagonist was at breakfast with his Staff as O'Connor entered and stood glaring from one to the other of them.

'Does anyone here speak English?' he demanded.

A bespectacled little officer sprang to his feet and clicked his heels.

'I do, Herr General,' he said, bowing stiffly.

'Then damn you – for a start!' O'Connor roared.

The story is probably apocryphal. Nevertheless, the Western Desert Force dearly loved it.

As soon as he had telegraphed Churchill of his decision to hold Tobruk, Wavell flew to the fortress, taking with him General Lavarack, Commander of the 7th Australian Division, whom he placed temporarily in command of the Western Desert Force.

Arriving in a raging sandstorm, Wavell was met by General Morshead and Colonel Lloyd, his GSO1. To their great relief, he informed these officers that Tobruk was to be held. He had come, he said, to plan with them how best this could be done.

There were enough stores and ammunition to sustain a garrison of some four brigades for four months. But already in the fortress was one brigade of the 9th Australian Division which had been there since its capture in January, so that altogether at this time there were about 36,000 men on the ration strength. But since approximately a third of that total was comprised of the base units, Libyan refugees, and prisoners, they added nothing to its fighting ability.

In spite of the hard work that had been put in during March, under Neame's orders, Wavell was far from satisfied with the state of the existing defences. As a whole, they lacked depth. The anti-tank ditch was still filled with sand in places and the wire was in bad repair. But even while Wavell and his commanders studied the map of the perimeter, Rommel's advanced units were moving into Derna, a mere seventy-odd miles away.

It was late in the afternoon by the time the Commander-in-Chief, accompanied by Major Earl Amherst, of the Coldstream Guards, to whom he had offered a lift, was ready to fly back to Cairo. By then the weather was worse than ever, and as the Lockheed-Lodestar taxied to the runway through the blinding sandstorm, one of its wheel-brakes seized up.

While this was being repaired, Wavell took refuge in a nearby hut on the airstrip. There he was joined by a party of Lysander pilots who had just flown back from the battle area and were cursing the visibility that had made any sort of reconnaissance impossible. They stared in wide-eyed amazement at their distinguished guest, who was sitting quietly reading a book. Then, hospitality overcoming embarrassment, they produced a few precious bottles of warm beer.

Sitting cross-legged on the sandy floor, eye-glass in eye, and , sipping his beer, Wavell explained to his young hosts the battle being fought a few miles away. Then he climbed back into the Lockheed and took off once more. A few days later the Lysandet Squadron received a case of champagne with the Commander-in-Chief's compliments and thanks.

After barely fifteen minutes' flying, the oil-pressure gauge on one engine dropped to zero, and the pilot was forced to turn back to a landing-strip near Tobruk. The sun was setting by the time the sand had been finally cleared from the filter and the plane was airborne again. But twenty minutes later the gauge was back to zero, and the pilot informed his passengers that he would do his best to carry on with one engine. However, it was not long before the latter began overheating, and the wretched pilot, sweating with nerves, announced that he was obliged to make a forced landing. This he managed skilfully, but owing to one brake seizing up the plane took a wild swing, tipped over, and ripped off the port wing and the greater part of the tail.

Except for the feeble light of the waxing moon, it was now dark, and the pilot seemed to have but little idea where he was.

But since Wavell was convinced that the RAF would come in search of him at first light, he declared that he would remain where he was. A cup of tea, brewed up desert-fashion, he suggested, was the immediate answer to their plight. But scarcely had a fire been lit when the headlights of a car appeared over the horizon.

Was it friendly or hostile?

Since it was driving directly towards them its occupants had evidently spotted the plane and the flickering fire. The situation was fraught with danger. After a hurried conference it was decided that while Major Amherst stayed with the pilot and crew, Wavell would set off in a northerly direction alone towards the coast. If the worst happened, a warning shot fired by Amherst might possibly allow the Commander-in-Chief time to make good his escape. The hope was a slender one.

Moreover, the vulnerability of high-ranking officers was upper-most in everyone's mind.

Some fifty yards from the plane the car halted. A giant figure carrying a rifle with bayonet fixed loomed out of the darkness, and a foreign voice challenged the little party clustered round the wrecked plane. Amherst shouted back hoarsely, for his throat was dry.

Slowly, cautiously, the soldier approached, and the car followed, covering him. His face was black and his teeth gleamed white as he grinned widely at them. A Sudanese of a desert patrol!

It was after one in the morning when Wavell arrived at the headquarters of the Town Major at Sollum to be told that he was more than six hours overdue, and the GHQ Cairo had been thrown into a state of near-panic lest the man responsible for the conduct of the war in the Middle East had followed his lieutenants into 'the bag'.

Undisturbed by his adventure, Wavell left that morning for Cairo. A few days later he flew back to Mersa Matruh to supervise its defences, and then on to Greece to explain personally to General Blamey why it had been necessary to send the 7th Australian Division to the desert.

Rommel was not the only general who could be said to be everywhere at once, except at his headquarters.

CHAPTER SEVEN

No Dunkirk

'There'll be no Dunkirk here. If we should have to get out, we shall fight our way out. There is to be no surrender and no retreat.'

In those words Major-General Morshead addressed his commanders when he informed them of the decision to hold Tobruk. As a young man before the First World War, the Garrison Commander had been a schoolmaster and his austere manner was still that of the classroom rather than the barrack square and therefore the more frightening. Nicknamed by his Diggers 'Ming the Merciless', he had taken part in the landing at Gallipoli, and was only in his early twenties when he had commanded a battalion in France. When the First World War ended he had been mentioned in despatches six times and awarded the CMG, DSO and the Legion d'Honneur. Then he had gone back to his native Sydney to the offices of the Orient Line, of which he was a branch manager. But all his spare time had been devoted to soldiering, he was a natural leader of men.

Now he had brought the 9th Division back from El Agheila to within the perimeter.

The 'Benghazi-Tobruk Handicap', as the soldiers called that retreat, had been a demoralizing experience for men who had recently arrived in North

Africa. They had come there full of heart and ready to fight. Instead they were forced to run away. 'We didn't know where we were going or why,' one young subaltern said afterwards, 'but running made us afraid.'

No man knew better than Morshead the unnerving effect of such a precipitous retirement. Harried by dive-bombers, out-gunned and outmanoeuvred by an enemy they scarcely saw, short of sleep, food, and water, and often lost in the strange featureless desert, he realized how easily this retreat could have disintegrated into a rout. Although they were tough fighters, he knew that his Diggers were bewildered by so sudden a set back. At the end of those seven days when they reached Tobruk, while mercifully their casualties had been few, they were tired men whose nerves had been severely shaken.

But now, Morshead told them, there would be no more running. Their task was to hold up the enemy's advance so that precious time might be gained to assemble reinforcements for the defence of Egypt. The sea at their backs was not an escape route. It was a line of communication, likely to become only one by which they would receive the tanks, guns, and ammunition vital not only for Tobruk's defence but for aggressive action against the enemy. From the start Morshead made it plain that if Tobruk was a fortress it was also a sally-port from which constant attacks were to be made on Rommel's *Afrika Korps*.

All this was just what the troops wanted to hear and, heartened by the news, they went to work on the strengthening of the defences with a will. There was so much to be done and yet so little time in which to do it.

On the morning of April 9th, Lavarack with Morshead and the brigade commanders made a rapid reconnaissance of the positions. The decision was taken that, until the whole defence system could be put in order and greatly increased in depth, an all-out effort must be made to improve and repair the old Italian perimeter. There, at least, were the series of concrete posts, the barbed-wire, the anti-tank ditch such as it was and what remained of the Italian minefields after many of the mines had been lifted or 'deloused' during the January assault.

For the immediately emergency the perimeter was manned by seven of the garrison's thirteen infantry battalions, each with a reserve company in support dug in about half a mile in the rear. With each company holding a front of more than a mile, Morshead had every reason to warn their commanders to expect penetrations. Nevertheless, every post was to be held to the last man and each foot of ground fought for.

Later, this defence system was greatly strengthened, and became known as the 'Red line'. Two miles behind it the garrison constructed a second defence system, the 'Blue Line'. This was composed of a continuous minefield covered by barbed-wire and the fire from anti-tank and machine guns dug into well wired and mined strongpoints. As the siege went on, so were these positions made stronger, and the area between the Red and the Blue so thickly sown with mines that the sappers themselves could no longer keep track of them.

But it was many months before this formidable defence system was finally completed, and at the beginning of April the fate of the fortress depended upon the cold courage of its troops rather than the strength of its defences. The garrison's armour at the outset consisted of a regiment of armoured cars, four 'I' tanks, twenty-six cruisers, and fifteen light tanks; these last being useless in an armoured battle. It possessed no medium artillery except a few captured Italian guns. Its field artillery was made up of three 25-pounder regiments from Cyrenaica, and one fresh from Egypt. In addition to these there were two anti-tank regiments, one Australian and the other British, both of which were a battery short. The harbour area was defended by an anti-aircraft brigade with sixteen heavy and fifty-nine light guns.

For two days while the stifling Khamsin lashed the surface of the desert into a raging sandstorm, wearing anti-gas goggles and with handkerchiefs over their mouths, the men of the garrison laboured ceaselessly, preparing the perimeter defences. Day and night the sappers laid minefields, infantry wrestled with rusting barbed-wire and hurled the sand from the concrete posts and the crumbling anti-tank ditch; gunners dug in their 25-pounders, the signallers unwound their miles of wire as they linked the posts one to another. Through the fog of driving sand, thicker than a London 'pea-souper', struggled the trucks carrying the ammunition and rations up the rocky escarpment to the gun-sites and forward positions.

Blinded, choking, their sweating half-naked bodies coated with sand, these men had no time to reflect that the very wind they cursed was their staunchest ally. For out in the desert its fury had brought Rommel's armour to a grinding halt and had pinned down his dive-bombers on their airstrips. Under cover of the storm the survivors of the 3rd Australian anti-tank Regiment, the 3rd Indian Motor Brigade and the 3rd Royal Horse

Artillery, who had escaped from the hell of Mechili, where they had suffered a hundred casualties, straggled into the perimeter bringing with them some forty guns to strengthen the lean defences.

For two days the sandstorm blotted out the sun, filling the water-cans and the dixies, driving into the shallow dugouts and through blankets and ground-sheets. Then, at about noon on April 10th, the storm abated and the dust cleared. The men in the advanced posts on the western end of the perimeter saw the enemy's tanks and trucks coming down the road from Derna. This was the signal for the sappers to blow the bridge over the road and for a battery of captured Italian 75s and 105s, manned by Australian infantrymen, to fire the first rounds in the garrison's defence.

By the morning of April 10th, Rommel had informed his Staff that the British force in the desert was but a rabble on the run, and had blandly announced that his next objective was the Suez Canal. At the same time he said that on no account must the British be allowed to break out of Tobruk.

On the following day the fortress was surrounded, but not precisely as he had planned, for, owing to the storm and a shortage of fuel, the *Afrika Korps*, which he had driven so relentlessly forward, was widely scattered. General Streich's 5th Division was already well to the east. Prittwitz's Group, its General dead and now commanded by Colonel Schwerin, came up from the south, while the Brescia Division was still to the west of the fortress.

Rommel ordered the 3rd Reconnaissance Unit on to Bardia, and having rounded up a mixed force with Lt-Colonel Knabe in command, sent it racing to Sollum, with orders to press on to Mersa Matruh.

While these units headed east to engage General Gott's Mobile Force, the 5th Panzer Regiment prepared to attack Tobruk. On Good Friday afternoon the first reconnaissance was sent out against the southern sector of the perimeter, held by the 20th Australian Infantry Brigade, commanded by Brigadier John Murray. Two of its battalions were spread out east and west of the El Adem road over a front of roughly ten miles, with a third battalion in reserve. All three were sadly short of arms, particularly the forward troops, who were without any anti-tank guns.

At first, as if contemptuous of the garrison's defences, the Germans sent forward a battalion of infantry. This was immediately pinned down by our artillery fire and was unable to move until joined by tanks. As soon as these appeared our gunners increased their fire. Again the infantry halted, but the tanks came on. Some seventy of them, including a number of heavy German Mark IVs armed with 75-mm guns, rolled right up to the anti-tank ditch, pouring shells into the Australian forward posts.

These tanks, supported by Italian M13s and light tanks, turning east, made their way along the perimeter, shelling each post in turn. But near the El Adem road they came under fire from two Italian 47-mm anti-tank guns, manned by a mortar platoon. One M13 was knocked out and others damaged, while the rest retreated south. At the same time an Italian light tank was put out of action by concentrated small-arms fire, at the junction of the El Adem road and the perimeter, and its crew taken prisoners.

The last enemy tanks probing the defences that afternoon were heavily engaged by eleven cruisers of the 1st Royal Tank Regiment. In a battle lasting about half an hour the latter accounted for a German Mark IV, while the artillery knocked out another. Altogether, the attackers lost seven tanks as against two of the garrison's.

That night in the moonlight more tanks came nosing up to the ditch searching for a crossing. They were followed by pioneers, with their tools and Bangalore torpedoes, whose task it was to blow up the wire and bridge the ditch. But they failed to find a likely spot and retired.

Throughout the next day the Germans continued their reconnaissances, but no attack developed since their tank and transport concentrations were bombed by the RAF and heavily shelled by the gunners.

Meanwhile, enemy dive-bombers, escorted by fighters, attacked the harbour, and were set upon by the six remaining Hurricanes from No. 75 Squadron and met by a fierce barrage from the heavy ack-ack batteries. Three *Stukas* were shot down.

As well as bombs, the raiders showered leaflets over the fortress. They read:

> 'The General Officer Commanding the German forces in Libya requests that the British troops occupying Tobruk surrender their arms. Single soldiers waving white handkerchiefs are not fired on. Strong German forces have already surrounded Tobruk and it is useless to try to escape. Remember Mechili. Our dive-bombers and *Stukas* are waiting for your ships which are lying in the harbour.'

This request, which delighted the garrison since it possessed no white handkerchiefs, was not only a clear indication of how badly Rommel had underestimated the morale of the defenders, but also that he had taken it for granted that the garrison was to be evacuated by sea. He was both surprised and angered by what had happened to his reconnaissance units, for he had expected a 'walk-over'. Furthermore, his Panzer troops had been shaken by the weight of our artillery fire, and already some of their arrogance had been knocked out of them by their first sight of the Australians' bayonets. Such weapons they had been taught were altogether outmoded.

CHAPTER EIGHT

Enter Some 'A' Lighters

On Easter Sunday morning, the anti-aircraft gunners at Tobruk, snatching a few hours' sleep after a long night's battle against the *Luftwaffe*, were suddenly awakened by the throb of petrol engines. Jumping from their bunks beside the gun-pits, they automatically searched the clear blue sky. But no planes were to be seen.

Then their sensitive ears picked up the direction of the sound, and looking to the eastward, across the harbour to the swept channel, they saw five strange craft steaming in line ahead led by a trawler and escorted by a small anti-aircraft sloop. The gunners rubbed their red-rimmed eyes and looked again.

What were they?

One, more sleepy than the rest, announced that they were 'five subs on the surface'. Another, who had a brother in the Navy, stated firmly that they were 'MTBs of sorts'. Their NCO said they were both wrong. But it was generally agreed that no one had ever seen anything like these vessels before.

The Aussies, having their morning swim in Anzac Cove, heard the throb of the motors too. Standing naked on the rocks, they shaded their eyes against the sun and stared.

'For –'s sake, what are they?'

No one knew the answer.

Indeed, there were not more than a dozen men in Tobruk who did know the answer. And a good percentage of that knowledgeable few was amongst the group of senior Naval and Army officers gathered outside Navy House watching the little procession making its way through the booms. Some of them, perhaps, even knew that they were seeing history made. But the chances were that they were all too delighted and relieved at the safe arrival of the craft and their escorts to realize it.

But, in fact, the vessels they were watching were Tank Landing Craft, and on that Easter morning in 1941 they were making their debut in the war.

Later, much later, they were to form the spearhead of our invasion of Europe; first at Sicily, Salerno, and Anzio, and then across the Channel to the Normandy beaches. But these five TLCs were the prototypes of all those hundreds of others building and yet to be built and they were arriving at Tobruk loaded with 'I' tanks, 25-pounders, Bren-carriers, and ammunition at a moment when those weapons were so desperately needed.

Eighteen tank landing craft (Mark I) had been shipped out to the Middle East in sections, bolted to the decks of merchant ships, and had arrived at Suez early in the New Year. Riveted together in the Suez Canal Company's yards at Port Tewfik and Port Fuad, they were intended to take part in the capture of Rhodes and the Dodecanese. But Fate had decreed otherwise. For during their convoy's long voyage round the Cape the situation in the Middle East had undergone a change.

Nevertheless, these craft came as mana from heaven to Admiral Cunningham, who gave orders that they were to be made ready for sea with every possible speed. 160 feet in length and powered by two 650-hp Hall-Scott petrol engines, the TLCs could carry five tanks in their holds, and were designed to beach and land their cargoes over the ramps forming their huge square bows. Although practically unsinkable because of their buoyancy tanks, they were clumsy, miserable sea-boats, and in any kind of weather their speed was reduced to a few knots. The accommodation for the two officers and crew of twelve was comfortless, and in the heat of the North African summer their little messdeck aft, measuring twelve feet by fifteen, was uninhabitable. But by far the most unpleasant features of those first landing craft were their twin petrol engines. Because of them, beneath their decks they carried 8,000 gallons of 87-octane petrol. These, when added to the leaking cased petrol, land-mines, tanks, and ammunition often crammed into their holds, formed, to say the least, a dangerous cargo with which to run the gauntlet of the *Stukas* along 'bomb alley' of Sollum and Bardia. Moreover, the noise of the engines, whose exhausts were carried up the squat funnel directly aft of the bridge, made it impossible to hear the approach of aircraft. so that from dawn till dusk the lookouts were ever on the alert, staring into the sun.

The crafts' only armament were two pom-poms mounted on either wing of the bridge. But as the battle against the *Luftwaffe* intensified, their crews acquired by devious and dubious methods an arsenal of Italian machine guns and small arms.

For reasons of security the TLCs in the Eastern Mediterranean at that time were dubbed 'A' lighters, and along their ugly slab-sided hulls were painted the large black letters WDLF, which, being interpreted, meant Western Desert Lighter Flotilla. But it was not long before their crews insisted that these initials stood for the grim slogan: 'We die Like Flies'.

The five 'A' lighters which arrived at Tobruk on Easter Sunday had loaded their cargoes at Alexandria in a matter of hours, and then sailed west escorted by the anti-aircraft sloop *Auckland* and the A/S Trawler *Southern Maid*.

Some thirty-six hours later they made the entrance of the swept channel leading to Tobruk harbour.

At this point it is necessary to pause briefly, for it was precisely at this point that my own life in the war became intimately involved with that of the fortress.

Having wearied of the monotony of minesweeping, I had volunteered for Combined Operations in October, 1940. Shortly before Christmas, I had sailed for the Middle East with the first flotilla of tank landing craft, and so came to be aboard A5 when we arrived off Tobruk on that Easter morning.

Contrary to all the rules and regulations of the Royal Navy, I kept a diary throughout the war. I wrote it at odd times and in odder places. Sitting on the bridges of minesweepers and landing craft at sea, alongside the jetty at Dunkirk, on a mountain top in Greece with the *Stukas* flying overhead, in hotel bedrooms in Alexandria, Port Said, and Famagusta, and in Navy House at Tobruk.

Fortuitously, the stout volumes, battered and dog-eared, survived the war, and from now on I shall quote from them. I have firmly resisted the temptation to edit them, lest whilst endeavouring to improve their English I destroyed their originality.

I described our first meeting with Tobruk as follows:

'April 13th, ominous date!

Our arrival off the entrance of the swept channel synchronized with the start of a terrific airraid. The sky was criss-crossed with streams of tracer and the saw-edged hills were silhouetted against the flashes of the ack ack guns and exploding bombs. Southern Maid signalled us all to stop, and then, as we lay there wondering what would happen next, the entire sky was suddenly bathed in the lurid tight of a great string of parachute flares. It was flat calm, and those bloody flares seemed to hang suspended above us like arc-lights!

Lying there with our engines stopped, above the racket of the batteries ashore we could hear the drone of the bombers. They sounded as if they were circling round right overhead. There we were, six sitting ducks! But by some miracle they didn't see us, and having plastered the landscape with bombs which started several huge fires, they cleared off.

Southern Maid led us all back out to sea, one supposed awaiting 'further instructions'. Just after dawn the planes were back again giving Tobruk another blasting and it wasn't until about eleven o'clock that we finally headed for the harbour feeling none too happy since it was fairly obvious by then that the Jerries must have spotted us.

As we came through the boom and caught our first sight of Tobruk, the sailors and our pongo passengers were all hanging over the side like trippers aboard a pleasure-steamer. Having stared at the wrecks littering the harbour and the bomb-shattered buildings, one of the sailors summed up the place pretty apty by remarking: 'Why the 'ell we wants to 'ang on to it beats me!'

There were wrecks everywhere; some half-rising out of the water like dying sea-monsters whose lungs had burst; others, beached, burnt-out and rusting; still others on the bottom, but plainly visible in the crystal-clear water. The little coves and bays around the harbour all seemed filled with floating wreckage and refuse covered in a glistening coat of black oil. Ashore, there wasn't a tree to be seen, or a green thing growing. The entire landscape was yellow-brown, except for the white houses, most of which appeared to have been blasted by bombs or torn apart by the fifteen inch 'bricks' our Fleet had burled at them during the bombardments in December and January yet, somehow, the blinding sunlight accentuated the fearful devastation. What's more, you could smell Tobruk as soon as you entered the harbour. An indescribable smell that was a mixture of burnt cordite, crude oil, drains, and I don't quite know what, unless it was sweat! The sweat of thousands of men who were rationed to half a gallon of water a head per day for all purposes. I wasn't certain about this until I got ashore, then I had no more doubts!

By the time we had nosed our way into the beach and lowered our ramp at the north-east corner of the harbour quite a crowd had gathered: 'Aussies' wearing nothing except slouch hats, ragged shorts and laceless boots, Libyans in tattered galabeyahs, a few sailors and a crowd of British soldiers, all of them sweating like pigs and covered with a coating of yellowish-grey dust. They swarmed aboard over the ramp like bees and some of the Libyans came within inches of being flattened out by the tanks as they trundled ashore.

It didn't dawn on me for a few minutes that this was an organized mob working like beavers to unload us as quickly as possible. Then I spotted the organizer – an elderly Lieutenant, who, although he was wearing a bush shirt and shorts, still managed to look every inch a cavalry officer. He introduced himself as O'Shaughnessy and in a rich brogue told me that he was the Chief Movement Control Officer in charge of the 'bloody rabble' on the quay. He took me into his office in a little white house without windows and pitted with bomb splinters. From a safe in the corner of the room he produced a bottle of Italian brandy and some delicious mineral water, called Recoaro. Pouring out a couple of stiff pegs, he handed me a glass, and raised his.

"Here's to your safe arrival," he said.

I told him that at one time I didn't think we'd make it as I was sure the Jerries had spotted us.

"They probably did. Hence the bloody rush!" he laughed.

Then back he went to the quay to curse his sweating troops to more vigorous efforts, while I climbed up the steep flight of steps to Navy House to make my number.

At Navy House I was introduced to 'Plonk' for the first time; a fearful concoction of Italian brandy and rum, a nice cooling tipple at high noon in North Africa! Then, since I hadn't to meet Peter Hutton[1] for half an hour, I took a walk round the town. Heaven knows, there wasn't much to see except battered, windowless white stucco villas, which could have had little charm even before the bombers got at them.

Wandering through the rubble, I found the Church of St Francis and walked into it. Long shafts of sunshine played through the holes in the roof, spotlighting the dusty altar, the overturned confessional box, smashed pews and broken statues. Just nearby I came across a small grotto, quite undamaged. In it was a statue of Our Lady and among the rocks at Her feet a china vase filled with flowers!

An 'Aussie' was kneeling in front of the grotto saying his rosary. I joined him and briefly thanked God for our safe arrival and put in a word or two for all of us for the future. It was a strange experience kneeling there in the dust surrounded by all the bombed houses and saying one's prayers to the accompaniment of the distant gunfire of the battle going on beyond the escarpment…

Back at Navy House over a plate of bully-beef, Peter told me we were bound for Suda Bay, in Crete, adding that he didn't know why. We were sailing just after sunset, and in the meantime were to fill up with fuel from a tanker in the harbour, going alongside her two at a time. To say the least of it, this struck me as a rash operation with the Jerry planes in the offing. However, it wasn't my job to argue the toss…

The Jerries came back! At about two o'clock I was down on the quay talking to Lieutenant O'Shaughnessy, when he glanced at his watch and said; "They're late today. They're always here by two." He seemed quite put out.

Seconds later, the ack-ack batteries opened up and the sky was patterned with little white balls of smoke. Then we spotted the planes. Thirty Ju 88s diving down out of the sun and weaving all over the shop, dodging the barrage.

One of them seemed to be heading straight for us, but O'Shaughnessy insisted we hold our ground.

"It doesn't look well to run," he said calmly.

Spellbound; I watched a very large bomb leave the plane's belly, and remarked that it looked like landing uncomfortably close to us. O'Shaughnessy disagreed. But as the bomb grew louder and larger and we saw the sunlight glinting on it, he changed his mind, and together we dived under a truck.

The bomb landed right in the middle of a building used as some sort of Army HQ and went off with a bang that shook the ground under us.

[1]Lt.-Commander. Peter Coates Hutton, DSC, RN, Flotilla Officer to the 1st TLC Flotilla.

Stones and flying debris fell like hail around us and the dust half-choked us. But we picked ourselves up just in time to see the bomber plunge into the harbour like a diving gannet. We stood waving our caps and cheering wildly like a couple of kids at a football match, but it made us feel braver.

The Jerries made a dead-set at the tanker alongside which two of the landing craft were fuelling and twice the little huddle of craft disappeared behind the great plumes of water thrown up by the sticks of bombs. I was certain they had bought it. But when the water subsided they were still there. One of them was badly shaken up.

They went for Auckland too, but she put up such a barrage that their bombs fell wide.

The raid was over in a matter of minutes. But in that brief space of time one merchant ship was sunk in the harbour and another alongside the quay set on fire. The gunners shot down seven planes.

When it was over, there was a mad rush to get the merchantman clear of the quay – the only quay – before she sank. The RAMC started collecting the dead and the wounded from the quay. Everyone seemed to know their job in Tobruk.

That evening as the sun went down behind the escarpment we were glad to leave for Crete – even though we had no idea what would happen to us when we got there…'

None of the five craft and but few of their crews ever returned to Alexandria. One of them, with Peter Hutton on board, was lost with all hands. But that is another story.

CHAPTER NINE

Night Attack

The wind that had whipped up the dust-clouds throughout the day had died with the sun. The night was still and the deep blue dome of the sky above the escarpment was bright with stars. The air was cold, and the men in their forward posts sat huddled with their greatcoats over their shoulders watching the young moon rise.

Except for the occasional stutter of a machine-gun, the line was quiet. Too quiet, for all day behind a veil of dust the Australians had watched the enemy's transports. Staff cars, and motorcycles darting about the desert. In the late afternoon German tanks followed by bunches of infantry had moved up towards the perimeter again, but were driven off by our artillery.

Now, the quiet was charged with tension; a tension that caused the men in the forward posts to talk in whispers, nervously fingering the triggers of their rifles and machine-guns. They had been warned to expect an attack that night. But when and where? Sitting waiting for it in the flea-ridden posts behind the rusting wire played hell with a man's nerves…

The mortar barrage which opened up at ten o'clock came almost as a relief to the waiting men, for they knew it was the overture to the night attack. For an hour they crouched in their posts while the mortar shells burst amongst the tangle of barbed wire in front of them and the machine-gun bullets ripped into the sandbags along the parapet. Then, as suddenly as it had started, the barrage stopped.

In Post 33, just west of the El Adem road, Lieutenant Mackell, the platoon commander, looked at his watch. The time was eleven o'clock. Beside him, Corporal Jack Edmonston, a sheep-farmer's son from New South Wales, peered into the darkness and the thinning dust cloud. He gave a low whistle.

'Jerries! A whole heap of the – s!'

Mackell's eyes followed the corporal's pointing finger. Vaguely he could see the Germans moving through a gap in the wire to the east of his post; twenty or thirty of them.

'Let 'em have it!'

As the machine-guns opened up, to Mackel's astonishment the Germans replied with mortars and light field-guns, plastering the post with shells.

Dug in about a hundred yards away, it was obvious that the Germans were determined to cover a bridgehead through which their tanks could pass. It was equally obvious that they could not be driven out by small-arms fire.

By midnight the situation was fraught with danger, and it began to look as if the line had been breached and that soon the enemy armour would come rolling through the gap.

Mackell decided to drive them out with bayonets and grenades.

With Edmonston and five others, covered by the fire from the post, he sprinted into the darkness, running in a wide semi-circle so as to approach the Germans from their flank. But almost immediately the enemy spotted them and turned all their guns on them, forcing them to go to ground.

A second dash brought the little party to within fifty yards of their objective. Once again they threw themselves down, and as they lay there panting they pulled the pins from their grenades. Then, with a wild yell, which was taken up by their comrades in the post, they charged. For a few terrible minutes the seven men came under a deluge of fire. Edmonston took the full blast of a machine-gun in his belly just as he hurled his grenade into the midst of its crew. Another bullet hit him in the throat. But he kept on running and, having thrown his second grenade, he went in amongst the Germans with his bayonet.

In a panic of terror they bolted out of their ditch, running blindly into the wire, to hang there screaming as their attackers bayoneted them.

Soon young Mackell was in difficulties, for as he fought with one German on the ground another came for him with a pistol. He yelled to Edmonston for help. With blood pouring from his throat, the Corporal dashed to his rescue, killing both Germans with his bayonet. In the hand-to-hand fighting which followed, Mackell, having broken his bayonet in a German's chest, clubbed another to death with his rifle-butt, while Edmonston and the five others killed a dozen more. The Corporal went on fighting until the last of the enemy had fled, abandoning their weapons. Then he collapsed, and the others carried him back to the post, where he died soon after dawn. He was awarded the Victoria Cross.

All through the night the battle went on. Although young Mackell's charge had routed the enemy's advance guard, by two in the morning the Germans had established a bridgehead several hundred yards inside the wire. In spite of being heavily shelled by two regiments of the Royal Horse Artillery, they held their ground.

Just after dawn, the first German tanks moved through the gap. By a prearranged plan the forward troops made no attempt to stop them, but lay in wait for the infantry. By 5.45 a.m. some thirty-eight tanks of the 5th Tank Regiment's and Battalion, which had made a name for itself in Poland and France, formed up for attack nearly a mile inside the perimeter wire. At the same time the 1st Battalion's tanks were moving up in the wake of the anti-tank and field-guns and infantry. Indeed, the attack was taking on the familiar pattern of all those other German attacks which had proved so invincible in Europe.

But this time the Panzer troops were in for a rude shock, for without suspecting it they had rolled into a trap. Ahead of them were the 25-pounders of the 1st RHA and the anti-tank guns of the 3rd Australian Regiment. To their left were the mobile anti-tank guns of the 3rd RHA, and to the right more mobile guns of the same regiment, as well as tanks of the 1st Royal Tank Regiment dug in, in hull-down positions.

The Germans first came under fire from the 25-pounders, sited just inside what were later to become the Blue Line defences. Our gunners engaged them over open sights at a range of less than 600 yards with devastating effect, one heavy tank having its armoured turret blown sky-high.

Altogether seven tanks were knocked out before the remainder disengaged and turned eastward in an attempt to outflank the batteries. Immediately they came under fire from the guns of the 3rd Australian anti-tank Regiment and suffered further casualties.

Baffled and battered, the Germans retired. But as they did so they were heavily shelled from both sides by the mobile guns of the RHA, mounted on 30-cwt. trucks, as well as the cruiser tanks.

At 7a.m. the Germans rallied for a further attack against the thin defences of the Blue Line, but were again driven off, for without their anti-tank and field-guns and the 8th machine gun Battalion they had no support. In fact, these units were still struggling to get beyond the gap. To their confusion, they were being savagely mauled by the Australian infantry, whom they had expected to surrender as soon as the tanks had broken through. Indeed, they had even called on the Australians to throw down their arms. But the Diggers answered them with everything they had got and bayoneted those who took refuge in the anti-tank ditch from the hail of small-arms fire. where before dawn some of the 8th machine-gun Battalion had established themselves in a ruined building. Early in the morning, Colonel Crawford, commanding the 2/17th Battalion of the 20th Australian Brigade, sent two platoons forward to clear the house. One section went in with bayonets and grenades, while the others gave them covering fire. The Germans returned their fire until the grenades started bursting amongst them and they saw the glint of the Australians' bayonets. Then half of them surrendered. The rest were already dead.

It was because of this and similar infantry operations that after daylight on the 14th no guns or infantry were able to break through to support the tanks. By seven-thirty that morning what was left of the German armour was fighting desperately to escape through the gap in the wire. Soon this retreat became a rout, as the tanks, gunners and infantry, in a swirling cloud of dust and smoke from burning tanks, fled for their lives. Into this rabble the defenders fired every weapon they possessed: 25-pounders, mortars, anti-tank guns, Brens, and rifles.

A captured Panzer officer described this ghastly shambles as 'a witches' cauldron'.

For many hours after the main battle had ended the mopping-up operations went on, and it was not until noon that the last of the enemy were rounded up. Some 250 dazed and bewildered Germans, many of them weeping with shame at their defeat, were marched back to the prisoner-of-war cage.

They referred to that Easter battle as 'the Hell of Tobruk', admitting that nothing like it had happened to them before.

'In Poland, Belgium, and France when our tanks broke through the soldiers gave in. They knew they were beaten. But at Tobruk you went on fighting,' they said, 'and fighting like devils out of hell!'

So certain had they been of success that some units – amongst them the 8th machine-gun Regiment – had advanced with their administration trucks ready to set up the headquarters in Tobruk. Undoubtedly, their repulse came as a great shock to those proud Panzer troops, and their morale was severely shaken. They had been assured that the garrison would surrender, Instead, the defenders had steadfastly held their ground, and to them must go the honour of winning the first battle against the Germans in the war.

After this setback, Rommel gave up any further attempts against the southern sector. Two days later, he personally directed an attack from the west, employing troops from the Ariete Division and the 62nd Infantry Regiment of the Trento Division. But, although urged on by German tanks, the Italians had little heart for their task and when the Australians counter-attacked they surrendered in their hundreds, advancing towards our lines waving white handkerchiefs.

Thus ended the opening rounds of Rommel's battle for Tobruk. But, while the enemy still staggered under these first severe blows. General Morshead sent out small patrols and sorties against them. One of these was carried out by a company from the 2/48th Battalion, supported by three 'L' tanks and a troop of the RHA It attacked a hill in the Ras el Medauar area, known as Hill 209, with the object of destroying a battery installed behind it. The objective was reached, two guns were knocked out, and 570 Italian prisoners taken. At the same time a company of 2/23rd Battalion carried out a raid across the Derna road, which resulted in savage fighting and heavy casualties. But the Australians brought back another 100 Italian prisoners.

These sorties so disturbed Rommel that he sent urgent signals to hasten the arrival of the 15th Panzer Division. He was, however, not the only one who viewed the situation outside Tobruk with concern. For the Italian *Comando Supremo* had sent a despatch to the OKW asking for the latter's agreement to call a halt to the advance into Egypt. Time was needed for the attacking force to be reorganized and for its badly strained supply line to be given a chance to recover.

General Halder, Chief of the General Staff, OKH, wrote in his diary that he was disturbed by the news from North Africa.

'Rommel,' he recorded angrily, has not sent in a single clear report, and I have a feeling that things are in a mess... All day long he rushes about between his wildy scattered units and stages reconnaissance raids in which he fritters away his strength... piecemeal thrusts of weak armoured forces have been costly... His motor vehicles are in poor condition and many of his tank engines need replacing... Air transport cannot meet his sensless demands, primarily because of lack of fuel... It is essential to have this situation cleared up without delay...'

To this end the OKW decided to send General Paulus, a Deputy Chief of the General Staff, to North Africa, whom Halder believed to be 'perhaps the only man with enough influence to head off this soldier gone stark mad'.

CHAPTER TEN

ATTACK AND COUNTER ATTACK

General Paulus arrived at Rommel's headquarters to find the stage set for a further assault against Tobruk. It was planned for April 30th. He withheld his permission for two days until he had discussed the situation with General Gariboldi. In the meantime he made it clear to Rommel that there was to be no more high-falutin' talk about Suez being the next objective. Thanks to 'Barbarossa', the OKH had no resources from which to supply any more troops or weapons to the Afrika Korps. That force's task was now to take Tobruk and if, and when, the fortress fell, to secure Cyrenaica by holding a line from Siwa to Sollum. Having given his impetuous junior time to reflect upon all this, Paulus then sanctioned the plans for the attack on Tobruk.

For this venture Rommel rushed up units of the 15th Panzer Division, amongst them the 104th Regiment, which had only arrived in North Africa twenty-four hours before. He also rid himself of General Streich, who had failed in the Easter attacks, replacing him by General Kirchheim, whom he summoned straight from a hospital bed in Tripoli to the front, to take over the command of the 5th Light Division.

The new attack was to be launched in the south-west in the environs of Ras el Medauar. Rommel's plan was that at 8 p.m. on the night of

April 30th, two German divisions, the 15th on the left and the 5th on the right, should make the breakthrough. Assault groups of the Ariete and Brescia Divisions would then advance through the breach to roll back the enemy's defences on both flanks. While this was being done, German troops pushing forward east would make reconnaissances to discover whether a main thrust could be made to the harbour. If this could be done, the flanks would then be held by the Italians, and the Panzer troops would attack again on the following morning.

At the section of the perimeter chosen, the line bulged in a salient. The twenty-two concrete posts to the north and south of Hill 209 were held by three companies of the 2nd Battalion of the 24th Australian Infantry Brigade, with a further company in reserve, approximately a mile east of the hill. On its left the 2/24th had the 2/15th, and on its right the 2/23rd. Behind them in the Blue Line was the 2/48th, supported by the 51st British Field Regiment, the Northumberland Fusiliers, with Vickers guns, and the anti-tank guns of the 3rd RHA and the 24th and 26th Australian anti-tank Companies.

During the lull between the attacks, the garrison had worked night and day strengthening the defences, and fortuitously had laid minefields between the Blue and the Red Lines in the south-western sector.

In addition to the 'I' tanks. 25-pounders, and Bren-carriers landed by the five 'A' lighters on the 13th, the Royal Navy had brought up during the past few weeks some 5,000-tons of valuable stores to the fortress. This had been done despite the incessant bombing of the harbour and the supply route, and with the loss of two valuable little passenger ships from India, commissioned by the Royal Navy, HMS *Fiona* and HMS *Chakla*. Commanded by RNR officers and with part-Indian crews, both these ships had been on the 'spud Run' since the capture of Tobruk. *Fiona* was sunk by dive-bombers off Sidi Barrani on April 18th and *Chakla* was bombed in the harbour itself in one of the heavy raids on April 29th which preluded Rommel's attack. Her loss was a warning to Admiral Cunningham not only of the increasing difficulties of running supplies into Tobruk, but also of the danger of using the harbour during the daylight hours, now that the enemy possessed all the airfields in the neighbourhood.

For the past two weeks the troops in the south-western salient had watched the dust-clouds rising between Acroma and Hill 209 as the enemy's lorry-loads of infantry, tanks and guns assembled some two miles beyond the perimeter. But on the morning of April 30th the dust-clouds thickened, and then in the afternoon the posts were heavily shelled and out of the red sunset a score of *Stukas* came screaming down to bomb and machine-gun the forward positions. Their ammunition expended, they turned away, to be followed by yet another formation which hurled its bombs on the barbed wire and the infantry positions around Hill 209. Then, as the last *Stuka* headed for home, its magazines empty, the Germans laid down a deadly barrage of artillery fire on the same positions and under cover of the dust and growing darkness, the 2nd machine-gun Battalion and sappers of the 33rd Panzer Pioneers raced forward to render safe the mines and blast gaps in the wire to the left and right of the hill.

The men in the forward posts had been so heavily bombed and shelled that they were unable to prevent the German penetrations between their widely dispersed posts or to stop them setting up machine-gun nests in their rear. Moreover, as a result of the bombing, the signal lines linking the company holding the hill with their HQ had been cut, so that their Commanding Officer, Lt-Colonel Spowers was without news of them.

Again and again he sent out runners and signalmen to try to make contact with the company through a curtain of machine-gun fire. Some failed to get through, others to get back. So concentrated was the enemy's fire that one signalman took four and a half hours crawling on his belly to cover the mile and a quarter between his company's post and the Battalion HQ mending the wire as he went. In the confusion, patrols got lost in their own minefields, and just before dawn the reserve company, a mile to the rear, reported enemy tanks and infantry to the east of the hill.

When daylight came a thick ground mist shrouded the desert. and since no one seemed to know where the Germans were, Colonel Spowers did not dare order the artillery to shell the hill. At eight o'clock, when the mist cleared, the situation was even worse than had been feared. The Germans had not only established themselves a bridgehead a mile and a half wide, but had overrun seven of the advanced posts around Hill 209, killing or taking prisoner the men holding them.

Soon after seven-thirty the German tanks which were to thrust eastwards to the harbour began forming up on the hill.

But because they were still without information our gunners left them alone. Heading east, forty tanks came straight for the 2/24th's reserve company's positions, blazing at them with cannons and machine guns. But near the Acroma road the first flight met the fire of the 24th Australian anti-tank Company, commanded by Captain Norman. One gun managed to knock out and set on fire a Mark III before it was itself set upon by eleven tanks and its crew all wounded. Two other guns were also silenced, and the tanks swept forward to within a few yards of the reserve company's positions where they ran into a minefield.

In a matter of minutes, seventeen tanks were brought to a standstill most of them with shattered tracks. But although they were sitting targets, all our anti-tank guns within range had been put out of action. Nor did the field-gunners dare to shell them heavily for fear of detonating our own mines and thus clearing a passage for the enemy.

However, after their initial setback the Germans made no further effort to penetrate the minefield, but turned away to the south.

By early that morning both Rommel's tank thrusts had failed. But he still had large reserves, and our reconnaissance aircraft reported a force of some 200 tanks in and around Acroma and Hill 209. Against this force all General Morshead could muster was twelve 'I' tanks and nineteen cruisers. So heavily out-numbered, his only chance was to hold his armour in reserve and rely upon his artillery and the minefields to reduce the enemy's strength. In fact, at this stage Morshead was in a dilemma so far as his tanks were concerned. He has been criticized for using his armour in 'penny packets' rather than in strength. But this is an injustice. His air reconnaissance was, to say the best of it, scrappy, and so he had no means of foreseeing from which direction Rommel's next thrust would come. Thus, in order to cope with the unexpected, he was obliged to keep some of his pitifully small force in reserve.

Even as it was, he took risks. On the afternoon of May 1st, for instance, he sent out a small force, consisting of five 'I' tanks and three cruisers, for the purpose of regaining control of the forward posts. This force was repeatedly attacked by superior numbers of German tanks. First, it came up against fifteen of them. Immediately a 'I' tank received a direct hit which killed all its crew except the driver, although the tank itself was not destroyed. As the seven others struggled to withedraw, they were set upon by another batch of fourteen Germans, and a further 'I' tank was knocked out and one of the cruisers badly damaged. In these two encounters the Germans lost four tanks. Neverthless, Morshead can hardly be blamed for holding his little force in reserve and depending upon his artillery, as indeed he had done with such marked success in the Easter battle. But Rommel was aware of these tactics and time and again he sent waves of *Stukas* to dive-bomb and machine-gun our gun-sites. But since they were well dug in, he failed to silence them, and before the battle was over they played havoc with his armour.

Although the defenders could not know it, by the end of the first day's fighting General Paulus had advised Rommel to abandon any further attempts to capture Tobruk and to be content with holding Hill 209 and the positions around it. And so, by the night of May 1st, the battle had resolved itself into a struggle for this hill. It was, from then on, a battle of attack and counter-attack, in which both sides fought doggedly, neither gaining nor giving ground.

Throughout May and in a thick sandstorm, the Germans fought desperately to hold the posts they had captured, suffering severe casualties in both men and tanks. On the night of May 3rd, General Morshead threw in his reserve brigade, the 18th in an attempt to retake Hill 209. The attack was planned as a converging one by two battalions. But as they assembled the Australians were so heavily shelled from the hill that zero hour had to be put forward until just before nine o'clock at night In the darkness, the attack quickly became a series of hand-to-hand skirmishes and individual bayonet raids on the enemy's strongpoints.

Typical of the night's fighting was an incident on the Acroma road when some Australians of the 2/9th, led by Lieutenant W H Noyes, saw three Italian tanks approaching. With Sergeant Hobson and three men, be crept on to the tanks and, lifting their hatches, dropped hand grenades inside, blowing them up,

In the early hours of the morning General Morshead called off the attack, since he did not wish his troops to be caught in the open after daylight.

Thus ended the second major battle for Tobruk. As a result of it, Rommel's troops had penetrated the perimeter defences to the depth of less than two miles on a front of nearly three miles. They had captured Hill 209, which gave them an excellent observation point. In achieving this the Axis had suffered more than eleven hundred casualties and had lost a large percentage of its armour. Paulus claimed the battle as an important success. Nevertheless, he gave definite orders that the attack on Tobruk was not to be renewed unless the garrison showed signs of evacuating the port.

There can be no doubt that at the time the defenders' courageous resistance to these attacks by vastly superior forces, employing the same *blitzkrieg* tactics by which they had conquered half of Europe, prevented the Axis Armies marching triumphantly on to Suez.

CHAPTER ELEVEN

THROUGH THE BACK DOOR

For Rommel Tobruk became an obsession, and for the next seven months its capture governed the conduct of his entire campaign in North Africa. As his contempt turned to rage, the annihilation of the ragged garrison which had thwarted his plans dominated his mind.

If his High Command forbade him to attack Tobruk, he would pulverize it with bombs and starve its defenders into submission by sinking their supply ships. These must be destroyed *en route* or in the harbour. No ship must be allowed to escape; not even hospital ships. All must be sunk, for so long as the British existed in Tobruk Rommel knew that they constituted a dangerous threat to his rear. Until he possessed Tobruk, his frontier flank would never be secure.

Yet, due to a number of circumstances beyond his control, Tobruk was to remain a festering wound in Rommel's side for many weary months; a wound which he could never forget since it needed constant attention.

Nevertheless, as Admiral Cunningham wrote: 'If that fortress was rightly described as a 'running sore' to the enemy, it was something equally painful to my Royal Navy.' For, throughout the siege which lasted for 242 days, it was the Navy's unenviable task to keep the garrison alive, as well as equipped with arms to defend itself and harass the enemy.

For Cunningham, the siege could not have begun at a worse time, for by the beginning of April the expeditionary force in Greece was in a precarious situation. Moreover, the Commander-in-Chief was being pressed by the Admiralty to bombard Tripoli, through which port Rommel was receiving the bulk of his supplies.

Cunningham was reluctant to undertake this operation because in his opinion such a bombardment was unlikely to result in any lasting damage to the port, while his ships would probably be heavily set upon by the *Luftwaffe* from Tripoli and Sicily. He reasoned that a squadron of long-range bombers could achieve effective results more swiftly. And in this he was supported by both Wavell and Longmore. The latter's request that such a squadron should be despatched to Egypt immediately was refused by the Chief of Air Staff on the grounds that there were no aircraft available.

Churchill, who described the situation in the Middle East at that time as 'chaotic', joined in the lists to give the full weight of his support to the First Sea Lord, Tripoli, he insisted, must not only be bombarded, but if possible the harbour was to be blocked.

To do this it was proposed that the old battleship *Centurion* should be used. But a few days later, to Cunningham's dismay, the Admiralty suggested that HMS *Barham* and a 'C' class cruiser should be sacrificed as block ships. He replied at length protesting against the idea, and having given his reasons and pointed out the fearful loss in officers and men that must inevitably be incurred, he ended: 'Rather than send *Barham* without support and with such slender chances of success I would prefer to attack with the whole battle fleet and accept the risks.'

This he did. *Warspite*, *Barham*, *Valiant*, supported by the carrier *Formidable*, and the cruisers *Pheobe*, *Calcutta*, and *Gloucester*, poured 530-tons of 15 and 6-inch shells into the harbour of Tripoli in forty-two minutes. But, as Cunningham had predicted, the results were disappointing.

Quite inaccurately, Churchill insisted that the same weight of bombs as the Fleet had fired in shells in those forty-two minutes might have been dropped by a squadron of Wellingtons from Malta in ten and a half weeks. In fact, only one cargo vessel loaded with bombs and fuel was sunk and one torpedo boat, the *Partenope* – damaged. The port and the town were severely knocked about, although many of the 11-inch shells failed to explode.

Cunningham, however, had no time to congratulate himself on having carried out this hazardous operation without loss, before his Fleet was involved in the evacuation of the expeditionary force from Greece. Between April 24th-May 1st, the Royal Navy with no fighter protection rescued 50,732 men from Hitler's clutches, carrying them back to Crete and Egypt.

Within a tragically short space of time, Cunningham's ships were called upon again to save a further 18,000 soldiers from Crete and to suffer fearful losses.

But in spite of all these commitments and the losses they entailed, units of the Royal Navy continued to maintain the garrison in Tobruk. The responsibility for this rested almost entirely with the ships of the Inshore Squadron. Formed in December 1940 for the purpose of supporting the Army's advance, the Squadron had already distinguished itself against the enemy. The old monitor *Terror* and the four little gunboats from the China Station, *Ladybird, Cricket, Aphis,* and *Gnat,* had thrown their salvoes into the enemy's troop and transport concentrations along the coast at Benghazi, *Dema*, Tobruk, Bardia, and Sollum in defiance of the *Luftwaffe*'s attacks. *Terror* was the first to go. After being severely damaged at Benghazi by dive-bombers, she was ordered to sail for Tobruk. On February 23rd, crippled by an acoustic mine, with her ancient plates leaking, she was again attacked by waves of *Stukas* and went down with her guns firing. The following day the same fate over took the destroyer *Dainty*.

Perhaps the heaviest burden was borne by the destroyers of the Royal Australian Navy – HMS *Stuart, Vampire, Vendetta, Voyager,* and *Waterhen,* – which ran a regular ferry service along the coast from Alexandria to Tobruk. The Captain (D) of the Flotilla was Captain H M L Waller, of *Stuart*. Month after month, these old destroyers carried on the 'spud Run', as the sailors called it, fighting heroic battles against the swarms of dive-bombers, more often than not without support from our own fighters as their losses rose, the jetty at Alexandria dockyard, alongside which they loaded their stores for Tobruk. was grimly christened by their ships' companies 'the Condemned Cell'.

After the evacuations of Greece and Crete, Cunningham was obliged to press all sorts and conditions of ships into service on the 'spud Run', including captured Italian schooners, ancient Greek merchantmen, and the 'A' lighters. Six of these last had been lost in Greece and Crete, but others joined the Inshore Squadron the moment they left the yards at Port Tewfik and Port Fuad, to carry tanks, guns, vehicles, and stores to the fortress.

In A5 I had been wounded at Nauplia and finally sunk off Monamvasia on the last day of the evacuation of Greece. After a spell ashore in Alexandria, I returned to the 'spud Run', duly recording the fact in my diary.

'With the resounding title of Senior Officer Western Desert Lighter Flotilla, I am now in charge of the TLCs operating between Alexandria and Tobruk,' I wrote early in May, 1941. 1 seem fated to wet nurse the soldiers, first Dunkirk, then Greece and Crete, and now the 'spud Run'.

At least, this time, we're maintaining the soldiery and not rescuing them I But for how long. Oh Lord, how long? Churchill insists that Tobruk must be 'held to the death'. Whose death? One can't help asking the question, for only this morning when I went to get our routing instructions, a nice Commander told me apologetically that we wouldn't have any fighter protection because there simply weren't any fighters. Then he added that the Stukas were pretty active around Cape Raz Azzas, near Sollum, and wished me luck. When I reflect how slow we are and that we are carrying a mixed cargo of ammunition, land mines, vehicles, and leaking cased petrol, I can't help feeling we shall need it. Incidentally, we had hoped to carry 'I' tanks once more, but, apparently, at the moment, there aren't any available anywhere in the Middle East. So instead, besides the cargo already mentioned, we're taking NAAFI stores, including shaving cream, to the beleaguered garrison…

The sailors are distinctly disgruntled at this job. They have decided that since the authorities dubbed lighters, we are fated to become 'beef-and-spud' boats. This they consider a comedown after what they had expected. They have listened to a lot of talk about the landing craft being the 'spearhead of an invasion force', worked themselves up over the prospect of capturing various islands whose names sound "like brands of toothpaste". Instead, they find themselves carrying stores to the pongos in Tobruk, and feel that is a bit of an anti-climax.

I hate pep-talks, but because of their mood I felt obliged to say a few words to the sailors about this job. I tried to explain to them how vitally important it is for us to hold Tobruk; far more important than taking the Dodecanese Islands. I also dropped a felt hints that they would probably see plenty of action before they were through, warning them that the RAF would be conspicuous by its absence. I was at pains to explain why, because after what happened in Greece and Crete, the RAF's stock has hit rock-bottom with the Fleet. I blame the officers for this, because many of them haven't bothered to tell their ships' companies that the only reason why they didn't see the RAF in the Aegean was because of the shortage of aircraft. What fighters there were in Greece were written off by the *Luftwaffe* before the evacuation began. Since the majority of the sailors have never been told this, they go around calling the RAF rude names. After Crete, they even started saying that RAF meant 'Rare As F – ', with ugly results in some of the bars in Alex!

Personally, I have no illusions about this job. What the *Stukas* did to us in Greece, they can repeat off the Libyan coast. Experience has taught me that in the battle between ships and dive-bombers the latter win every time, provided their pilots have the guts to press home their attack, and no one can accuse the *Luftwaffe* boys of being lacking in guts.'

As the 'nice Commander' predicted, on this particular passage the two TLCs were to suffer their initiation into the perils of the 'spud Run'.

'In the Med. at this time of year it's so damned easy to forget one's at war,' I wrote in my diary. 'The sea is so blue and the sun so warm, and between the two, one is lulled into a sense of false security. But this morning about noon we had a grim reminder that we weren't on a pleasure cruise. We passed the split body of a German airman. Floating in the calm sea in his yellow life-jacket and fringed by his trailing entrails, he looked like a giant jellyfish. Nobby Sub-Lt EL Oarke, DSC, DSM, RNVR wondered whether we ought to pick him up in case there were papers in his pockets, but I decided to leave him where he was...

Some of the hands, drinking tea and hanging over the after rail, spotted the body as it bobbed by in our wash, and I remember a stoker calling out: "Game to the last! Arse up 'ards!" Nevertheless, after a couple of weeks of peace and plenty in Alex, the sight of the dead man had a sobering effect on all of us...

To keep the sailors alert, I promised ten bob to the first man who spotted a plane. Early in the afternoon I parted with it to Leading Seaman Newton, our coxswain. He spotted a Dornier flying high over us. A bird of ill-omen! It kept us company for quite a while and then droned off to the south west, obviously to whistle up his pals. After that, there was no need for further bribes! But nothing happened until about 1800, when we sighted four Ju 87s heading for us. Nobby sounded 'Action Stations' and rang down for full-speed on both engines. As the guns' crews closed up, I told them not to fire until I gave the order, reminding them once again that the best chance of bagging a *Stuka* is in the moment that it pulls out of its dive…

We had plenty of time to reflect as the planes flew high over us before turning in a wide circle in order to get between us and the sun. This was to be my first dive-bombing attack since being sunk off Monamvasia. and I remember wondering with butterflies in my stomach how I would take it. I know nothing more terrifying or demoralizing than being dive-bombed, especially at sea. On land, it isn't nearly so personal but at sea, you're left in no doubt as to who is the target. What's more, there's no question of taking cover. Probably it's the noise that frightens one most of all. The shriek of the diving planes, the scream of the bombs growing louder and louder, the crump of them exploding, and the ear shattering crash of the guns seem to tear one's nerves apart. So far as I'm concerned, I'm always conscious that the sailors are watching me. Maybe it's just imagination. But whatever it is, the fear of appearing afraid only adds to the agony of being dive-bombed. Sometimes I wonder, if we survive, whether any of us will ever be quite sane again…

As the first of the *Stukas* peeled off from the formation, Nobby shouted; "Hard a-starboard!" down the voicepipe to the coxswain. We'd spent a lot of time planning the best evasive action to take in just such a situation, and now we were putting our theories into practice, I was fascinated to see how they would work, so fascinated that I forgot to feel frightened! I even found time to look astern at Dennis (Sub-Lt Dennis Peters. DSC, RNVR) to see what he was up to. He was swinging away to port…

I could hear the scream of the *Stuka*'s engine above the roar of our exhausts. Foxed by our alteration of course, it dived at us cock-eyed, and its bombs straddled us. As he pulled out of his dive, I yelled, "Fire!" and both pom-poms let fly together. Our shooting was pretty wild, but at least the lads kept firing. For most of them this was their first taste of action, and they stood up to it well…

Just as the second *Stuka* came for us, the port pom-pom jammed… I saw the bombs falling from the plane. One burst off the port bow, the other, seeming to graze the wing of the bridge, went off with a deafening crash alongside our starboard quarter. The explosion lifted our stern right out of the water, as I hit the deck, I heard the spent cartridge cases clattering past me, cascading over the side. Then a great geyser of water hurled up by the bomb poured over us.

I clambered to my feet, drenched to the skin, in time to see one of the planes diving at us with its machine-guns blazing.

As I ducked, I saw the bullets ripping through the tarpaulin over the hold and felt, sick as I thought of all that leaking cased petrol slopping about in our bilge…

The whole show was over in a matter of minutes, quite miraculously no one was hurt. But the near miss had given the lads in the engine room a fearful shaking. When I saw one of the motor mechanics retching his heart up over the rail, I decided it was time for a tot of rum all round…

As a result of the near miss, the starboard motor packed up, its filters filled with muck. But fortified with rum the stokers and the motor mechanic got it going again, and we were able to proceed at maximum revs in order to reach Tobruk in accordance with our ETA (estimated time of arrival)…

As we reformed, Dennis called us up on his Aldis lamp to inform us that "We have just passed through Bomb Alley!"

This ordeal was by no means unique. During the first two months of the siege scarcely a ship reached Tobruk without being attacked, many fared worse than these two 'A' lighters. For a time when the garrison's food reserves ran dangerously low, every ship arriving with supplies left loaded with prisoners and surplus personnel, until by the end of May some twelve thousand men had been evacuated.

CHAPTER TWELVE

THE FORTRESS FROM WITHIN

The fortress of Tobruk may be said to have been divided into two parts; the perimeter defences and the harbour area. The whole covered an acreage of roughly the size of the Isle of Wight and was inhabited by an exclusively male population of approximately 30,000.

While it is difficult to generalize about the living conditions within the fortress, since they varied from one area to another, it is true to say that every man's comfort depended largely upon his own ingenuity and resourcefulness. The men quartered in the town lived in reasonable comfort by comparison with those in the forward areas. Generally speaking, the nearer a man lived to the perimeter, the worse was his lot and the more he suffered from the violence of the North African climate. the lack of water, the torment of flies and fleas, the misery of the dust churned up by the wheels of the trucks and tanks. But dust storms, flies and fleas were plagues common to all men in Tobruk.

At the end of the siege a sergeant of an anti-aircraft battery, who had spent seven months in the fortress, wrote:

'Almost worse than the bombs as a tribulation to the flesh and the spirit were the fleas. The desert fleas are famous and ours were obviously in the pay of the enemy. How we cursed them on the nights when the moon was late up and we hoped to catch a couple of hours' sleep before the inevitable procession of night bombers started. The fleas marched and counter marched up and down our twitching bodies until we thought we would go crazy… We needed those hours of sleep, for when the moon was up we would get mighty little rest. Twenty-one alarms in one night was our record; and it was nothing to have half-a-dozen night after night…

No wonder we looked forward to our periodic "day off" by the sea. Even then we had to keep an eye open for the bombers and dive into the caves for shelter from swooping *Stukas*, but it was heaven to wash ourselves and our sweaty clothes in the clear blue water, and lie naked on the sand and dream of home, beauty, and beer…

We had our "quiet days" when the wind howled and the dust devils swept over the desert so that one could not venture out without goggles or eyeshields; as we lay in our shallow dug-outs dozing and reading some tattered paperback, the dust would settle in a floury yellow veil over face, hands and blankets. We ate it and breathed the stuff so that in the end we scarcely noticed it… Mostly our grouse was plain boredom, week after week, month after month, the same eternal desert, the same discomforts, the same raids. Danger itself becomes tedious after a while…'

None knew better than General Morshead that boredom could demoralize the spirit of his garrison more rapidly than even Rommel's *Stukas*. So living up to the nickname of 'Ming the Merciless' which the Diggers had given him, he kept his troops constantly working and in continual contact with their besiegers. His infantry battalions were moved every few weeks from the concrete posts in the Red Line back to the Blue Line where they worked on the fortifications and then into reserve.

After a few days' rest, swimming, sun-bathing, washing clothes, they were usually sent up to the Salient sector, where a night seldom passed without patrols being sent out across no man's land to the enemy strongpoints.

Overlooked by the Germans on Hill 209, conditions in the Salient during the early days of the siege were the hardest of all to endure. The positions, due to the rock beneath a shallow layer of sand, were part weapon pit and part sangar, since they were provided with no sort of cover overhead, their occupants were exposed all day to the heat of the desert sun. The majority of these section posts were not even connected by crawl trenches, so that the men were forced to crouch or lie face downwards in what were little better than open graves.

Throughout the long hours of daylight bully beef and biscuits formed their staple diet, while the bitter, chlorinated water in their bottles became so warm that it no longer eased their burning throats. Only by night was any movement possible, and then under cover of darkness the ration-truck came forward and a hot meal was issued and a further supply of hard rations left for the following day. Thus, the men had their breakfast at 9.30 p.m., a hot lunch at about midnight, and dinner before dawn. After a week of such living the troops left their sangars thin and weak and often racked with dysentery.

Typical of life in the Salient is this description written by Major G D Evans, of the 2/13th Australian Infantry Battalion:

'After a bare week's rest we were placed under the command of the 18th Brigade and sent back to the line, this time on the left of the Salient in relief of the 2/ist Pioneer Battalion. The Pioneers had been rapidly converted to infantry and given a sector of perimeter posts and a portion of the Salient to hold. They had been doing this since the unsuccessful counter attacks of the 18th Brigade on May 3rd...

A heavy mist hung like a pall over the part of the front which Company entered and it helped considerably. The outgoing Pioneers advised great caution in dealings with the enemy we would see when first light came. Certain men, they said, acting as decoys for the Spandau gunners, would stand up on their sangars and shake out their blankets in a most brazen manner. The infantrymen of the 2/13th smiled and thanked the Pioneers for the warning...

Daylight on the 12th (May) saw the commencement of the aggressive action that was to spread to all units around the Salient and force Rommel to keep that area packed with his most reliable German troops. The Pioneers had spoken the truth. When first light came the German Spandaus rippled out their morning welcome, as if bidding the new troops opposing them to stand to with alacrity. There followed the spectacle of enemy soldiers shaking out their dust filled blankets and moving about as if they were anywhere else but within small arm's range of Australian infantrymen. There came the sudden crack of rifles and the angry chatter of Brens. The next use for many of the blankets was as shrouds…

On the night of the 26th, A Company went forward again and commenced digging new positions. Before first light the diggings had not been completed, so the Company withdrew. The intention was that A Company would come forward again the following night, complete the diggings and move in. This decision, however, was to lead to an unexpected dash with the enemy. The A Company men commenced their task of improving their positions when the ration truck arrived with the hot meal and 'everything stopped for tea'. The Germans, who had heard this digging on these two consecutive nights, apparently guessed what their adversaries were up to and determined to take advantage of it. When Staff Sergeant Doug Robinson was feeding A Company we assumed that the enemy imagined that work was finished for the night. They set off in strength to occupy what they fancied to be unoccupied, partly completed, positions, perhaps to stay, perhaps to provide a welcome when A Company should return the following night. The movement was immediately observed by the small covering party that A Company posted while it ate its meal this party skillfully withdrew and alerted both A and B Companies. The unsuspecting Germans pressed on until met on two sides by merceless, point blank fire. They fled in the wildest disorder.

In the morning large numbers of enemy dead were observed on the front. Soon enemy ambulances appeared and under cover of a white flag, began to move out to collect their dead and wounded. This they were permitted to do.

The men of A and D Companies took fall opportunity of this short truce and stood up and stretched their legs and had their first look at the front in daylight. In all, five German ambulances were found necessary to collect their casualties.

Some of our stretcher bearers went out to assist the Germans and got within fifty yards of the enemy lines in the process.

They reported that the enemy appeared to be operating from two-man weapon pits which were surrounded by trip-wires of single-strand barb. When the last German vehicle had departed a salutary burst from a Bren declared it on again.

This closer contact with the enemy was a new experience for the Battalion. It was a regular thing, during those first few days, to hear the Germans singing in their positions. Their favourite song appeared to be 'We'll Hang Out Our Washing on the Seigfred Line', which they would follow up with shouts of laughter and obscene advice. As the days passed the singing became very scarce and even the obscenities disappeared, it became too dangerous to advertise a collection of troops, many a discussion was interrupted by a hand grenade from an unheard patrol.'

Rommel clung tenaciously to Hill 209 and the ground he had captured immediately to the east of it, since be looked upon it as a weak spot in the garrison's defence through which a way could be forced when the moment came to renew his offensive, But to hold the Salient he was obliged to use a third of his total infantry strength.

For Morshead, too, this sector of the perimeter was a constant source of anxiety. Before the enemy's attack on May 3rd-4th the garrison had held three and a half miles of the old perimeter, well mined and wired and covered by fire from the old Italian strongpoints. Now it had to hold a front of nearly five and a half miles without wire or minefields, the whole length of which 'was overlooked by the enemy'. Ten companies of infantry were required to defend a sector which had previously been held by only two.

In spite of the fact that he had been reinforced by the arrival of the 2/23rd Battalion by sea, Morshead was hard put to it to hold the Salient. But since his chief role was to keep the greatest number of German troops pinned down outside Tobruk, he never lost an opportunity of taking aggressive action. Now, he took it to shorten the front in the Salient so that he could hold it with two infantry battalions. But, owing to the enemy's complete air superiority at this time, reinforcements were so slow in arriving that Morshead was obliged to draft men, like the Pioneers and the RASC from the docks, into the infantry battalions. He also resorted to cunning. By a series of patrols into no man's land by night which came to grips with the enemy, by sending out wireless messages that hinted at a forthcoming attack, and by driving trucks and light tanks backwards and forwards from the docks to the western sector of the perimeter in a cloud of dust, Morshead was able to convince the Germans that he was about to launch an attack in force against Hill 209.

This ruse succeeded with the result that Rommel withdrew troops from the Sollum area to meet the threat to the Salient, while his sappers and pioneers hurriedly set about strengthening the positions around the Hill itself. But although he did manage to shorten his front line by the end of June, Morshead was never able to drive the enemy from the high ground overlooking his fortress.

Life all along the perimeter was tuned to harrying the enemy. Except in the Salient where our positions were within easy range of the *Afrika Korps'* mortars and machine-guns, our troops in the forward area were free to move about in daylight in comparative safety and our trucks could drive up almost as far as the Red Line without risk of surprise attack. This freedom of movement was largely due to the patrols which kept Rommel's troops so far back that no man's land along the greater length of the perimeter was never less than a mile wide and at some points as much as four miles of open desert lay between the opposing forces.

After the May battles, this no-man's-land virtually belonged to the garrison, or, at least, our troops had the free run of it. For a while, the Australians and the Indians shared it between them. Amongst the Indians were a number of Rajputs, warrior caste Hindus from Jodpur, of whom the enemy went in terror. They could move through the darkness without a sound and never returned from a raid without claiming a high score of Germans and Italians. Indeed, so successful were they that their senior officer became suspicious and lectured them sternly against over estimating the number of enemy dead. A few nights later, when the patrol returned through the wire just before dawn, its leader, saluting smartly, laid two small sacks at the senior officer's feet. They contained irrefutable, if macabre, evidence of the night's operation. For in one were sixteen right ears, and in the other sixteen left ears, all still oozing with the blood of their former owners.

Apropos of the stealth with which these Indians moved by night, I remember the alarming experience of a South African sapper Major while lifting German mines under cover of darkness near Sollum.

'It was one of those nights,' he told me, 'when the desert was as quiet as the grave. I was on my knees dealing with a detonator when suddenly a hand was clapped over my mouth and a thin arm wrapped itself round my neck. I was so numb with fear that I couldn't move. But my hair stood on end! I felt someone running their fingers over me; feeling the buttons on my tunic, my revolver, my pockets. When they reached the crowns on my shoulders, they seemed to hesitate. Then, just when I'd made up my mind that I was as good as dead, I was released. I heard a voice whispering, but I couldn't hear what was said because the blood singing in my ears deafened me. But I did catch the single word "Sahib". I don't know, but I may even have passed out in sheer terror. But when I pulled myself together, I was still kneeling on the ground staring up at two bearded Sikhs. They were out on patrol and since I was in the Jerry minefield, I'd had a pretty close shave. I still get the trembles every time I think of it!' the Major told me with a shiver.

Every night our patrols went out from Tobruk across no-man's-land and as the siege lengthened, the men became better and better equipped for their task. In the early days, the Diggers set out with socks over their boots and even in their stockinged feet, while the Indians made themselves special sandals from the rubber of old motor tyres. Later, the patrols were provided with thick desert boots with soft rubber soles, and special one-piece patrol suits reinforced at the elbows and knees as protection against the thorn bushes and stony ground.

The patrols usually consisted of between ten and twenty men, each with a rifle with fixed bayonet, and carrying two or three hand-grenades. In every patrol there was at least one man with a Bren, which he fired from the hip, often as many as six armed with Tommy guns. Usually, they were supported by a Bren or mortar earner to give covering fire as they withdrew and when necessary, to pick up the wounded. Fortified with a hot meal and a tot of rum, they set out in the darkness, moving on a compass bearing across the featureless desert to the enemy's lines. To achieve surprise, it was their practice to attack a strongpoint from the flank or rear; a manoeuvre which called for very accurate navigation by the patrol leader.

One of the main objects of these night raids was to capture a prisoner for interrogation.

One moonlight night when two officers and fourteen men of the 2/23rd Battalion were out on patrol on the Bardia road sector, they had a strange experience.

'As we went forward,' their leader. Captain Rattray, told afterwards, 'we saw the shadowy figure of a soldier moving out from the forward enemy position to the patrol… Every few yards he would stop and give a low whistle. When he whistled the third time, McMaster whistled back. The figure turned towards us and as he got nearer we could hear him calling: *"Herr Leutnant! Herr Leutnant!"* McMaster called back *"Si, si, Comradio!"* and the Eytie walked right into our arms. We had been sent out to get a prisoner and so now we could go back. ...Next day we all had badly lacerated knees and elbows, but if we had the unusual distinction of having whistled a prisoner in.'

Such patrols played havoc with the enemy's nerves, particularly the Italians, and to protect themselves against the night raiders the Germans sowed the ground round their strong points with mines and booby traps linked together with trip wires. They also covered their whole front with an ever increasing number of mortars and machine-guns. But through out the siege they were never able to prevent the nightly sorties made against them. They were constantly on the alert and forever in fear that one of these night patrols might be an overture to a full-scale breakout from the fortress. Indeed as time went on, the Axis radio tried to make propaganda to the effect that these raids were desperate attempts by the garrison to escape from the 'hell of Tobruk' 'The progressive and systematic work of the Axis land and air forces,' Rome Radio announced, 'The destruction of warehouses and the blocking of supplies to the stronghold render the British situation at Tobruk more unsupportable, difficult and precarious with each passing day.'

The garrison's position was difficult and precarious, but it was never unsupportable so far as its troops were concerned. Morshead and his men might have been content to have settled down to hold their fortress. But they never were.

'Tobruk,' one of them said, 'was a dagger in the flank of the Axis forces in Libya and we never lost a chance to twist that dagger.'

The enemy's opinion of the defenders can be judged from the following captured document:[1]

---

[1] 'This document was sent to the author by Lt-Colonel A B Millard, who wrote: 'I enclose a photostat of an original Western Desert Force Intelligence circular which came into my hands in 1941. At the time I was Troop Leader in 'C' Squadron 6 Aust. Div. Cavalry Regiment, which did not go to Greece. We were part of the 7th Armoured Brigade of the 7th Armoured Division at the time and were up against Rommel's armoured forces on the Libyan border when his main forces were attacking Tobruk.
'The document is a translation of a German assessment of the Australian troops' in Tobruk. Whether it was written by Major Ballerstedt, or to him. I do not know. I should imagine that it is the only such document which came into Australian hands...'

In the Field
7 June, 41

Major Ballerstedt.
  O C 2 Bn, 115 Lorried Inf. Regt

Report on the Situation and Operations in AFRICA
Infantry Positional Warfare in the Desert

Enemy

The Australians, who are the men our tps. have had opposite them so far, are extraordinary tough fighters. The German is more active in the attack but the enemy stakes his life in the defence and fights to the last with extreme cunning. Our men, usually easy going and unsuspecting, fall easily into his traps, especially as a result of their experiences in the closing stages of the Western campaign.

The Australian is unquestionably superior to the German soldier:

(i)   In the use of individual weapons, especially as snipers.

(ii)   In the use of ground and camouflage

(iii)   In his gift of observation, and of drawing correct conclusions from his observations.

(iv)   In every means of taking us by surprise:
Immediately taking up of alternative positions after the fire-fight, even with heavy Inf. weapons.
Daily changes of the forward sentry trenches Posts held sometimes strongly.
Sometimes weakly and possibly only feigning to hold them.
Firing from guns of different troops and different calibre at the same time
Forward btys. firing from an artificial dust cloud made by MT (this has often been observed).

The enemy allows isolated individuals to come right up to his positions, and then fires on them. Enemy snipers have astounding results. They shoot at anything they recognize. Several NCOs of the Bn. have been shot through the head with the first shot while making observation in the front line.

Protruding sights in gun directors have been shot off, observation slits and loopholes have been fired on, and hit, 'as soon as they were seen to be in use (i.e. when the light background became dark). For this reason loopholes must be kept plugged with a wooden plug, taken out for use, so that it always shows dark.

The enemy shoots very accurately, with his high angle Inf. weapons. He usually uses these in conjunction with a sniper or a MG. The greatest mistake in such cases is to leave cover and try to withdraw over open ground. What is necessary is to dig several alternative positions connected by crawl trenches.'

A young Australian gunner writing home to his mother from Tobruk in the summer of 1941, summed up the fighting qualities of his fellow countrymen somewhat differently.

'I'm proud to be an Aussie,' he wrote from his dug out beside a gun site on the perimeter, 'there's something different about them. The Huns fight with grim determination, the Tommies fight by numbers, but the Aussies tear about like kids at a picnic, swearing and laughing the whole time. They knock some b – , then lean against a rock and roll a cigarette.'

In another letter this same gunner described a strange encounter beyond the wire and sandbags of his gun position.

A *Stuka*, hard hit by the Bofors of an ack-ack battery, came skimming over the escarpment from the direction of the harbour, its engine spluttering, to crash-land near the gun-site. Out of the wreck scrambled its pilot, shaken but unhurt, to be confronted by a long-legged Australian armed with a rifle.

Pulling off his goggles and flying helmet, the German threw his revolver on the ground, and stared at his captor. Then he laughed.

'You're quite a hero when you have a rifle in your hand!' he taunted. 'I wonder how you'd get on without it?'

For a full minute the two men stood glaring at each other. Then, slowly, the Australian laid his rifle on the ground and threw his slouch hat down beside it.

'Okay, if that's the way you want it,' he drawled.

As the German stripped off his flying kit, tunic, and shirt, the rest of the gun's crew clambered out of their pit and came running across the sand. Soon, they were joined by others from the nearby slit trenches and dug outs, to form a circle round the two men, now both naked to their waists. They were about the same weight and height; both broad shouldered, lean, and darkly tanned by the African sun. And scenting a well matched fight, the soldiers pressed close around them as they squared up to each other.

'Come on, boys! Get back a bit. Let' em have a fair go!' a brawny sergeant shouted.

Then, surrounded by a ring of cheering Australians, the blond young *Luftwaffe* pilot and the lanky Digger went for each other with their bare fists. Both knew something about boxing and both were game fighters, and the soldiers yelled themselves hoarse as they fought it out in a whirling cloud of dust.

For twenty minutes without a break, the two men pounded each other until the sand was spattered with their blood. Then, the German's knees sagged and his arms fell limply to his sides.

'All right. You didn't need that rifle!' he grinned, wiping the blood from his mouth.

'I'm certain that if the Hun had won, the boys would have let him return to his own lines,' the young gunner wrote home to his mother, describing this strange interlude in the desert war.

CHAPTER THIRTEEN

DEDICATED MEN

It was the spirit of the men in Tobruk which defeated Rommel. Yet that spirit which inspired the garrison is hard to define.

'Throughout all those months,' an officer wrote of it afterwards, 'it so permeated the whole atmosphere of the place as to be almost tangible. Everywhere one was as conscious of it as the very sand that filled the air we breathed, the food we ate, arid the vile brackish water we drank. It manifested itself in the manner of the men. Although most of them looked like scarecrows and many of them, owing to the lack of fresh vegetables and in spite of the vitamin-C tablets, were covered in suppurating 'desert sores', they bore themselves with pride. Instinctively, one recognized them for what they were; dedicated men, resolutely, grimly determined to endure fear, discomfort, hardship and, if needs be death, rather than surrender. Rommel couldn't hope to defeat such a spirit any more than he could understand it. When he came up against it, he was confounded by it. Those ridiculous pamphlets he showered on us from the sky calling on us to surrender proved that.

Up to April, 1941, when the *Afrika Korps* chased us into Tobruk, the German Army had been invincible. Its Panzer Divisions had rolled over

Poland and the Netherlands, and had hustled us out of France. Even while we were sorting ourselves out in Tobruk, other British troops were being defeated by the Germans in Greece and Crete. For a year and a half they had had everything their own way. Then they came up against the fortress of Tobruk and battered themselves senseless against it. Then the *Afrika Korps* were fresh and newly equipped while we, who had already fought Graziani's Army, were pretty weary and sadly lacking the weapons with which to defend ourselves. In the long run and what an interminably long run it seemed, it was the spirit of the men within the fortress that won the Battle of Tobruk.'

That spirit was epitomized by such men as Captain Smith, the Naval Officer in Charge and Major O'Shaughnessy. Of Smith Admiral Cunningham wrote:

'Whenever the place is mentioned my mind goes back to the Naval Officer in Charge, Captain Frank Montem Smith, DSO, RD, RNR, outstanding among gallant men. Except for a few weeks when he had to be withdrawn for illness, he was at Tobruk throughout the siege. When he was in hospital in Alexandria I went to see him and offered him command of a ship; but in his quiet voice he firmly replied, "No, sir, I'd like to go back to Tobruk," and he went.'

In my diary I recorded an incident which illustrates the extraordinary courage of both Smith and O'Shaughnessy.

'One evening, O'Shaughnessy and I were sitting sunning ourselves on the old green bench outside Navy House which commanded a wonderful view over the harbour. He had just told me that there was a chance that he might be relieved, and that while he wanted to rejoin his old regiment, he dreaded the thought of leaving Tobruk before the end of the siege. At that moment, our conversation was cut short by a shattering explosion. Out in the harbour one of the lighters unloading petrol alongside a merchant ship blew sky high. It was a ghastly sight. We could see the water burning all round her, and hear the dreadful cries of her crew, some of whom were burning like torches. A second later, we saw smoke pouring from the forepart of the merchantman.

O'Shaughnessy raced down the steps to the quay, and old Smithy came rushing hell-for-leather out of his office. Together, they jumped into a launch and were off out to the burning ship…

I shall never forget how the pair of them worked that night. Two of the oldest men in Tobruk, they were the first ' aboard and the last to leave. Unconcerned for their own safety, or the fact that at any moment the ship might blow up under them, they manned the hoses and directed operations from the red-hot deck. They were still struggling to get the fire under control and save the ship when the enemy planes came over and plastered the harbour with bombs. But neither of them took the slightest notice of the bombs or the shell splinters falling all round them. Yet the ship was a sitting target in the moonlight. Their only thought was to save her precious cargo. In the small hours of the morning they came ashore with their clothes scorched, faces blackened, eyebrows singed, and feet blistered. But they had accomplished their task and saved not only tons of petrol going up in smoke and flames, but a merchant ship worth her weight in gold.'

Some time later, Major O'Shaughnessy, as he was by then, was awarded the George Cross for that night's work. When he finally left Tobruk at the end of the siege he had also added a Military Cross to the row of ribbons on his bush jacket.

Of this gallant Irishman I wrote in my diary:

'I never came to Tobruk without seeing O'Shaughnessy, for he was always down at the water's edge to speed up the unloading and in his office, over a glass of Italian brandy or Chianti, he would tell me about his latest adventures. From time to time, to break the monotony of his life in the fortress, he would take his truck and drive up to the front line, where his activities were cloaked in mystery. But seldom did he return empty handed from these jaunts. Sometimes, he came back loaded with Italian machine-guns, revolvers, and ammunition, so that his bedroom was a veritable armoury of captured enemy weapons. The Nazi flag hanging on his office wall was a souvenir of one of these excursions.

On one occasion he drove back in triumph with a huge barrel of Chianti and several cases of brandy to replenish his dwindling stocks. Another night, he and his friends drove just a little too far and fell in with a German mechanized patrol. They had to fight their way out of a singularly tight spot and the holes in their truck showed the accuracy of the enemy's fire.

The spoils of war play a great part in the lives of the men in Tobruk. NOIC (Captain Smith) has a penchant for thin very black Italian cheroots and equally strong, black Italian coffee. I often long to ask him the source of his apparently inexhaustible supply of both, but have never quite had the nerve! "Plonk", that devilish mixture offered to visitors in the Bombe and Blaste Inne at Navy House, is concocted from Italian brandy, laced with rum. Some say the siege will end when the supply of "wop" brandy runs dry!

The men of Tobruk dream of three things; cigarettes, drink, and women, in that order! As a Digger remarked to me the other day: "Brother, that's the natural sequence of events!"

How we have to watch those Diggers whenever we arrive with a few cases of canned beer in our holds! Unless they have spies in Alex and Mersa Matruh, I shall never know how they discover that we have such creature comforts aboard, but they always do. Perhaps, not quite always, for not long ago their "intelligence" slipped up badly,

I was sitting on the bridge of Nobby's craft under the camouflage netting, watching the unloading, when I spotted three Diggers walking nonchalantly ashore, their bellies bulging like pregnant mothers. Since I knew there was no beer on board, I wondered what they had scrounged and sent a sailor to find out. He reported thats a case of medical lime juice had been broken open, so I hurried after the Diggers and ordered them to disgorge. They didn't in the least mind being caught with the swag, but were thoroughly disgusted with themselves for mistaking the lime juice for beer...

This scrounging very soon became a serious problem for us and I was forced to complain to very senior officers about it. I'm afraid the Aussies are the worst offenders. However, even my own sailors aren't above suspicion, since for a few cigarettes or bottles of beer it is possible to acquire a pair of desert boots, an Italian motor-bike, or a Leica camera. The other day, one of the 'subs' was offered a little Fiat in exchange for a bottle of gin! The temptations are great and I have to keep reminding them that not only does the cargo not belong to them, but that we haven't risked our necks bringing it to Tobruk simply to use it as Black Market currency! Yet it's hard to refuse these poor devils anything, if they'd only ask instead of helping themselves. Most of them look wretchedly thin, and although nearly all of them try to bluff one that they don't give a damn for the bombers, their faces are drawn and their eyes bloodshot from staring into glaring desert sun. It's one thing to put up with bombing when there is plenty to drink and you've got a comfortable bed and a woman to sleep with. But it's a different story when you have to be brave on chlorinated water and snatch what sleep you can on a straw mattress in some vermin infested cave…'

Yet Tobruk cast something very like a spell over the men who lived there, so that years afterwards they remember it with nostalgia. It would be easy to say that time had lent enchantment to the scene, were it not for the fact that at the height of the siege there were men who wrote home with genuine affection for their beleaguered fortress.

Returning from a twenty-four hour stint in his battery observation post, the young gunner who described the stand up fight between the Digger and the German pilot, wrote home of his 'day off' by the sea.

'It's my turn down to the beach tomorrow, so I'll have a good scrub and do some washing,' he told his mother. I'm black or at least grey this sand gets everywhere and my clothes stand up by themselves when I get undressed. Sweat and sand make good concrete. I won't have much washing to do, only pants and socks. I don't wear anything else.

Furthermore, I'll have to walk around in my boots until my clothes dry. It's nothing here for the boys to walk around stark naked for half the day as most of them have nothing else to wear while their clothes are drying, so at meal times they line up with nothing on but their boots and hats…

The sea was like a mill pond when we got there, the day glorious, so things couldn't have been better. At night, another chap and I lit a fire and cooked some tinned food and then lay in bed and had a good feed… You know, when lying there in bed I remarked to my mate that I wouldn't swop beds with anyone in the world and he agreed. It was beautiful lying there on the sand about five yards from the Med., a lovely still night with every star visible. We were wonderfully warm and comfortable and hadn't a care in the world. . . .

You women back home sit and worry about us. You don't realize the good times we have, days that we have at the beach or days when Jerry is quiet and we have a euchre party at threepence a game. …

I awoke the next morning feeling great, just crawled out of bed, stripped off and had a swim before breakfast…

I'm extremely happy here; I don't know why! There ain't no bird to sing, no flowers or lawns or trees or rivers to look at, but I'm just happy…

I suppose I enjoy company and I enjoy the wonderful feeling of comradeship in Tobruk. We are more or less cut off from the world, and we have one job and one job only that is, to hold this place. This is an experience I shall always relish. It will be a privilege later to say "I was there..."

Those simple words written home during the summer of 1941, sum up the spirit of the garrison of Tobruk.

CHAPTER FOURTEEN

THE LEAN ARMY

The rumours current in Alexandria that there were no tanks available for Tobruk in the early spring of 1941 were well founded.

In Wavell's own words, the Western Desert Force was 'living on its lean'. In a telegram to General Dill on April 20th, he stated frankly that the future outlook would cause anxiety for some time, owing to his weakness in tanks, especially cruiser tanks. He pointed out that desert warfare depended largely upon armoured strength.

> 'I have one weak unit in Tobruk of mixed cruiser. Infantry, and light tanks, and in the Matruh area one squadron of cruisers… The best I can hope for by the end of the month is one cruiser regiment less one squadron and one Infantry tank regiment less one squadron, to assist defence of Matruh. During May I may get another thirty or forty cruisers out of the workshops… and some Infantry tanks which will probably be required for the close defence of Alexandria against possible raid. I cannot count on getting any tanks back from Greece…'

Wavell then added that he had received disquieting intelligence reports from Tripoli that a German armoured division had arrived there to reinforce the *Afrika Korps*. 'If this is so,' he wrote, 'the situation is indeed serious… I will cable again when I have digested this unwelcome news.'

In another telegram despatched on the same date, the Commander-in-Chief stressed the parlous state of his armour. He could expect only two regiments of cruiser tanks by the end of May and no reserves to replace any losses, although he had enough trainee men to man six tank regiments I consider the provision of cruiser tanks vital, in addition to Infantry tanks,' which lack speed and radius for desert operations. CIGS please give your personal assistance,' he pleaded.

Churchill read these telegrams sitting up in bed in the country and found them 'alarming'. He reacted to them with characteristic resolution.

By good fortune, a convoy carrying armoured reinforcements was about to sail for the Middle East via the Cape. It included five 6-knot transports loaded with tanks and Hurricanes. These vessels Churchill determined, in spite of strong opposition from the Admiralty, would now proceed to Alexandria through the Mediterranean. He insisted that such a risk was justified since the fate of the war being fought in the desert as well as the Suez Canal depended upon the swift arrival of a 'few hundred armoured vehicles'.

The Chiefs-of-Staff were opposed to the scheme. The odds against passing five large merchant ships through the Central Mediterranean were heavily against us. They would be constantly bombed in the Narrows and in all probability attacked by the Italian Fleet once they had passed Malta. General Dill, in spite of Wavell's plea, protested vehemently against Churchill's suggestion that an additional hundred cruiser tanks should be despatched with the convoy. These could not be spared without seriously weakening our defences at home. However, when confronted by their determined leader, the Chiefs-of-Staff wavered and Admiral Pound gave his support to sending the convoy through the Mediterranean. Operation 'Tiger', as Churchill called it, was launched. But the frantic efforts to load a sixth ship with sixty-seven cruiser tanks so that she might sail with the convoy failed.

Churchill despatched an enthusiastic telegram to Wavell telling him of the reinforcements that were on the way. With typical optimism, he declared that if the convoy got through 'the boot will be on the other leg and no German should remain in Cyrenaica by the end of June'.

But the 'Tiger' convoy had scarcely sailed before Wavell telegraphed the sobering news that Rommel had already been reinforced by the 15th Panzer Armoured Division. Unlike ourselves, the Germans had been able to clear up Benghazi harbour and were using it regularly in conjunction with Derna, Sollum and Bardia. In spite of its losses crossing the Mediterranean, this new division was moving forward and several of its units were already in the Tobruk-Capuzzo area. This, Wavell pointed out, indicated that Rommel's supply situation was considerably better than our intelligence had led us to believe. If such were the case, the 15th Panzer Division, the 5th light Motorized Division and two Italian divisions – the Trento and Ariete – would be ready to strike at any time after the middle of June.

On May 6th, the *'Tiger'* convoy, consisting of the motor ships *Clan Lament*, *Clan Chattan*, *Clan Campbell*, *New Zealand Star*, and *Empire Song*, turned east to pass through the Straits of Gibraltar.

They had sailed in the greatest secrecy and every measure had been taken by the Royal Navy and the RAF to safeguard these precious ships on their perilous voyage. For the western half of its passage the convoy was escorted by *Renown*, *Ark Royal*, *Sheffield*, and nine destroyers of Admiral Somerville's Force H as well as the battleship *Queen Elizabeth* and the cruisers *Fiji* and *Naiad*, which were on their way to join the Mediterranean Fleet. The cruiser *Gloucester* and units of the 5th Destroyer Flotilla sailed from Malta to escort it through the dangerous Narrows by night, while at dawn Beaufighters from the island were overhead to give it fighter protection. From Malta eastward, it was handed into the care of *Warspite*, *Barham*, and *Valiant*, the carrier *Formidable*, the cruisers *Ajax*, *Orion*, and *Perth*, and every destroyer that Cunningham could muster.

During the hours of daylight on May 8th, Fulmars from the *Ark Royal* drove off several air attacks by enemy aircraft from Sardinia and Sicily. At dusk, the main units of Force H withdrew to the west leaving their charges in the care of the *Queen Elizabeth* and the cruisers and destroyers bound for Alexandria. As they entered the Narrows in bright moonlight the warships formed up in close support of the convoy to protect it from submarines and motor torpedo boats.

At midnight, the convoy was shaken by a heavy explosion as a mine went up in one of *New Zealand Star*'s paravanes causing her slight damage. A few minutes later, there followed two more violent explosions as the *Empire Song* struck two mines in quick succession. As she began to drop astern, she signalled that her ammunition hold was ablaze. At four in the morning, she blew up and sank, after her crew had been taken off by one of the destroyers. With her to the bottom went fifty-seven tanks and ten

Hurricanes.

During that same night a single torpedo bomber attacked and narrowly missed the *Queen Elizabeth*.

With the dawn came the Beaufighters and although enemy aircraft were seen on the radar screens, no attacks developed.

From Malta onwards throughout the greater part of its voyage the elements contrived to protect the convoy; low cloud and occasional rain squalls hid it from the waves of bombers sent out to attack it; at times fog reduced visibility to less than two miles.

On the afternoon of May 12th, Cunningham's Fleet escorted the '*Tiger*' convoy up the Grand Pass and into Alexandria harbour. Two hundred and thirty-eight out of the 295 tanks and forty-three out the fifty-three Hurricanes thus arrived to reinforce our dwindling strength in the Western Desert.

While awaiting the arrival of the convoy Wavell decided to attack Rommel before the latter had time to bring up the 15th Panzer Division in full strength, for until then he knew that his enemy's supply lines were stretched to their limits. Wavell's plan was to take Rommel's front line troops by surprise and drive them out of Sollum and Cappuzzo. If dus Operation '*Brevity*' as it was called, was successful, he intended that the Western Desert Force and the Tobruk garrison should combine to drive the Germans west of Tobruk.

The operation, which began on May 15th under the command of Brigadier 'Straffer' Gott, was an ill fated adventure. Having intercepted our signals, Rommel was forewarned of the attack which he immediately suspected to be an all out attempt to relieve the garrison in Tobruk. He therefore strengthened his eastern flank against a possible sortie from the fortress and at the same time was prepared to resist in the frontier area.

The result was that the operation achieved little beyond the capture of Halfaya Pass for the loss of some eighteen 'I' tanks as well as six fighters of our small Desert Air Force. Moreover, our tenure of the Pass was short, for ten days later Rommel retook it, having inflicted heavy casualties on the Coldstream Guards and knocked out all but two of our tanks. Still convinced that our intention was to relieve Tobruk, he proceeded to occupy the positions round the Pass in strength.

On May 20th, Wavell reported to Whitehall that a tank battalion of the 15th Panzer Division had arrived in the forward area and so the chance of defeating Rommel before he was reinforced was lost.

Meanwhile, the Royal Navy continued to run supplies into Tobruk through the back door and to harass Rommel's lines of communication by bombarding Benghazi and troop concentrations in the coastal area. Wellingtons from their bases in the Canal Zone also bombed the enemy's supply ports and forward airfields.

During May, 1,688 men were landed at Tobruk and some 5,000, including prisoners, were taken away, while the ships of the Inshore Squadron carried in a daily average of eighty-four tons of supplies. But the toll of ships sunk on the 'spud Run' rose steadily.

Within the fortress itself the garrison was given no respite from the fury of Rommel's dive-bombers. Day and night they set upon the ships in the harbour. Almost without warning the *Stukas* came screaming down out of the sun to bomb and machine-gun the quay which was often packed with wounded and prisoners awaiting shipment to Egypt. Ignoring the Red Cross, they attacked the hospital ship *Vita*, severely damaging her. Twice they deliberately bombed the hospital. Since, the Germans have tried to excuse their conduct on the grounds that the British used the Italian barracks as a hospital. It consisted of several buildings forming a hollow square in the centre of which was a huge Red Cross painted on canvas laid out on the ground so as to be conspicuous from the air. Other similar crosses were painted on the flat roofs.

Nevertheless, the *Luftwaffe* cold bloodedly attacked the hospital.

Chaplain J C Salter, Baptist Padre to the Australians, describes the worst raid as follows:

'A simultaneous attack was made on both sections of the hospital, and from quite low level. This was the most disastrous day in the whole of our experience as a hospital.

'Two of our medical officers and two of our orderlies were killed at their posts, and a great number of patients were killed or wounded in their beds. The two medical officers were men who stood high in their profession, their loss was a very sad blow to the hospital. This raid happened late in the afternoon. I was doing a round of the wards on the surgical side at the time, when suddenly I heard the roar of a plane diving down on the area, at the same time the scream of descending bombs. The whole stick fell on the medical wards across the square from where I was.

'Rushing over, I plunged with many others of our staff through the acrid fumes and blinding, choking dust and smoke. There, where a few seconds before had been a neat and tidy ward full of cheerful men well on their way to recovery, was now a scene of indescribable disorder and stark horror.

'Some things I saw that day, as I stumbled with the others over the debris and litter, will never fade out of my memory. Great gaping holes appeared through walls and roof, letting in the brilliant sunshine upon the ghastly disorder that was scattered on every hand. The moans and groans of the wounded and the dying filled the air.

'Our first thought was for the wounded. Many unfortunately were already beyond human aid. I have seen many busy days at the hospital at Tobruk. but never such another day as that. For hours that stream of wounded passed from the casualty ward to the operating theatres and back to other wards. The worst-bombed one was allowed to remain in its grim isolation for the time being, as we could not ask men to go back there again.

'Whilst many were busy with the wounded, others were reverently removing the dead and trying, amongst all the litter and confusion, to identify each body. But this was no easy task where beds had been thrown together by the violence of the explosion and identity discs torn away and lost.

'Whilst taking water to some of the wounded I heard a voice saying, "It's your turn now Padre", looking closely through the dust and dirt in which he was smothered, I saw the face of an English laddie who had attended me as an orderly in a British hospital where I had myself been a patient a few weeks previously.

'The next day… we made our way with all our dead out to the little strip of desert two miles or so along the Bardia road, that had been set aside as a war cemetery.

'A strong wind was sweeping across the desert, bringing with it blinding clouds of dust that made it extremely difficult for the drivers to find their way… When at last we did arrive there, we had to stand in that swirling, blinding, stifling dust storm while we committed to that inhospitable bit of earth the broken bones of the victims of this the most tragic experience which came the way of the hospital during the whole of our sojourn in Tobruk.'

When it is considered that this and other equally savage attacks on our hospital ships could not have been carried out without Rommel's knowledge and authority, it is impossible to think of him as the dashing, chivalrous General whose photograph graced Montgomery's desk. Rommel has been glamorized by his biographers and by Hollywood since his death. Even during the war there were those who toasted him as a sportsman in the bar of Shepheard's. In fact, he was a Nazi who owed his rapid promotion to Hitler. So long as his Führer's star was in ascendancy, Rommel never lost an opportunity of basking in its light. Courageous to the point of fanaticism, arrogant and ruthless he was a typical product of the Nazi regime. The graves of our soldiers killed in their hospital beds at Tobruk yet remain to bear witness to these facts.

CHAPTER FIFTEEN

THE RELIEF THAT FAILED

If '*Tiger*' comes through it will be the moment to do and dare,' Churchill telegraphed to Wavell on May 8th.

Four days later, by a miracle '*Tiger*' arrived in Alexandria. Jubilant the irrepressible Churchill immediately proposed sending more fast merchant ships with more tanks through the Mediterranean. But, this time, their Lordships flatly refused to cooperate. '*Tiger*', they said, had been favoured by luck and to repeat the experiment would be tempting providence too highly. Grudgingly, Churchill bowed to their decision, growling that he would not have done so but for the fact that Wavell himself had not pressed for further reinforcements by such perilous means. 'In spite of our defeat in Greece and the impending disaster in Crete, Churchill's resilient spirit soared as he contemplated those hundreds of tanks rolling westward. With the 'tiger cubs', as he called them, the Western Desert Force should be able to give 'those Hun people' a savage trouncing.

But the 'cubs' suffered from teething troubles from the moment they arrived. From the docks, they went to the workshops to be fitted with sand filters and to be camouflaged and many were found to be in need of major engine repairs before they could be thrown into battle. Moreover, once they were ready, their crews still needed time to learn to handle them, for it was now three months since the 7th Armoured Division had existed as a fighting unit.

All these tiresome delays infuriated Churchill and he bombarded the unfortunate Wavell with telegrams. Wavell patiently replied to the CIGS explaining the situation in detail. He was perfectly aware of his enemy's position. Intelligence reports had told him that Rommel's armour was halted in the desert owing to lack of fuel and had warned him of the arrival of the 15th Panzer Division in Tripoli. He knew, too, that the enemy had managed to get the harbour at Benghazi into some sort of running order. He was, he pointed out, conscious of the urgency of the situation. Nevertheless, it would be fatal to go off at half cock.

He had learned lessons from Operation '*Brevity*'. Our 'I' tanks were too slow for desert war and had suffered heavy casualties from the fire of the enemy's anti-tank guns which were superior to ours. The cruisers were really no faster than Rommel's medium tanks, while our armoured cars were too lightly armoured to stand up to the cannon shells of the German fighters and, having no gun, were powerless to defend 'themselves against the Axis eight-wheeled armoured cars. This last fact greatly hampered our reconnaissance.

For these reasons the outcome of Operation '*Battleaxe*', which was to be launched against the *Afrika Korps* with the object of driving the latter west of Tobruk and re-establishing land communications with the fortress, was doubtful.

'We shall not be able to accept battle with perfect confidence in spite of numerical inferiority, as we could against the Italians', Wavell stated with complete frankness.

Due to the 'cubs' teething troubles and the time required to give the 7th Armoured Division at least some training, '*Battleaxe*' had to be postponed for two weeks.

This respite was just what Rommel needed, for it enabled him to bring up the newly arrived 15th Panzers, replenish his fuel tanks and call up more heavy anti-tank guns.

'*Battleaxe*' was a brief encounter between the opposing armies in which we achieved nothing. After fighting with the greatest bravery, our troops were driven back to where they had started. Of the 100 odd 'I' tanks and ninety cruisers with which we had begun the fight sixty-four 'I' tanks and twenty-seven cruisers were either knocked out or broke down. Thirty-three fighters and five bombers were destroyed. Rommel lost about fifty tanks in all and ten aircraft.

The operation failed largely for those very reasons which Wavell had foreseen. The armoured units were heavily penalized through lack of training. Our two brigades – one of cruisers, the other of 'I' tanks – had no time to practise combined tactics.

Our losses in the air too, were due to lack of experience and training. There was also a sorry lack of cooperation between our air and ground forces that resulted in our fighter strength being frittered away to little purpose.

But the cause of our final defeat was the enemy's skilful employment of their heavy anti-tank guns – particularly the 88-mm, firing a 16-pound shell. Primarily an anti-aircraft weapon, but also designed for low-angle fire, the Germans had already proved this gun's effectiveness against tanks in France where they tested it against our captured Matildas.

In 'Brevity', when Rommel recaptured Halfaya Pass and decided to hold his positions on the Egyptian frontier, he had given orders for a few of these 88-mm guns to be dug in, in that area. These were so carefully concealed and camouflaged that their presence in the front line was not even suspected by us. And since they were deadly against our tanks at a range of as far as 2,000 yards, during 'Brevity', our wretched crews had little or no idea what had hit them. When the battle was over, we were in no position to make a close examination of the stricken tanks.

It was probably during 'Battleaxe' that Rommel foresaw the extreme value of using these guns in cooperation with his tanks. At that time he had not more than a dozen 88-mm in the forward area, Nevertheless, his tanks were armed with 75-mm and 50-mm guns, which were more powerful at long range than our 2-pounders. Our only effective anti-tank weapon was the 25-pounder, but we had yet to mount this and use it as a mobile gun.

From both operations 'Brevity' and 'Battleaxe' the British could have learned profitable lessons. Yet it is doubtful whether they did. They should, for instance, have benefited from Rommel's use of tanks as weapons with which to deal with infantry and soft-skinned vehicles rather than other tanks. The destruction of the tanks he left to his heavy anti-tank weapons. In both these encounters, Rommel used his tanks to lure our armour within range of his heavy artillery. Over and over again, we fell into such cunningly baited traps with dire consequences.

The failure of *'Battleaxe'* came as a bitter disappointment to the garrison in Tobruk whose troops had been within ear-shot of our guns for the second time within a few short weeks, Its result also had a demoralizing effect upon the officers and men of the Western Desert Force. All had fought with high courage, and had been forced to retire by the superior weapons of their enemy. The men in our tanks had suffered dreadful wounds from the heavy German guns often without being able to retaliate.

The Navy too, were bitterly disappointed that the tanks they had risked so much to deliver had failed to drive the Axis force westward from Tobruk and so relieve the Inshore Squadron of its fearful burden.

For the toll of ships on the 'spud Run' was mounting daily. In April, we had lost six ships, and in May eight, amongst them the gunboat *Ladybird* which had rendered such gallant service to the Army by bombarding the Axis-held ports and troop concentrations.

The old gunboat from the China Seas fought her last fight before the eyes of hundreds of men of the garrison.

It was shortly before three o'clock in the afternoon of May 12th when the *Stukas* flew in from the south-west and *Ladybird's* alarm bell clattered, calling her crew to 'Action Stations'. She was lying at the western end of the harbour not far from the shore and while some of the raiders went for the ack-ack batteries, the rest of the Ju 87s came screaming down out of the sun to attack the gunboat.

Almost immediately she received a direct hit in the stern which killed the crew of her after pom-pom and wounded the men manning the two 8-mm Fiat guns.

Another bomb crashed through the deck and burst in the boiler-room, blowing out her ancient plating. Its force hurled some of the men at the 20-mm Breda gun amidships overboard but Chief Petty Officer Thornton-Allen and some of the crew kept this gun firing until they received orders to abandon ship.

The First Lieutenant reported to his Commanding Officer, Lt Commander Blackburn, that the explosion had started a raging fuel fire which was spreading rapidly to the after magazine. Steam could not be raised nor could the flooding valves be reached and soon the ship was listing heavily to starboard, the burning oil pouring from her sides. Blackburn gave orders for the wounded to be landed in the motor sampan while the forward guns continued to engage the enemy.

That afternoon, T W Pulsford and one of his mates of the 2/15 Australian Infantry Battalion had driven down from the perimeter to see friends in the underground dressing station near the docks. They had hardly parked their truck when the air raid warning sounded and the red flags fluttered above the shattered. buildings.

'Everyone working on the docks ran for shelter in the main entrance of the hospital which was blocked off by a thick wall of sandbags,' Pulsford wrote. 'From behind this wall, by standing on a table. I could obtain a view of the harbour and the docks. A few minutes after the sound of the sirens had died away we heard the first enemy planes flying high. All our thoughts were concentrated on 'what will be the target?' We knew that the centre of the raid would be on the town and docks. But where? This question was soon answered by the ack-ack guns, the quick pumping sound of the Bofors and the sharp ripping sound of the light machine-guns.

By looking over the wall I could see the dive-bombers coming down from the blue sky through the white puffs of the ack-ack barrage. Yes, their target was the harbour. But what ship? Then I saw her, HMS *Ladybird*, her ack-ack guns blazing, men moving quickly about her deck; no panic there, just steady unhurried action…

Ladybird was an old friend of ours. Her work up and down the coast had earned her a great name among all the troops and many times we had heard the shells from her guns screaming over our heads to crash into the Hun positions outside the perimeter. But no more for today her end was near.

The first *Stuka* had let go its bombs and was coming out of its dive almost at water level. The bombs fell with an ear-splitting crash. *Stuka* after *Stuka* came screaming out of the sky. I lost count of them, for all my thoughts were on *Ladybird* as she lay fighting for her life…

As I watched a great sheet of flame and smoke rose from her decks. In a few minutes she was burning fiercely and the oil from her tanks was running into the water. She was surrounded by sheets of flame licking greedily at her sides. I saw some of the crew begin to leave her, leaping from the blazing decks into the blazing water below, while bombs were still falling all round her...

A small tugboat and a pulling boat, ignoring the bombs and the flames, put out from the shore to pick up the survivors...

We ran down to the beach and watched those men from the Ladybird being brought ashore, many being carried with great pieces of skin and burnt flesh hanging from their chests, arms, and legs...

Others had been hit by bomb splinters. One man had lost both his legs. As the little group of survivors gathered, several of us moved amongst them offering cigarettes and feeling helpless in the face of such need. I watched those men lighting their own and their mates' smokes with hands as steady as rocks. One giant of a man was standing there stripped to the waist with a great hole in his side from which the blood was running down his body and legs on to the ground. In a clear calm voice he turned to the others and said, "Never mind, mates, we'll have another bloody ship next week!"

I turned away from this little group of men blasted and burnt and dying but still possessed of a spirit that could not be crushed by bombs or fire. And to me these men will always represent the men of His Majesty's Navy possessing the calm courage that is beyond description, and every "Tobruk Rat" knows what the Navy did during the eight mondths siege. They evacuated our sick and wounded, returning again and again with ammunition, stores and reinforcements, and finally, to crown it all, to bring enough fresh troops to relieve almost the whole of the eight-months-old garrison...

It is over a year since the sinking of the *Ladybird*, but the details of that action in Tobruk Bay are deeply impressed in my very soul, and these impressions and scenes will remain with me to the end.'

Ladybird went down fighting, but she never really died for the gunners of Tobruk continued to man the 3-inch gun under her bridge and her foremost pom-poms.

Of this, her last action, Captain Poland, R.N., Senior Naval Officer Inshore Squadron, wrote to Admiral Cunningham:

She has been credited with two and a possible third air craft within the last ten days. The *esprit de corps* in the *Ladybird* was very high... It was good to see guns in action in spite of the bomb explosions and the fire raging.'

It is inspiring to remember too that some of those very guns that the men fought with such courage they had salved from the deck of HMS *Chakia* which had been sunk by dive-bombers in Tobruk harbour a fortnight before.

CHAPTER SIXTEEEN

THE 'MUDDLE' EAST

'*Battleaxe*' was Wavell's last offensive against Rommel. Its failure was too bitter a pill for Churchill to swallow. At enormous risk and in the face of stern opposition, he had ordered the '*Tiger*' convoy through the Mediterranean. After its safe arrival he had frankly confessed himself thoroughly dissatisfied with the arrangements made by the Middle East Head quarters Staff for the reception of his precious 'Tiger cubs'.

When these had been so savegely mauled. Churchill declared that Operation 'Battleaxe' had been 'ill-concerted', and was angered that no sortie had been made by the garrison from the 'Tobruk sally-port as an indispensable preliminary and concomitant'.

For all this, Wavell, as Commander-in-Chief, had to 'carry the can'. The Chiefs-of-Staff considered the moment ripe to say that he was a tired man, and remembered that Eden had reported some months before that after his Army's flank had been breached in the desert Wavell had 'aged ten years in a night'. In a sudden flash of anger at that time Churchill had growled that 'Rommel had torn the new-won laurels from Wavell's brow and thrown them in the sand'. 'This,' the old man wrote with regret after the war, 'was not a true thought, but only a passing pang.' Nevertheless, as the direct result of the failure of '*Battleaxe*', Churchill decided that the time had come to relieve Wavell of his command of the armies in the Middle East.

There was, in fact, nothing new about the Prime Minister's dissatisfaction with the situation in that theatre. It had nagged at him for many months. Early in May, Longmore had been called to London for discussions concerning the state of the Air Force in the Middle East. When, well satisfied with the outcome of his journey and with the promise of strong reinforcements, he was about to return to Cairo, he was suddenly told he was to stay in London. A few days later, it was announced that he had been succeeded in his command by his deputy. Air Marshal Tedder, and would himself become Inspector-General of the RAF. While the new post was an important one, it was not comparable with that which he had held since the outbreak of hostilities with Italy.

Such behaviour by the War Cabinet was to say the least high-handed, particularly so since the public announcement of the change in command coinincided with the débâcle in Crete.

Longmore had held his appointment for a year and, like Wavell, he had achieved remarkable results with weapons that were few in number and obsolete in pattern. Again like Wavell, he had been called upon to fight simultaneously in East Africa, the Western Desert, Greece, Crete, Syria, and Iraq, often against his wisdom and experience. Together with Wavell, he had incurred Churchill's displeasure by doubting that the utmost aid was being given to him, and was constandy criticized for not making the best use of his material.

Both men went the way of so many British commanders whose doubtful honour it was to find themselves in high places at the outset of the war. Theirs had been the invidious task of making bricks without straw. Over and over again, they had drawn the attentions of the War Cabinet and the Chiefs-of-Staff to the almost insuperable difficulties of maintenance in Egypt and in this they had been fully supported by Eden.

Randolph Churchill had even talked Miles Lampson, our Ambassador in Egypt, into allowing him to telegraph his father at length, pointing out that he did not see how the war could be won in the Middle East until we had some 'competent civilian on the spot to provide day-to-day political and strategic direction'. Although Churchill admits that it took this telegram to clinch matters in his mind, a year before Wavell himself had requested dial someone should be sent to Cairo for precisely this purpose. In this he had been supported by both Cunningham and Longmore, for all three of them had been impressed by how quickly things had been accomplished during Eden's short sojourn in the Middle East, Then, not only had the endless delays been avoided, but the Foreign Secretary had borne the brunt of the spate of telegrams arriving from 10 Downing Street. But Wavell's proposal was flatly turned down, and, ironically, it was not until he had been relieved by General Auchinleck that Oliver Lyttelton arrived in Cairo as Minister of State in the Middle East.

So, by the early summer of 1942, Admiral Cunningham alone remained of the original triumvirate which had begun the war together in the Mediterranean. For many months he continued to hold Mussolini's Navy at bay while his own little Fleet harassed the Axis lines of communication to North Africa and kept alive the garrisons in Malta and Tobruk. The supplying of these two fortresses put an almost unbearable strain on Cunningham's slender resources. For while the Royal Navy commanded the sea, the *Luftwaffe* dominated the sky. To escape the dive-bombers, supplies were carried to Malta by submarine, and only destroyers whose high speed made it possible for them to accomplish the trip to Tobruk during the hours of darkness were employed on the 'spud Run'. In daylight, the *Luftwaffe* attacked every ship afloat until not even hospital ships conspicuously marked by their red crosses were safe.

After their deliberate attack on the *Vita* just outside Tobruk harbour, the Germans went for the *Karapara*, killing many of the casualties aboard her, including their own wounded. On May 8th, south of the Kaso Strait, they set upon the hospital ship *Aba*. The cruisers *Phoebe* and *Coventry* on patrol in the vicinity picked up her SOS signals and proceeded to her assistance. As these ships arrived on the scene, they were themselves set upon by a swarm of *Stukas*. In the first attack on *Coventry* a Ju 87 carried out a steep dive-bombing assault, at the same time spraying the ship with its machine-guns. The bombs fell harmlessly in the sea. But as the result of the machine-gunning. Petty Officer Sephton, who was in B director as layer, was fatally wounded. The bullet, having passed through his body, also wounded a communications rating, Able Seaman Fisher. Sephton reported to his control officer that he had been hit, but insisted that he could carry on. In fact, owing to the cramped space in the director and the difficulty of access, he knew that he could not be relieved until the attack was over. Although in great pain and bleeding profusely, he stayed at his post until the end of the action. When it was over, he refused any offers of help and climbed out of the director by himself, but collapsed on the deck below from loss of blood. The next day he died. He was posthumously awarded the Victoria Cross.

After these three attacks on the hospital ships, the wounded from Tobruk were evacuated by destroyers.

In June, General Morshead sent urgent signals to Cairo for petrol. His supplies were running so dangerously low that unless they could be replenished his vehicles would be immobilized and the soldiers on the perimeter would starve in their outposts. To meet this emergency it was decided to send the little petrol-carrier *Pass of Balmaha* to Tobruk. On June 3rd, by a miracle, she arrived there safely, escorted by HMS *Auckland* and the South African trawler *Southern Maid*.

A few weeks later, Providence was tempted again, and the *Pass of Salmaha* set out once more for Tobruk with her dangerous cargo escorted by the anti-aircraft sloops *Auckland* and *Parramatta*. The three ships left Alexandria on June 22nd. All went well until the morning of the 24di when the convoy was shadowed by a single Savoia 79. *Auckland*, immetately opening fire, drove off this intruder. But soon after nine o'clock, another S 79 appeared and dropped two bombs about five hundred yards from the *Parramatta*. Then just before noon, three more S 79s came in to attack. While one acted as a decoy to draw off *Auckland's* fire, the other two carried out torpedo attacks on the petrol-carrier and the *Parramatta*. At 1.15, another S 79 turned up and dropped four bombs round the convoy.

These high-level attacks were but a prelude to what was yet to come, for at half past five *Auckland* picked up a large formation of enemy planes on her radar. Almost before she had time to flash a warning to the others, three formations of sixteen *Stukas*, escorted by a flock of Me 109s and Me 110s, came winging in from the south-west.

Climbing into the sun, they prepared to attack as the two little sloops, putting up a thick barrage, patterned the clear blue sky with black shell-bursts. But the *Stukas* came screaming down through this screen of fire to concentrate their first attack on the *Auckland*. Within seconds, she was struck by a heavy bomb which blew her stern above water to pieces. Although her wheel jammed at 50 degrees of port, she took a wild list and for some unaccountable reason turned 180 degrees to starboard. The explosion silenced the after guns, killing and wounding their crews. But with the forward guns still firing and moving through the water at ten knots, *Auckland* appeared out of a thick cloud of smoke, to charge straight at the *Parramatta*. Only by putting her helm hard over did the latter manage to avoid *Auckland* as she passed across her bows, her after guns still pumping shells amongst her attackers.

Then, *Auckland* was hit by three heavy bombs in quick succession. The first crashed through the skylight of the sick bay, the second went through the bridge, killing everyone on it, and bored its way into the bowels of the ship before exploding. The third burst somewhere amidships; no one quite knew where.

As the first waves of bombers flew homewards, the stricken *Auckland* lay stopped and heeled over until her port gunwale was awash, and as she appeared in imminent danger of capsizing, orders were given to abandon ship. But at that very moment, even as some of her crew were leaping overboard, there was an enormous explosion which lifted the little sloop five feet out of the water. She continued jumping through the air for approximately twenty seconds, and those aboard the other ships could see that her back was broken. Survivors and those in *Parramatta* who witnessed this horrifying spectacle believe that it was caused by the bomb which had penetrated through the sick bay and which was fitted with a delayed-action fuse. For a little while *Auckland* lay torn apart and listing heavily to port, flames and black smoke pouring from her. At six-twenty-nine she sank.

The violence of the explosion had hurled many of her crew into the water and also killed and wounded many of those already swimming near the ship, wrecking the skiffs, whalers, and overturning the rafts crowded with men.

Parramatta closed and stopped to windward of *Auckland* as she sank. But even as she did so, a further wave of dive-bombers appeared. Lt Commander Walker of the Royal Australian Navy, *Parramatta's* Commanding Officer, was immediately faced with the awful problem of either risking his ship to rescue the men in the water or killing many of them with his screws as he gathered speed to avoid his attackers.

Plainly it was his duty to protect the petrol-carrier and this he could only do by abandoning those men and zig-zagging to dodge the bombs and torpedoes which were being hurled at him.

Now the reddening sky was filled with aircraft; S 79s carrying torpedoes, dive-bombing *Stukas* and swarms of fighters. And to add to his predicament, Walker saw that the *Pass of Balmaha* had stopped and her crew were taking to their boats, for in the previous attack she had been so seriously damaged by near misses that they expected her cargo to blow up.

As *Parramatta* gathered way, her guns blazing, her crew threw overboard rafts, lifebelts, and Carly floats to the swimming men shouting and floundering in her wake. Then, the fighters swept out of the setting sun to spray the men struggling in the water and huddled in helpless bunches on the rafts and Scats with cannon shells and machine-gun bullets. The sky seemed filled with diving and screeching planes. While one formation came in to attack, there was always another waiting its turn overhead, and a third coming in low across the water like fighting ducks to launch their torpedoes.

For the best part of half an hour *Parramatta* fought the attackers. With her high-angle 4-inch guns she scored a direct hit on one *Stuka*, blowing it to pieces and before the final attack was over, she sent two more enemy planes plummeting into the sea, and winged a couple more.

After what seemed an eternity the sun sank like an elliptical orange below the horizon, and the bombers with their escorts turned for home.

Between noon and sunset more than one hundred planes had attacked the convoy.

As dusk closed in, *Parramatta* and the *Pass of Baimaha*, alone in a calm copper-coloured sea littered with the debris of the sunken *Auckland*, splintered upturned boats, and the shattered mutilated bodies of dead and dying men, sighted the destroyers *Waterhen* and *Vendetta*. Taking courage, the crew of the petrol-carrier rowed back to their ship. But in spite of their efforts, they could not start her engines. So *Waterhen* took her in tow. *Parramatta* gathered up some 160 survivors from the *Auckland* and carried them at full speed back to the underground hospital at Mersa Matruh.

Waterhen, under cover of darkness, brought the *Pass of Balmaha* with her cargo of 750-tons of petrol to Tobruk. This was the last of the old destroyer's many gallant runs, for a few days later, she followed *Auckland* to the bottom in 'bomb alley'. Perhaps her finest exploit was when she attempted to save the hospital ship *Vita* by taking her in tow. When this failed, she rescued 437 patients, six doctors, six nurses, and forty-seven sick-berth ratings, and carried them in safety back to Alexandria.

CHAPTER SEVENTEEEN

HIGH COMMAND

Churchill and Wavell were strangers to each other until the General flew to London in August, 1940, to discuss the conduct of the war in the Middle East. Then, the two men had several long conversations together, which resulted in Churchill stating that he was not in full agreement with the Commander-in-Chief's use of the resources at his disposal. It was a view that shocked Eden and Dill, both of whom held the General in the highest respect.

A sensitive and intuitive man, Wavell was quick to realize the Prime Minister's lack of confidence in him, and this feeling was strengthened when on returning to Cairo he received Churchill's General Directive on the situation in the Middle East, containing numerous suggestions as to the disposition of his forces. This lengthy document, whose opinions ran contrary to his own views as well as those of Cunningham and Longmore, was the first of a sheaf of telegrams Wavell was to receive.

As Minister of Defence, Churchill was never satisfied solely to direct the high strategy of the war, but insisted on concerning himself with the details of its conduct. Whether or not this policy was a wise one or, in fact, fostered the war effort is open to doubt. It is certain, however, that Churchill's habit of bombarding his Commanders-in-Chief with telegrams greatly added to their burdens. Many of those closest to Wavell believed that his weariness in the early summer of 1941 was not solely due to the strain of campaigning, but was greatly increased by all those telegrams from Downing Street concerning matters of detail that could best have been left to the man-on-the-spot.

Both Cunningham and Longmore came in for their share of these despatches, and were hurt by their inference that they were not fighting the war audaciously enough to please the Prime Minister.

Wavell's sudden removal from Egypt to India was extremely unpopular throughout the Middle East, especially with the Desert Army. He was essentially a soldier's soldier. Not only did the men admire his calm fearlessness, but he possessed a personal magnetism which surmounted his many reversals of fortune. His officers, particularly those on his Staff, trusted his cool judgement and profound knowledge of war.

A man of few words, his long silences and tersely apt comments encleared him to his subordinates. His favourite expression, 'I see,' often made on hearing some disastrous news, became a catch-phrase amongst them when things went wrong.

The sight of him playing golf at Gezirah or as the host on Sunday evenings in his home, surrounded by his large and youthful family, his sudden descents from a rickety Lockheed or little Lysander into the whirling sandstorms of battle, made him a legendary figure throughout the Middle East. Every soldier felt that he knew the immaculate General with the eyeglass personally, although Wavell never sought popularity by playing down to his troops.

Wavell's successor, Claude Auchinleck, who arrived in Egypt in June, 1941, was a man of an entirely different calibre. A strict, almost ruthless disciplinarian, it was typical of him that, since the rank-and-file of the Army were not allowed to bring their wives to Cairo, he stepped out of his aeroplane alone, having left his wife behind in India.

One of his first acts was to turn the large rambling house at Gezirah, which in Wavell's time had so often been filled with flowers and gay young people, into a bleak barracks and officers' mess. The son of a gunner, Auchinleck was born at Aldershot, the cradle of the Army, and in the natural course of events entered Sandhurst. He was twenty when he took his commission in the 62nd Punjabs and went to India. In the First World War he had fought against the Turks in the Middle East and afterwards returned to India where he took part in the fighting on the North-West

Frontier. After a spell at the Imperial Staff College, he was back in India again to rise steadily from Colonel to Brigadier, and then from Major-General to Lieutenant-General.

At the beginning of the Second World War he had commanded our expeditionary force in Norway and played his part in preparing the southern defences of England against invasion. Then, once more, he went back to the East to become Commander-in-Chief, India. While there was nothing spectacular about his career, he had climbed painstakingly to the top, so that when the decision was made to replace Wavell. Auchinleck seemed the obvious man. Indeed, there was only one man who had any doubts about him. But, since that man was Churchill, those doubts inevitably cast their ominous shadow across the tortuous path ahead of the Commander-in-Chief.

Churchill had declared himself in disagreement with Auchinleck's attitude to the Norwegian campaign. 'He had seemed,' he wrote afterwards, 'to be inclined to play too much for safety and certainty, neither of which exists in war.'

These views were to lead to a spate of telegrams. The first arrived almost before Auchinleck had had time to sit down at his desk at GHQ, Cairo. It placed squarely on the Commander-in-Chief's shoulders the responsibility for deciding when the new offensive in the Western Desert should start and advised him to have special regard for the situation at Tobruk. Churchill added that the 'vexatious dangers' of allowing the operations then taking place in Syria to flag should be carefully considered.

The very next day, he again stuck a finger into the pie to suggest that, as soon as the situation in Syria had resolved itself, General Wilson, commanding in that theatre, should be moved to the Western Desert. Thus, from the very start, Auchinleck was given a clear indication of the shape of things to come.

To these and other telegrams the new Commander-in-Chief replied expressing his views, which were in conflict with those a held in Downing Street. There, the greatest importance was attached to the opening of an offensive in North Africa while the Germans were preoccupied with their newly launched Operation 'Barbarossa' against the Russians. The Soviet strength was an unknown quantity. There was no telling how Stalin's armies would stand up to the German onslaught. But in the opinion of the Defence Committee, it was politically as well as militarily important that we should take the initiative in North Africa at the earliest possible moment. If the Russians repulsed Hitier's hordes, they would undoubtedly boast that they had won the war while we sat and watched. On the other hand, if they were quickly defeated, they would revile us with leaving them to their fate. But far worse than these recriminations would be the fact that, once the Russians were beaten, Hitler would be able to deploy his vast forces and sweep through Turkey, Syria, and Iraq, capturing Cyprus on his way to Suez and the Persian oil fields.

Apart from such alarming possibilities in the future, there were other immediate reasons for an early offensive in the desert. Our intelligence reports showed that Rommel was becoming anxious about the losses inflicted upon his supply ships by the RAF and our submarines based on Malta. He was short of ammunition and fuel. The tanks he had lost during '*Battleaxe*' had not been replaced. His supporting fighters and dive-bombers had been reduced in numbers since the opening of the campaign against Russia.

Having taken all these facts into account, the Defence Committee urged Auchinleck to open his offensive not later than the middle of September. Until then, it seemed probable that he would have superiority on the ground and in the air. At any time after that there could be no foretelling what might happen; Russia might collapse, the invasion of England might become a reality instead of a threat and the *blitzkrieg* from the north might destroy us in the Middle East.

There can be no denying that these were strong arguments in support of an early offensive. But while Auchinleck agreed with them in theory, he replied that it was his considered opinion that his Army would not be ready for any offensive for three months. Upon further reflection, he stated that it would be four-and-a-half months before he would be fully prepared to drive Rommel out of North Africa.

This decision brought down upon his head an avalanche of telegrams from the Chiefs-of-Staff as well as Churchill. But it was soon apparent that the situation had resolved itself into an *impasse* which could not be solved by remote control. So Churchill telegraphed to Auchinleck asking him to come to London, bringing with him one or two of his Staff Officers. Accompanied by Tedder, Auchinleck arrived in England on July 29th.

There followed long talks in London and at Chequers, during which, according to Churchill, the Commander-in-Chief placed himself in 'harmonious relations with members of the War Cabinet, with the Chiefs-of-Staff, and with the War Office'. Nevertheless, no amount of argument could shake Auchinleck from his resolve to wait until November before launching his offensive. He fully appreciated the urgency of the situation and the necessity of relieving Tobruk, the supplying of whose garrison was becoming so costly in shipping. He understood, too, that two or three months hence the strategic value of that fortress might no longer exist. No man wished to begin the new offensive more than he. But what one wished to do and what one could do were two entirely different matters.

At the moment, the two armies opposing each other in the desert were having a 'breather', since neither had sufficient superiority of armour to launch a full-scale offensive. Rommel had two modified armoured divisions, one partially armoured Italian division, one Italian motorized division, and four infantry divisions.

Auchinleck said that he needed two, if not three, fully equipped and trained armoured divisions to defeat his adversary. He had, in fact one – the 7th Armoured Division. His other, the 2nd, after the evacuation of Greece and the long retreat from Benghazi, no longer existed as a fighting unit, Admittedly, apart from light tanks which had proved themselves useless against the Germans, he had 500 tanks. But half of that number were heavy, lumbering 'I' tanks which could not stand up to Rommel's armour.

Because of these shortcomings, he pointed out that all the 'I' tanks had been withdrawn from the 7th Armoured Division. The latter now had one brigade equipped with cruiser tanks, and the other – the 4th – for which there were not enough cruisers, waiting to be armoured with American Stuart tanks. By the end of September there would still not be enough of these Stuarts. Moreover, while they were good tanks, ammunition for them was in short supply, and before they were fit for desert fighting, they would have to be subjected to a number of modifications.

All these, as well as many other practical difficulties, Auchinleck pointed out to Churchill, the Defence Committee, and the Chiefs-of-Staff. Nothing, he said, would persuade him to go, off at 'half-cock'. For that very reason 'Battleaxe' had failed. Tanks, anti-tank guns, and aircraft were the deciding factors in modern war – not mere infantry strength – and nowhere more so than in the fluid war waged over the rolling expanses of the Western Desert.

Having listened to his arguments, it was decided to send the 22nd Armoured Brigade – of the 1st Armoured Division – to the Middle East; a proof that the Chiefs-of-Staff were convinced by what they had heard. Only Churchill remained sceptical. Nevertheless, he admitted that the

General's 'unquestioned abilities, his powers of exposition, his high, dignified, and commanding personality, gave him the feeling that Auchinleck might after all be right'. With considerable reluctance he yielded to the decision that Operation '*Crusader*', as the new offensive was called, should be launched in November.

Thus, having won possibly the toughest battle of his career so far, Auchinleck flew back to Cairo.

While we were changing our Commanders-in-Chief and appointing a Minister of State in the Middle East, the Axis Powers, on the basis of General Paulus' report, were also reorganizing their High Command and discussing the date for their new offensive in North Africa.

In June, Hitler and Mussolini had met once more on the Brenner Pass to consider negotiations with the Vichy Government. While they were talking, Field-Marshal Keitel, the Chief of the OKW, took the opportunity of conferring with General Cavallero, the Chief-of-Staff of the Italian forces. The two soldiers did not see eye to eye about the capture of Cyprus at some future date, or the wisdom of demanding that Pétain should throw open the Port of Tunis to their supply ships. But they were agreed that there was no chance of beginning a new offensive in North Africa before the autumn.

Cavallero pointed out that his forces in the desert had suffered heavy losses and must be reinforced. Keitel countered by saying that, thanks to the RAF and the British submarines, it was difficult enough supplying those troops already there. The experience of the 5th Light Panzer Division had proved that the quality of a unit – its armour and its supply organization – was more important than mere numbers of men. A suitable force for the new offensive, he said, would be two German armoured divisions, with the Trento and Ariete Divisions brought up to full strength, and two or three motorized divisions, together with the troops to safeguard the long lines of communication. It went without saying that more anti-aircraft artillery, fuel, supplies would be necessary and of course, fighters and dive-bombers. As for the *Fliegerkorps X*, it could not be used to better advantage than from the airfields in Crete.

Both Keitel and Cavallero agreed that more heavy and medium artillery must be ranged against Tobruk, while every effort must be made to put Benghazi harbour in full working order and the port strongly defended against air attack. It was also agreed to run single supply ships from Brindisi and Bari to Benghazi as well as from Piraeus as soon as the railway traffic to the Greek port could be got going again.

Ten days after Auchinleck had assumed command in the Middle East, General Gariboldi was replaced as Commander-in-Chief in Libya by General Bastico. The latter was a tough soldier whom the Italians hoped would be able to stand up to Rommel better than his predecessor.

Rommel, who remained in command of the *Afrika Korps*, still declared that he intended taking Tobruk before the end of the year. But, he insisted, the Italian Navy must do far more to protect his Mediterranean supply routes before he could consider an all-out offensive against Egypt in February, 1942. Even to take Tobruk he would need all the reinforcements already promised to him and could not begin that operation until they landed in North Africa complete with their vehicles, fuel, ammunition, and rations. Taking everything into consideration, he said that the attack on Tobruk could not take place before the beginning of October at the earliest.

This view was supported by Field-Marshal von Brauchitsch, the Commander-in-Chief of the German Army. The taking of Tobruk and the advance to the Nile depended upon the flow of supplies, and this would never be adequate unless both Malta and Gibraltar could be reduced to ruins. German strategy, he said, must therefore be based on an attack on Egypt from both directions simultaneously, as well as an advance from the north towards the Persian Gulf. All this should start in October. But, in view of the Russian resistance, it would not be practical to begin the double attack on Egypt before the spring of 1942. The advance on the Persian Gulf would have to be postponed until October of that year. But before either of these campaigns could become possible, Malta must be destroyed by the *Luftwaffe* from Sicily; Gibraltar must be attacked and Tobruk captured. All this, von Brauchitsch said, should be accomplished during the autumn of 1941.

The German Naval Staff was in complete agreement with these views, and backed them up by ordering Admiral Dönitz to despatch U-boats to the Mediterranean.

CHAPTER EIGHTEEN

ORDEAL FROM THE SKY

Hitler's preoccupation with Russia and the lull in the Western Desert brought no respite to the garrison in Tobruk. If elements of the *Luftwaffe* had been withdrawn to the eastern front, neither the men in the perimeter outposts nor those working down at the harbour were conscious of this fact. As for the crews of the ships on the 'Spud Run', their ordeal by bombing grew daily harder to bear.

But of all the garrison, none were under more continuous strain than the crews of the anti-aircraft batteries ringing the harbour. Month after month, day and night, they were in action against the *Luftwaffe* almost without cessation from every form of attack – high-level bombing, combined dive – and high-level bombing, dive-bombing, and minelaying.

From April until September, 1941, Headquarters 4th AA Brigade RA was commanded by Brigadier J N Slater and then by Brigadier J S Muirhead. Some units were relieved from time to time, but 153rd and 235th Heavy AA Batteries RA, Headquarters 14th Light AA Regiment RA and the 39th, 40th, and 57th Light AA Batteries RA were in Tobruk throughout the siege. For 242 days their gunners defended the fortress against all Rommel's attempts to bomb it into submission. In the end, their courage and the accuracy of their shooting broke the morale of his pilots.

But this victory was not speedily or easily won. The struggle between the ack-ack guns and the bombers was bitter and protracted.

With the exception of the 8th Battery of the 3rd Light AA Regiment, which was Australian, all the guns were manned by British troops. Their weapons, especially in the beginning, were a mixed collection made up of British 3.7s and Bofors and captured Italian 102-mms and Bredas and when the siege started there were only sixteen 5.7s and six Bofors to defend the fortress. And between April 10th and June 2nd, the harbour and town were raided in daylight by 807 dive-bombers. By June, the gunners had engaged more than fifteen hundred enemy aircraft of which all but a hundred had struck in daylight.

Slowly – painfully slowly it seemed to the gunners – the 'A' lighters and other ships brought more guns and ammunition to Tobruk, until by the end of June there were twenty-eight 3.7s and a dozen Bofors. By then too, the garrison's fire-power had been increased by some forty Italian guns of various calibre.

The crews lived beside their guns. The pits themselves were solid. Their foundations were of stone and concrete and were protected by a wall of 40-gallon oil-drums filled with sand and rocks. On top of these drums was a parapet of sandbags more often than not filled with condemned Italian flour, which when mixed with sea-water became as hard as cement.

The men slept on old Italian iron bedsteads under the camouflage netting, and when off duty in some nearby cave, if there was one. But they seldom slept for long, for whenever there was a 'Red Warning' they had to stand-to, and there were days when they stood-to more than thirty times and were in action a dozen or more. At the peak of the blitz, their only respite came on moonless nights or when the dust storms blotted out the sun.

At the beginning of the siege, the *Luftwaffe*'s attacks were directed on the shipping in the harbour, or, when there were no ships, on the jetties on the north shore and the town itself. To defeat these, Brigadier Slater put up an umbrella barrage at about 3,000 feet. But the *Stuka* pilots had guts, and either dived through the barrage, under it, or round it. The bravest of them came down to less than 500 feet before releasing their bombs, and, at first, the majority of them got away with it.

So Slater tried new tactics. As more guns arrived, he thickened the 3.7s' barrage and staggered its ceiling, so that the *Stukas* had to come down through a curtain of fire extending for 3,000 feet. He also kept the barrage moving back and forth across the harbour so that the pilots never knew where the fringe of the curtain would be and those who were still brave enough to take a chance had to face the concentrated fire pumped out by the Bofors.

Then, the attackers, too, changed their tactics. They sent over Ju 88s, escorted by Me 109s, flying high. While the heavy ack-ack guns were concentrating on these planes bombing the harbour from 20,000 feet, the *Stukas* came screaming down to attack the gun-sites from the four points of the compass.

The first time this happened, most of the guns' crews were taken completely by surprise, for above the thunder of their own guns they never heard either the diving Stukas or the high whine of their falling bombs. Some coolly went on firing at their target. Others dashed for shelter as the bombs burst round their pits and the machine-gun bullets tipped into the sandbags and ricocheted off the metal drums.

It took cold courage to go on firing without flinching as the bombs burst choking and blinding the men at the guns.

A Tobruk gunner described one of these first surprise attacks one blazing hot afternoon early in May. They had picked up a formation of enemy planes flying in from the sea.

At first, they were out of range. Then, as they swung slowly towards the harbour, their height was read off on the height finder.

'Twelve, nine hundred,' orders the GPO to the predictor.

'Steady!'

'Fire!'

There is a rattle and clang from the guns as the long shells are rammed home; a pause, and then the air is torn with the crash of a salvo. This is followed by another pause that seems to last for ages. Then four little round puffs of smoke appear near the leading planes. Again the guns crash out, and this time – a plane staggers and then plunges into a steep dive.

'Suddenly a yell; "Pla-ane!" cuts through the din. Even as the look-out shouts his warning, the whoo-sh of the falling bombs tells us what has happened. A squadron of *Stukas* has come in from behind and is diving on us out of the sun.

'Cr-aash! go the bombs like the splitting of a thousand trees, and those of us who are not already on the ground, are hurled flat. Cr-aash! Wurr-mp! Cr-aash come the bombs again and again and again!

'We are blinded, suffocated; the breath knocked out of our bodies as the earth heaves beneath us. The world seems to be collapsing round us and burying us in black darkness. We claw the ground and pray. Nothing can live in such an inferno. It is going on for ever and ever…

'Suddenly everything is still. As the clouds of smoke and dust drift away, we pick ourselves up, scarcely believing that we are still alive. But not all of us…

'From the reeking gunpit stagger tattered, grimy gunners carrying limp, bloodstained forms. A blackened figure stumbles towards us, its clothes hanging in rags. It's my buddy, Phil, shouting that his gunpit is afire and his ammunition exploding. He has already dragged a couple of his wounded from the blaze…'

Yes, it took cold courage to go on firing under such conditions. But those who kept their guns in action, even though they could not see their target, often came through unscathed. It was the men who ran for shelter who were killed and wounded.

When this first attack was over Slater called his officers and NCOs to his headquarters and gave his orders. In future every gun was to remain in action when set upon by dive-bombers. No man was to run for shelter. Those who were not actually manning the guns were to engage the *Stukas* with light machine-guns and rifles. The first duty of the gunners was the defence of the harbour and so no gun-site was to use more than one gun for his own protection. As soon as possible he would see that each battery should have one light ack-ack gun near its emplacement.

Since it was obvious that the guns themselves were to become the targets, Slater ordered that the pits must be dug deeper and their parapets strengthened to resist a 1,000-pounder exploding ten yards off. Dummy gun-sites must be built near the ack-ack positions, manned by dummy men and surrounded by dummy trucks and ammunition dumps and to fool the attackers these dummy guns must not only produce convincing flashes but clouds of dust, timed to synchronize with the fire of the real guns. As a final piece of deception, Slater ordered that the dummies and the real guns must be interchangeable.

A regular gunner, he was a master of improvisation, and under his leadership the morale of his guns' crews soared.

During the height of the battle they destroyed over a hundred enemy planes and damaged nearly twice that number for the loss of a dozen killed and some seventy wounded. But more important than the number of aircraft destroyed was the fact that the gunners of Tobruk killed so many of

Rommel's best pilots that he was forced to call a halt to the dive-bombing by day.

For a while he tried to replace these pilots by Italians, but they had neither the nerve nor the skill to press home their attacks through Slater's roaming barrage. 'Gestapo' planes accompanied them to see that they fulfilled their mission, but such was the reputation of the ack-ack gunners that these pilots preferred to face disgrace rather than the flak.

So for a time, Rommel had to resort to high-level bombing which became less and less effective as the anti-aircraft defences were strengthened. In July, for the first time for many weeks. General Morshead sanctioned the unloading of ships in the harbour during daylight.

Ironically, as a direct result of the growing efficiency of the ack-ack batteries, the lot of the ships on the 'Spud Run' worsened, for if Rommel was prevented from sinking the supply ships in the harbour, he was determined to destroy them *en route*. Thus. the battle of 'bomb alley' intensified as the *Luftwaffe* swooped like hawks on every vessel sighted. Steadily, the toll of our ships rose, until Cunningham said that it was asking too much of the same few ships to continue on the Tobruk run week in and week out.

By June it was possible for the RAF to provide a certain amount of fighter cover during the day for the destroyers on the 'Spud Run'. So Cunningham decided they should be sailed from Alexandria in order to reach Tobruk under cover of darkness, unload their cargoes of men and stores and sail again to be well clear of 'bomb alley' before daylight and in time to rendezvous with our fighters.

But Alexandria swarmed with enemy agents and in no time at all Rommel knew of these nocturnal visits, he sent over bombers at night to sow magnetic mines in the harbour and the swept channel while others flew out to sea to search for our ships in the moonlight.

These night attacks at sea placed the destroyer captains in a dilemma. In order to keep to their strict time table they were obliged to proceed at high speed, with the result that in the brilliant Mediterranean moonlight their wake, sparkling with phosphorous, could easily be spotted by the enemy. If on the other hand, they slowed down, or even started to zig-zag, they could not deliver their cargoes and be away from Tobruk before dawn. So the destroyers just kept going and trusted to luck. But often the soldiers crowding their decks arrived soaked to the skin; drenched by the ghostly plumes of water thrown up by near misses.

A British six-pounder gun crew opening fire on enemy motor transport.

German artillerymen stockpiling shells beside an 88mm Flak gun.

South African troops salvage food supplies from a dump in the desert.

German Infantry struggle through wind-blown sand, North Africa 1941.

A German 88-mm anti-aircraft gun being used in an anti-tank role.

Australin Infantrymen operating from a front-line dug-out.

A British tank put out of commission at the Halfaya Pass.

German Panzer III's, advancing over stony desert terrain.

British field gun and a German tank, both knocked-out.

A member of the Afrika Korps, *protecting his face from the blowing sand.*

A British 5.5 field gun, during the advance towards El Agheila, January 1942.

Allied officer inspecting destroyed German '88' anti-tank gun.

A British SAS raiding party returning by jeep from behind enemy lines.

Allied infantry advancing past a destroyed DAK. Mark III Panzer.

A truck-load of British troops crossing the border from Egypt into Libya.

The wreckage of British ships in Tobruk harbour.

German infantry, waiting for the artillery barrage to lift before attacking Tobruk.

Alleid officers and men wait for transportation to PoW camps, June 1942.

Finally, this bombing of his destroyers by moonlight became so accurate that Cunningham could not afford to risk his ships except during the moonless periods. Then, by sending two and sometimes three destroyers each night and the fast minelayers *Abdiel* and *Latona* once a week, he kept his promise that the Navy would supply the garrison at no matter what cost. In August, during the moonless period, the destroyers made twenty-nine trips to Tobruk and the minelayers seven.

But moon or no moon, in daylight and in darkness, with or without fighter cover, the 'A' lighters and the little ships of the Inshore Squadron continued the 'Spud Run'.

One of the 'A' lighters – *A 14* – was an early victim of the magnetic mines laid in the harbour, when she blew up while approaching her berthing place. Her crew and Commanding Officer survived, but the latter. Lieutenant Mullins, RNR, was later murdered by thugs in a side-street in Alexandria. Two other landing craft, Also, commanded by Sub-Lieutenant Thom, DSC, RNVR and *A8* (Sub-Lieutenant Wright, RNVR), were set upon by dive-bombers off Sidi Barrani. For four hours they fought a Homeric battle with the *Stukas*, firing over a thousand rounds apiece from their pom-poms. Then, having been repeatedly hit by bombs and machine-gunned, *A8* sank and as she did so, the door leading from the wheelhouse jammed. Since this was also the only exit from the engine-room, all her crew not already killed on the bridge were imprisoned within her. One seaman, determined not to be drowned, forced himself through a small scuttle from the wheelhouse and survived with all his ribs crushed.

A tug came to the rescue of Thom's stricken craft and tried to tow her to Tobruk. But she was so torn to pieces by bombs that she sank before she reached harbour.

By June, 1941, the 'A' lighters were based on Mersa Matruh, and there they loaded their cargoes of tanks, guns, petrol, land-mines and vehicles for Tobruk and to Mersa they returned – if, indeed, they returned at all – bringing back damaged tanks, anti-aircraft guns, prisoners, and often their own wounded, for during that summer they seldom managed to evade the dive-bombers.

While the 'A' lighters and the destroyers brought the weapons, ammunition, and soldiers, the garrison's food supply depended largely upon the safe arrival of a small fleet of merchant ships – all very old – and four captured Italian fishing schooners. The most famous of the latter was the schooner *Maria Giovanni*. Even more famous was her captain,

Lieutenant Alfred Palmer, DSC, RNR. A burly Australian, he was affectionately known to the garrison as 'Pedlar'. Once he had been a merchant seaman, but had come to rest in China, where he had been a steward in the Shanghai Club, and in his spare time had commanded a company of Chinese Lancers in the Shanghai Volunteers.

'Pedlar' was a dedicated man, for he believed it his sacred duty to save his fellow Diggers in Tobruk from starvation, and he had managed to instil this faith into his crew. He was also a man of cunning.

Loaded to the gunwale with stores and often with live sheep on deck, he would sail his schooner to sea from Alexandria or Mersa Matruh and during daylight head for Crete to 'fox' the enemy that he was just another Italian schooner. Then, when darkness came, he would shape a course for Tobruk. But throughout the long hours of daylight he kept a weather-eye open for the *Stukas* and was always ready to tack towards the enemy's territory. Not that he was afraid to fight, for his ship was bristling with captured Fiats and other guns, but because he was at sea to bring food and the odd bottle of rum to his 'cobbers' in Tobruk.

He was a true seaman, but his navigation was rusty and his ship's compass erratic, so that he boasted that at night he sometimes took a running 'fix' on the headlights of the German lorries on the coast road near Bardia. And he was not ashamed to admit that he was happiest when he had sighted the shaded green light marking the entrance to Tobruk harbour.

But the Germans played poor 'Pedlar' Palmer a cad's trick by placing another shaded green light along the coast to the east of the harbour. And one night, when the off-shore wind brought with it a mist of driving sand, 'Pedlar' sailed into the trap. With all sail set, the old *Maria Giovanni* ran hard ashore.

When the Germans captured her captain and crew they were all over the side up to their necks in the water digging a channel in the sand to refloat their ship.

'Pedlar' was shot while making a dash for it, and two years later he was repatriated to Australia with but one arm.

CHAPTER NINETEEEN

FORTRESS UNDER FIRE

Rommel stood on Hill 209 and looked at Tobruk through his field-glasses. The white houses, pock-marked by bomb splinters, sprouted out of the dun-coloured desert like little clumps of mushrooms. Feathers of dust marked the tracks of the lorries grinding up the escarpment to the perimeter. Over the still blue surface of the harbour motor launches darted like water beetles. A small merchantman rode at anchor, her derricks swung outboard above the lighters lying in her shadow. Further east, at the entrance of the harbour, two whalers steamed side by side trailing their long tails behind them. Suddenly, the water astern of them rose in a white plume. Seconds later, the reverberating rumble of a detonated mine rolled across the desert to the little group of officers standing on the hill. One of them, General von Ravenstein, glanced furtively at Rommel and saw the muscles of his jaw twitch with anger. Then, as the last echo of the distant explosion spent itself, the Commander of the *Afrika Korps* turned his back on Tobruk and walked to his waiting car.

That night orders were issued from Rommel's headquarters to bombard the fortress with heavy artillery.

A few days later, the first shells came hurtling over the escarpment to crash into the town and harbour and Tobruk's ordeal by gunfire began. It lasted from mid-June until the siege was raised. The Germans installed huge 6-inch siege guns in the Wadi Belgassen near Bardia, some eight and a half miles from Tobruk. The first of these was christened 'Bardia Bill' by the garrison. Other heavy artillery was sited on the escarpment near El Adem and behind Hill 209, from where two big guns known jointly as 'Salient Sue' lobbed their shells into the main pumping station in the Wadi Auda.

'Bardia Bill' was the greatest menace. Directed by high-flying spotter planes, its gunners shelled the shipping in the harbour and very quickly had the range of all the wrecks alongside which the landing craft used to hide-up. Two wrecks in particular were heavily bombarded; the *Marco Polo* and the *Liguria*. Beached on the south shore, their towering, rusting hulls gave protection to the lighters and little ships. '*Bardia Bill*' poured its huge projectiles into them, but with, little effect.

A particular bugbear to the German gunners was *Eskimo Nell*. She was one of six little sponge-fishing vessels which we had captured early in 1941; four in Tobruk and two in Dema. The Navy dubbed them the 'F' Class and used them for all manner of harbour duties such as ferrying troops to the destroyers and salvage work.

One by one they all fell victims to the violence of the enemy and the elements. *F1*, having been damaged by near-misses, was moored alongside a wreck and lived on for a time as a gun-site for two 20-mm Bredas manned by the 38th Light AA Battery. But one day after she had been repaired, 'Bob' Blackburn, who had been captain of the *Ladybird*, took *F1* out to sea to save the crews of two landing craft that had been bombed. It was blowing hard and no sooner did she strike the seas than her stern post fell to bits and she sank. Blackburn and his crew were left swimming well within range of 'Bardia Bill'. But the latter's gunners had the decency to leave them alone to be rescued by a minesweeper.

F2 was destroyed by the *Stukas* while hauled up on the slips, *F3* blew up on a mine, while *F5* and *F6* were wrecked in a sand-storm. But *F4*, old *Eskimo Nell*, survived the siege.

When Derna fell to Rommel, Lt Comander Douglas Duff, RNR, set sail in her eastwards with three 7-mm Bredas and a 7-pounder anti-tank gun mounted on her deck. On the voyage she fought a duel with an Italian submarine and forced it to crash-dive. Later off Bardia, she was mistaken for an enemy by the gunboat *Aphis* and came within an ace of being blown out of the water. In this action Duff was wounded, but *Eskimo Nell* again survived to reach Alexandria. Refitted, she sailed for Tobruk with a mixed cargo, which included a consignment of land-mines, and ran the gauntlet of the *Stukas* in 'bomb alley'.

There was something about her high prow and rakish stern that appealed to the eye of Captain Smith and caused him to keep her at Tobruk. She was a proud little ship, and her name which was inscribed on her wheelhouse was fashioned in metal studs from Army boots. She was known to every man in the garrison, and since she ferried thousands of soldiers ashore on their arrival and carried them out to the destroyers when they were relieved, she was their first and last link with the fortress.

During her life she must have survived more bombs and shells than any other single ship in the Royal Navy.

It was 'Bardia Bill's' habit to welcome any ship entering the harbour at night. Although they did little damage and caused but few casualties, the distant roar of the huge gun and the shriek of the mighty shells, tearing through the darkness and plunging into the harbour to throw up great spectre-white columns of water around the ship, was a terrifying experience for the soldiers packed tight on the deck. Such a baptism by fire played the devil with the nerves of the men who had just reached the end of a perilous voyage along the North African coast.

To counter this night shelling, the 2/12th Field Regiment set up four 60-pounders and the 104th RHA four 25-pounders and two 149-mm coastal defence guns on the shore to the east of the town. Their crews were always closed-up whenever there was shipping in the harbour or due to arrive. Although 'Bardia Bill's' position was constantly shifted, these batteries eventually pin-pointed most of them so that the Germans seldom got off more than a dozen rounds before they were forced to move.

Meanwhile, up on the perimeter, the artillery under the command of Brigadier L E Thompson were ceaseless seeking out Rommel's gun positions and the heavy ack-ack were taking their toll of the high-flying reconnaissance planes. By night too, infantry patrols, accompanied by sappers armed with explosives, crept through the enemy minefields and wire to raid the gun-sites near the El Adem road and in the Salient.

A typical 'guns patrol', as they were called, was carried out by the Australians of the 2/13th Battalion. It was known that the Germans had brought up heavy artillery which was sited somewhere between El Adem and the sea. For several nights prior to the raid. Lieutenant John Martin had made a series of trips to locate the weak spots between the enemy positions. It was during one of these that by good luck the German guns had opened up on Tobruk, so that Martin had been able to take a compass bearing on the flashes while another patrol had also managed to take bearings for cross-reference.

Two nights later a patrol of fifty men, including six sappers, led by Captain O M Walsoe and Lieutenants John Martin and Ross Bucknell, set out to destroy the gun-sites. Undetected, they passed through the gap cleared and taped by the engineers in the minefield and wire, and reached what was obviously the tracks cut in the crusty surface of the desert by the German supply lorries. Across these, they discovered signal wires, which they cut. Having marked the gap in the severed wire with a large 'V' sign scratched in the sand, the patrol moved in for a further 500 yards. Then, according to plan, they split up into three parties. Walsoe and a few men stayed at 'headquarters', while Bucknell led his section forward to cover a German strongpoint. Martin, with the remainder, moved stealthily forward on the compass bearing to the gun-sites.

But they had scarcely covered fifty yards when the desert was flooded by Very lights and parachute flares. Hurling themselves flat, the Australians lay still waiting for the inevitable burst of machine-gun fire.

The flares drifted away on the night breeze, flickered, and died out. In the silence, Martin raised himself on his elbows. In the darkness, he could only just see Bucknell's party moving forward again. But he could hear them clearly. At every step he could hear the small, brittle shells covering the surface of the desert crunching under their boots and it was obvious that the Germans could hear them too, for even as he listened, another string of flares burst in the sky, forcing him to duck.

'Off boots!'

Cursing under their breath, the Diggers took off their boots and then climbed gingerly to their feet.

For two hours Martin's party moved painfully over those knife-sharp shells in their stockinged feet hunting for the gun-sites. But they found only empty pits, shell-cases, abandoned ammunition boxes and finally, more wheel tracks that showed that the guns had shifted their positions.

Martin fired the green Very light which was the signal that he was moving back to join Walsoe. Bucknell, too started to withdraw, but as he did so his party came under heavy fire from the strongpoint and were forced to go to ground. As they lay there, Bucknell counted his men. Two were missing. Crawling back on his belly, he found them. Their feet bleeding, and swearing fearfully, they were scouring the desert for their lost boots!

That night the patrol had nothing to show for their painful adventure except a coil of German signal wire. But often these 'guns patrols' reached their objectives. When they did, the raiders returned with the vital parts which were fitted to the captured guns used by the 'Bush' Artillery in the fortress. At the beginning of the siege, the regular gunners laughed at the Digger infantrymen who manned these weapons. But as time went by, they grew to respect both their shooting and their courage, for many of these guns burst when shells exploded in their barrels. But the Diggers went on firing others like them with the aid of a length of rope.

The garrison's artillery, which consisted of some of the finest units in the British Army, was never able to silence Rommel's guns, simply because he had so many of them and so, all through the burning heat of the summer, the Germans poured shells into Tobruk.

Then, suddenly and witthout warning, the *Stukas* were back again. Before their return, Rommel stepped up the night raids on the harbour, and while some of his bombers were drawing the fire of the ack-ack batteries, others were laying mines. The latter were so successful that for a brief period they actually closed the harbour to the supply ships.

It was August when the *Stukas* came back and by then the Navy had lent a hand at strengthening Tobruk's anti-aircraft defences. This they did by sending to the fortress three remarkable weapons called officially Unrotated Projectiles, or 'UPs' for short. They were multi-barrel rocket projectors, capable of firing twenty rockets into the air simultaneously. These burst open to release small parachutes from which trailed a length of piano wire armed with a small bomb.

Some months before the 'UPs' were installed. I recorded in my diary meeting the officer in charge of them, Lt Commander Sanderson, RN. During one of my stays in Tobruk I shared his room in Navy House. He had furnished it with ingenuity from the various wrecks in the harbour. From one he had taken a wash-basin, from another a handsome dressing-table, linen sheets, and strips of carpet, and from yet another the table around which we sometimes sat down to a four of bridge. Where he had acquired the large framed colour-print of Churchill that hung in splendid solitude on the wall, I never discovered.

We had met before at Dover, where the 'UPs' were tried out for the first time to defend the harbour against the tip-and-run dive-bombers which nipped across the Channel from the nearby airfields in occupied France.

The 'UPs' were one of Churchill's pet devices and I happened to be in Dover in my minesweeper on the day when Churchill arrived to watch a demonstration firing. A hard easterly wind was blowing when the 'UP' went off with a thunderous roar, hurling its missiles into the sky. One was reputed to have entangled itself outside the windows of Vice-Admiral Sir Bertram Ramsey's quarters at Dover Castle, before exploding. Another drifted over the town to do considerable damage. One I know, because I watched it with growing apprehension, fouled the rigging of a minesweeping trawler before pursuing its startled crew as they raced for safety along the Southern Railway jetty.

After this alarming display, Ramsey declared that he had little faith in the 'UP' as a weapon of defence, and so Sanderson sailed for the Middle East in search of sites for his monsters.

Tobruk was an ideal spot for them with its encircling hills and prevailing off-shore wind and so he installed three 'UPs' there, each one sited to give the best possible protection to the ships in the harbour.

The weapons were in the charge of Lieutenants G E E Somerset and Lambton Burn, RNVR. These young officers and their sailors had their first chance against the *Luftwaffe* on August 10th. At dawn that morning the *Maria Giovanni* was alongside the jetty just below Navy House unloading stores and the 'UPs' were ordered to give her the maximum protection. All day long the Ju 88s and Savoias were bombing the harbour, but none came within range of the new weapons. But as the sun sank towards the horizon, eighteen *Stukas* lined up to make a dead-set at 'Pedlar' Palmer's little schooner. As they dived, Somerset gave the order to fire. Thirty rockets roared up to meet the *Stukas*. A second later another salvo of thirty was hurled skywards. The diving formations split up to take violent avoiding action, the pilots letting go their bombs in panic as they twisted and turned to escape the trailing wires with their dangling *charges*. Thrown into confusion by this new and mysterious weapon, the Stukas fled for home. But not all escaped. One plunged into the desert, two more were hard hit by the Bofors, while a third made off with a 'UP's' wire trailing from its rudder. Not a single bomb fell anywhere near the little schooner.

After several attempts to get through the 'UPs' barrage, the *Stukas* gave it up and turned their attention to targets beyond the range of all the Unrotated Projectiles.

CHAPTER TWENTY

THE DIGGERS DEPART

There was a monotonous sameness about the letters which the men of the garrison wrote home to their wives, families and sweethearts. They told of the fleas and flies and sandstorms and the lack of women and beer and cigarettes and because there was little else to do, the men wrote a great many letters as they sat in their caves in the wadis, their sangars out on the perimeter, under the camouflage nets beside their guns and on the beaches at the edge of the sea.

But as the months dragged by there crept into those letters an insidious note of resignation – an undertone of philosophic contentment – towards their utterly unnatural existence. They wrote almost with affection about the fly-blown Libyan port in which they were virtually prisoners. In spite of the *Stukas*, the shelling, the eternal bully beef, the brackish water and the absence of women, they said they were happy. They didn't know why, but there was somthing about Tobruk, the blue of the Mediterranean by day and the dark indigo of the desert sky by night, even its detachment from the rest of the world, that tugged at their heartstrings.

Perhaps, they wrote, this was all to the good, since they looked like growing old there!

Life was hard and often dangerous. But hardship and danger forged strong bonds of comradeship, binding men together. Besides, in time a man could get used to anything. Even to a world without women! Thus wrote the men in Tobruk telling their folks not to worry about them.

But thousands of miles away in Australia the wives, families and sweethearts of the men of the garrison became afraid. Particularly, the wives and sweethearts.

What would become of their men cut off in that filthy desert fortress, lacking good wholesome food and fresh vegetables, clean clothes and fresh water for washing? They were living like savages, going around stark naked, their bodies pitted with desert sores and sleeping cheek-by-jowl in caves. What was more, they wrote that they were happy. Happy to play interminable games of cards, sleep, swim and fight. Happy in each other's company and able to get along without women. What would these men be like when they got home? If they ever got home!

Fanned by the fulsome praise lavished on the fighting qualities of the Diggers in the British Press, as well as the German propaganda accusing the British of waging the war with Dominion troops, such fear swept across Australia like a bush fire until it finally destroyed the Menzies Government.

Menzies had given his word that when the AIF sailed for the Middle East, the divisions of the Australian Corps would be kept together. But Menzies had broken faith with the people. At a moment of crisis the Corps had been split up.

In order to pull Churchill's political chestnuts out of the fire, some of the Australians, under Blamey, had been sent to Greece. Others under Morshead, had been rushed to Cyrenaica to save the British Army from defeat in the desert. Blamey's troops had been chased to the beathes of the Aegean, and Mors-hcad's men had been pursued headlong into Tobruk.

Practically the whole of the 9th Division and a brigade of the 7th were shut up in the fortress, where they were kept alive not by the British Navy, but by a flotilla of little destroyers belonging to the Royal Australian Navy.

According to the English newspapers, the *BBC* and 'Lord Haw-Haw', the men in Tobruk – the 'Rats' – were nearly all Diggers, supported by Indians, Cypriots, and Palestinians. The Tommies were sitting on their backsides in the old country waiting for Hitler's invasion.

Such views were commonly and openly expressed in Australia in the early summer of 1941. It was known there too that when Menzies had flown to London in May, he and Churchill had not seen eye-to-eye about the conduct of the war. Menzies had suggested that an Imperial War Cabinet should be formed containing representatives of the four Dominions. Churchill had flatly turned down the idea.

Blamey had met with no better success when he proposed to Wavell the relief of the Diggers in Tobruk so that they might join up with the rest of the Corps in Syria and Palestine.

When Menzies returned after visiting Canada, he was forced to resign in favour of Fadden. Then Curtin's Labour Party ousted Fadden. But each in turn, under pressure from the electorate, insisted that their troops be withdrawn from Tobruk.

Churchill did his level best to dissuade the Australian Government from its resolve in a long series of telegrams to Canberra. He felt certain, he cabled Auchinleck, that the Australians would play the game if the facts were put to them squarely. But he was wrong.

Having put the facts squarely to Fadden, he said: 'I trust that you will weigh very carefully the immense responsibility which you would assume before history by depriving the Australians of the glory of holding Tobruk till victory is won, which otherwise, by God's help, will be theirs for ever.' Even this eloquent and stern warning failed. The Australian Government remained obdurate.

In a further long telegram to Auhinleck, Churchill said that he had long feared the dangerous reactions on Australian and world opinion of our seeming to fight our battles in the Middle East with Dominion troops.

He might well have added that such reactions were largely the fault of the British Press and the *BBC*, whose correspondents consistently ignored the existence of British troops in that theatre. The public were never told, for instance, about such units as the 153rd and 235th Heavy AA Batteries of the Royal Artillery, without which Tobruk would not have survived for a single week.

Churchill, however, chided Auchinleck for having recently ordered the newly arrived 50th British Division to Cyprus instead of to the desert and smarting under this rebuke and deeply offended by the attitude of the Australian Government, Auchinleck proposed tendering his resignation on the grounds that he did not have the latter's confidence.

Churchill then got in touch with Oliver Lyttelton and confessed that he was astounded at the Australian Government's decision, for he was sure that it would be repudiated by the people themselves if the true facts could have been made known to them. But for reasons of security it was not possible to tell either the Australians at home or the soldiers in Tobruk the truth; namely, that in a matter of weeks. Operation '*Crusader*' was to be launched to relieve Tobruk and drive Rommel out of Cyrenaica. In the circumstances, all that Churchill could do was to continue to press, first Fadden and then Curtin, to change their minds. But by then, no Prime Minister could hope to remain in office by running contrary to the will of the people who were determined that the Australians should be withdrawn from Tobruk.

In the fortress the Diggers took little interest in the political changes taking place in their country. On most evenings before dark on the perimeter, those who could would gather round to listen to the *BBC* news, relayed to the Company posts a few yards from the front wire by the Battalion HQ Signals. One sweltering summer night, the dusty, sweating, bearded men suddenly heard that Menzies was out of office and that Curtin was forming a Government. There were neither cheers nor groans. The news was received in silence. Out there on the perimeter, facing the enemy across no-man's-land, party politics had no meaning.

Nevertheless, the sultry summer air over the fortress was rife with rumours; rumours that many of the Diggers refused to believe and moreover, did not want to believe. Since the failure of '*Battleaxe*' they had resigned themselves to waiting until another operation was launched, when they would triumphantly link arms with the advancing troops outside the perimeter defences. It simply did not occur to them that they could get out of Tobruk by any other route, least of all by sea. 'Ming the Merceless' had told them that to leave Tobruk they would have to fight their way out and all this talk about being withdrawn to Palestine was so much balderdash.

In the blazing heat of the North African summer the men of the garrison moved slowly about their business. Dysentery and desert sores were sapping their vitality. Sickness had thinned their ranks until the infantry battalions faring the enemy were reduced to less than seventy-five per cent of their normal strength.

That summer the convalescent camp in the Wadi Auda was always full and the destroyers seldom made the return trip to Alexandria without evacuating their quota of lean, weary soldiers, the pus suppurating through the bandages round their legs and arms.

The handfuls of men coming up to Tobruk to replace the hospital cases, arrived with fresh stories about the impending withdrawal of the Division.

Blamey, they said, was again demanding that the entire 9th Division should be sent to Palestine and Blamey, as Deputy Commander-in-Chief Middle East, meant business. He insisted that after all those months in Tobruk the 9th was in danger of becoming a wild, undisciplined collection of bandits. Officers and men alike needed rest, re-equipping, and training. The new Government, led by Curtin, fully supported Blamey and 'Ming the Merceless' had twice travelled to Cairo to discuss the Division's future.

Although such stories had a ring of truth about them the Diggers listened to them with incredulity. Thoughts of being in Haifa again, of drinking iced beer in a bar, eating fresh oranges and meat, dancing in night-clubs with pretty girls and swimming at Tel Aviv without concern for the *Stukas*, were tantalizing. But it was useless to daydream, the facts must be faced. What of Tobruk? If the 9th left, who would defend the fortress against Rommel?

The answer came: The Poles!

Then, one morning towards the end of July, three strange officers presented themselves at the 9th Divisional Headquarters. They wore grey shirts and shorts, comical little pith helmets and glittering silver insignia. They were very smart, clean, freshly laundered and they smelt slightly scented. Clicking their polished heels, they saluted and shook hands with everyone in sight and then saluted again. They were Poles! And one of them was a general called Kapanski.

Even when the advance party of the 1st Battalion of the Polish Carpathian Brigade arrived, the Diggers had their doubts whether they had come as reliefs or reinforcements. But by mid-August it was confirmed that the Poles were there to release the 18th Brigade. But still there were sceptics who were prepared to wager a month's pay that the old 9th was destined to stay in the fortress until the siege was raised. They were not pessimists, but wishful thinkers.

CHAPTER TWENTY-ONE

A Night to Remember

The Polish Carpathian Brigade had been formed in Syria by General Kapanski. It consisted of regular soldiers who had fiercely resisted the German invasion in 1939 and a large number of volunteers. The majority of the former had been officers who, having escaped from Hungarian, Rumanian and German prison camps, had made their way to Syria to join the Brigade as NCOs and private soldiers. The rest were patriots who, rather than live under the Nazis, had left their homes and families and suffered ghastly hardships tramping across Europe in order to fight for the Allied cause.

When France capitulated, Kapanski, ignoring orders from Vichy, marched his force into Palestine, taking with him all the arms, equipment, and vehicles supplied by the French. For more than a year the Brigade had remained in Palestine and Egypt, it had been camped outside Alexandria for several months before the decision was made to send it to Tobruk to relieve the 18th Australian Infantry Brigade.

There were Staff Officers in Cairo who predicted that this move was doomed to failure from the start. Everyone knew, they said, that the Poles were raring to kill Germans. But they also had quite a reputation as lady-killers, and so were what was technically known as a 'bad security risk'.

Even if their leave were stopped prior to departure, there were bound to be those truants who would sneak out of their camp at Agomi to take passionate leave of their lights o' love in Alexandria. There would be wild farewell parties in the Monseigneur Bar and Pastroudi's, these Staff Officers warned the Navy and every Axis agent would know exactly what was afoot.

The Navy shrugged its shoulders and remarked that conveying the Poles to Tobruk looked like being a sticky business. So they gave the operation the code name 'Treacle'.

But no one, least of all Cunningham, really treated this undertaking lightly. The evacuations of Greece and Crete were still fresh in his memory and although 'Treacle' was not an evacuation, it nevertheless entailed the withdrawal of large numbers of soldiers from under the very nose of the enemy. The risks were enormous and the odds even more heavily weighed against his ships than they had been during those desperate days in the Aegean, for now the *Luftwaffe* were in possession of the Cretan airfields as well as those around Tobruk.

To succeed, 'Treacle' would have to be a combined operation in the fullest sense of that term. Its success would depend upon split-second timing and perfect planning by the Staff Officers of the three Services in cooperation with Morshead, the Fortress Commander, Poland, the Senior Naval Officer Inshore Squadron and Smith, the Naval Officer in Charge, Tobruk.

It was fortunate indeed to have these three able, level-headed officers in Tobruk at such a time; officers who not only inspired confidence in those under them, but who were masters of improvisation and in Tobruk, where there were no facilities for the quick unloading of ships and handling large numbers of troops, a positive genius for improvisation would be needed.

Morshead had twice left the fortress to confer with the planning staffs in Cairo and was confident that his Transport and Movements Control Officers, together with Smith and his staff at Navy House, could cope with their end of the operation. He had given orders that extra mobile 3.7s were to be moved in from the perimeter to strengthen the harbour defences and had arranged with Poland that the 'A' lighters and other small craft arriving in Tobruk should be retained there to ferry troops between the ships and the shore. His pioneers, sappers, and the Docks Group had further improved the berthing facilities alongside those wrecks used as wharves by the destroyers. The men leaving would take with them only what they could carry on their backs; the rest of their equipment, including vehicles, would be left behind for the Poles.

No amount of planning, however thorough, could insure against all the hazards of an operation involving so many lives. It was for this reason, therefore, that Operation 'Treacle' was an experiment. If it succeeded – and that was a very big 'if' – Cunningham, Auchinleck, and Tedder were prepared to repeat it until the 15,000 Australians in Tobruk had been replaced by a like number of British and Polish troops. But in no event could this relief be allowed to delay the start of the new offensive in November, before which all the available destroyers, 'A' lighters and other ships of the Inshore Squadron would be engaged in carrying tanks, guns, ammunition and supplies to the fortress. Auchinleck made this point clear in his telegrams to Whitehall, and Churchill, who loyally supported his decisions, forwarded them on to Canberra.

A great deal, therefore, depended upon 'Treacle'. Everyone concerned knew that if the operation was to work it must do so with clockwork precision. Yet in their hearts, few believed that Rommel would allow it to work. He had vowed that he would either overwhelm the garrison or starve it out. Now that his reputation was at stake, it was inconceivable he would permit the Diggers to escape without making a supreme effort to destroy them.

'Treacle' began on the first day of the moonless period in August when three destroyers and the minelayer *Latona*, loaded with nearly a thousand troops and some two hundred tons of stores, sailed from Alexandria, escorted by other destroyers. All during the day relays of fighter squadrons flew over the ships. Then, as darkness fell and the Hurricanes turned for home, the first of the bombers and long-range fighters set out from their bases in Egypt, heading west for the Axis airfields. Their task was a dual one; to bomb the runways and then circle the airfields so that the Germans would not dare to light the flarepaths for their pilots to take off into the inky darkness.

As the convoy approached Tobruk other bombers roared out of the east to Bardia to drop bombs and flares over the German long-range guns. As they did so, a destroyer was detached from the convoy to fire salvoes into the gun positions. Then, as the three destroyers and the minelayer neared Tobruk bay and swung to port, the batteries of 60- and 25-pounders opened up on 'Bardia Bill' and his mates. The timing was superb. Blinded by the smoke-shells and under a deluge of high explosive, the German gunners could see nothing, while the star-shells bursting in the sky guided the ships up the narrow swept channel into the harbour.

In Tobruk the Diggers waited. They stood shoulder to shoulder on the only jetty, on the rusting decks of two half-sunken hulks, packed like cattle in the cavernous holds of the 'A' lighters, and on the decks of launches and tugs. On the quay below Navy House and at the edge of beaches, the lorries waited. All round the harbour, the crews of the 3.7s and the Bofors and the 'UPs' waited.

It was a night to remember. Yet in retrospect, to many of those who were there it must appear like a dream. But for the evidence of my diary, I could easily believe I had imagined the whole business. Like a nightmare, it seemed to last a lifetime. Infact it was all over in the space of half an hour.

I watched it sitting on the old green bench outside Navy House. I had known about the operation for some weeks before it started and I was one of those who did not believe it could succeed.

To start with, so many people were involved in it that it seemed ridiculous to imagine that the spies in Alexandria would not get wind of it and inform Rommel what we were up to. How could we possibly spirit away a thousand men from Alexandria of all places, pack them into warships and put to sea without anyone knowing? Even assuming this could be, I felt convinced that the ships would be spotted *en route* and bombed to blazes. Of course, they would have fighter protection. But it was so simple for the Germans to launch an attack from their nearby airfields at the exact moment when our own fighters had reached the limit of their range. Experience had taught me that if the *Luftwaffe* set its heart on sinking a convoy, nothing would stop it. Besides, there was a strong possibility the ships would encounter U-boats, for there was little doubt that these were by then in the Mediterranean. Only a few weeks before, Lieutenant Brodie, RNVR, who was in charge of the R-boats at Mersa Matruh, had been shot up by a German submarine off Sollum. The authorities had been disinclined to believe him, but he had assured me he was not mistaken. He had clearly seen the U-boat silhouetted against the rising moon.

Finally, 'Treacle' seemed to me such a cold-blooded piece of audacity that I could not believe the Navy would get away with it!

With a sense of foreboding, I recalled all these doubts as I sat that evening on the old green bench looking across the harbour. It had been a day of unbearable suspense which the burning heat had intensified to a pitch almost beyond human endurance. The muscles in my neck and shoulders ached dully and my eyes smarted from staring into the glaring sun in search of enemy planes. My nerves were so stretched that they recoiled violently to the slightest sound. When a truck back-fired on the quay below, I had jumped half out of my skin. Even the familiar roar of one of the landing crafts' engines starting up I had mistaken for a squadron of *Stukas* winging their way over the escarpment.

But now, at last, the sun was setting and it would soon be dark – pitch dark, for tonight there would be no moon. Tobruk was strangely quiet. Usually at the end of these stifling summer days, the port came to life with a sigh of relief. The crews of the landing craft came ashore, the Aussies working on the quay ambled off to wash their sweating bodies in Anzac Cove, the Indian troops, who had been unloading stores, began to chatter like starlings and a few of the staff of Navy House brought their 'Plonk' into the evening air. But this evening Tobruk appeared like a ghost town. Then, as the sky grew dark and the stars came out, the still air was filled by the rumble of approaching trucks. Operation 'Treacle' had begun.

Below me, although I could not see them, I knew the Aussies were clambering down from their lorries, rifles slung over their shoulders and were humping their kit on to the jetty, into the launches and tugs and over the ramps of the landing craft. I marvelled that so many men, keyed up with excitement, could make so little noise, and listened for the sound of their tramping feet against metal decks. Then I remembered that they were wearing their rubber-soled desert boots.

Suddenly, I heard the distant drone of aircraft. All day long I had waited for that sound and now that I heard it I felt sick. Getting up from the bench, I gazed into the starry sky, expecting at any second the rhythmical hum of the distant planes to be drowned by the ear-splitting crash of the ack-ack batteries. Instead, I heard the far-off thud of exploding bombs and saw their flashes like summer lightning in the southern sky beyond the escarpment, so that I knew the RAF must be bombing El Adem airfield.

The reverberating drum-beats of those bombs were the opening notes of an Olympian symphony that I felt was composed by Thor himself. They were joined by the pulsing beat of diesel engines and the throb of giant petrol motors and as the tempo quickened, this wild orchestra was swelled by the crash of heavy artillery, the shrill whistle of speeding salvoes and the staccato crack of bursting shells. The very earth trembled as the symphony soared to a mighty crescendo.

Awed and dazed by this cataclysm of sound, I watched the great pall of smoke rising like a curtain over Bardia change from black to deep crimson and saw silhouetted against it the shapes of the approaching ships. I saw too, the jagged wrecks rearing out of the water like dinosaurs.

Slowly, *Latona* glided up the harbour and lost way, and the onyx water sparkled with phosphorus as her anchor cracked its surface. Through my night-glasses I watched two of the destroyers until they vanished into the shadows of the wrecks crowded with waiting troops. The third nosed her way towards the quay, to come to rest alongside yet another wreck. I could see the soldiers lining her deck four deep and heard above the thunder of the bombardment the clatter of gangways.

Almost before the shore parties had secured her lines, the Indians were aboard off-loading boxes of ammunition, while down the narrow gangplanks the Poles came ashore. As the last of them landed, the Aussies swarmed aboard. There was no noise, no shouting, no flashing of torches, not even a lighted cigarette to be seen; and no confusion.

In less than ten minutes some 350 men had left her deck and another 350, including wounded on stretchers, had taken their places and the destroyer was going astern on her engines.

Within thirty minutes the four ships were heading for the harbour entrance. High over their masts screamed the salvoes from the 60- and 25-pounders as one by one they merged with the darkness.

When the firing ceased and the drone of the planes died away and the engines of the craft bearing the troops ashore became silent, I sat down on the old green bench outside Navy House conscious only of an overwhelming feeling of relief, but too emotionally exhausted to realize what had happened.

Later that same night I wrote in my dairy: 'the first night of Operation 'Treacle' went off without a hitch and without a single casualty. Thank God!'

CHAPTER TWENTY-TWO

RACE AGAINST TIME

Operation ,Treacle' was a noble victory for Cunningham, Auchinleck and Tedder and an ignominious defeat for Rommel. For all the latter's bombast and boasting, the 'Rats of Tobruk' escaped. They did not leave behind them a sinking ship, but a fortress as strongly defended as ever. Indeed, they left like fine fighting men in accordance with their orders, to rest re-equip, train and finally return to the desert to help drive the *Afrika Korps* into the sea.

Whether or not Rommel's spies had informed him in advance will never be known. However, as soon as he found out about 'Treacle', he did his best to put a stop to it. There were moments when he met with a measure of success. There were, for instance, nights towards the end of August when the moon set late and the ships ran a desperate race against time. It was then that the enemy bombers reappeared in force. But the very fact that they came by night and in the pale light of the waning moon was an admittance of defeat. Even then, they scurried off as the moon set to get back to their airfields before the RAF arrived and the moment the moon disappeared, the destroyers and the minelayer steamed into the harbour, their guns cocked in the air and their crews at 'action stations'.

It was the timing and the perfect co-operation between the Navy, Army and Air Force that beat Rommel.

On the last night of '*Treacle*', Just before dusk, the *Luftwaffe* was over Tobruk in strength and every gun round the harbour was firing as the lorryloads of troops ground their way down the escarpment, for the Diggers were in the front line until a few hours before sailing. The sky was filled with the drone of Ju 88s and Savoias flying high and the screech of diving *Stukas*, as the men jumped down from the trucks and were hurried into the shelters tunnelled under Navy House. But thanks to the barrage, the bombing was wild.

When the planes left the long-range guns opened up and although their huge shells drew up geysers of water dangerously close to the craft ferrying the troops out to the wrecks, there were no casualties. But those last units of the 18th Infantry Brigade certainly underwent their final ordeal by fire in Tobruk that night, and the hours dragged by interminably as they waited for the ships. When they did appear, the Diggers were strangely quiet as they embarked. But as the convoy turned and headed out to sea, the whistles from the men in the ships brought answering whistles from all round the harbour. Then, as the throb of the last destroyer's engines faded, a long 'Coo-ee!' echoed through the darkness.

Operation '*Treacle*' was followed by Operation '*Super-Charge*', which was undertaken during the moonless period in September. Earlier in the month, the cruisers *Ajax*, *Neptune*, and *Hobart*, of the 7th Cruiser Squadron, had embarked some 6,000 men of the British 70th in Beirut for Alexandria. The cruisers then acted as a covering force for the minelayers *Latona* and *Abdiel* which with eleven destroyers made altogether nine trips to Tobruk. They also added the weight of their shells to those of the Royal Artillery to pound the German gun emplacements and troop concentrations at Bardia. Throughout the operation the RAF provided strong fighter protection for the convoys, while the bombers went out each night to raid the Axis airfields.

In this operation 6,308 troops were landed with 2,100-tons of stores, and 5,444 Australians and over 500 wounded were brought back to Alexandria.

In mid-October, when the moon once again served our cause. Operation '*Cultivate*' was launched. It followed the pattern of its predecessors, and was carried out by *Latona* and three destroyers, which ran into Tobruk every night. *Latona* carried 150-tons of stores and twenty-five men westward, while the destroyers took either 450 men and 15-tons of stores, or seventy-five men and 50-tons of stores. Altogether 7,138 men were taken to Tobruk and 7,234 men and 727 wounded embarked for Egypt.

On the last night of '*Cultivate*' the 2/13th Australian Infantry Battalion was due to leave. In the early hours of the morning of the 25th, they had handed over their positions on the perimeter to the 2nd Battalion of the Yorks and Lanes Infantry. By half-past-five that evening the Diggers had eaten their last hot meal and downed their last tot of rum on the perimeter and were clambering into their transports. All were wearing desert boots or sand shoes and field service uniform for the first time for many months.

As the sun tipped the horizon, the *Stukas* came over and dropped a few bombs and then hurried off for home. The Diggers merely jeered at them. At the outskirts of the town, the convoy was held up for a while, in case the *Stukas* returned in the moonlight to bomb the wharf area, and it was not until 11.30 that they reached their embarkation points.

Then, they settled down to wait. Unable to smoke, the troops just sat about in the dark, forever glanding at their watches, talking in whispers and peering into the night to catch the first sight and sound of the ships.

That night *Latona* and the destroyers *Hero, Hotspur,* and *Encounter* were scheduled to carry the battalion back to Alexandria.

Midnight came and passed, and there was still no sign of the ships. If they did not show up soon, the know-alls said, there would not be time to clear 'bomb alley' before daylight. If they did not show up soon, the pessimists foretold, they would not come at all.

' – , the Navy always comes!'

By half past twelve, the waiting men were growing restive, the rumour started that the ships had been attacked *en route* and as it spread through the ranks of anxious soldiers it gathered credence.

The Battalion had been in Tobruk since the beginning of the siege, there was not a man who did not know how long it took fast ships such as *Latona* and the three destroyers to make the passage from Alexandria. So now, as the minutes ticked by, they knew that something must have gone wrong; seriously wrong, for nothing short of disaster could have prevented the Navy from keeping its appointment.

At 1.15 the order came to collect kit and move back to the waiting transport. The ships would definitely not be arriving.

Silently, the Diggers shouldered their rifles and gathered up their kit-bags and turned their backs on the harbour. Another month would pass and another moon wax and wane before the ships would come again.

Before dawn the convoy was back at Eagle Corner where to add to their wretchedness, a sandstorm was raging. Later, as the men ate a scratch breakfast provided by the Durham Light Infantry, they were told what they had already guessed; *Latona*, *Hero*, *Hotspur*, and *Encounter* had been set upon by enemy bombers. The faithful minelayer had gone to the bottom. *Hero* had been damaged by near-misses, and *Encounter* had returned to Alexandria loaded with survivors.

The four ships bringing the Polish Officers' Legion to the fortress had been attacked five times during the afternoon of October 25th. But by taking violent evasive action and putting up a fierce barrage, they had come through unscathed.

They were only forty miles from their destination when, by the light of the waning moon, they were again attacked. Although the weather was fine and clear, with their high speed the ships were by no means easy targets. But as they raced through the night, one bomb came whistling out of the darkness to tear through *Latona's* side and burst in her engine-room, killing every man in it. The explosion shattered the starboard main steam-pipe, threw the dynamos off the board and plunged the ship into darkness. At the same time the flash started a fierce fire in the engine-room which spread to the cargo of ammunition and landmines stored on the mining deck aft.

With light and power cut off and the pumps out of action and with nothing but buckets and hand extinguishers to fight the flames, the fire was soon beyond control. Moreover, with her after-deck ablaze, the minelayer was a sitting target, so *Encounter* was called alongside to take off the soldiers and half the ship's company. Even as the men jumped for the destroyer's fo'castle, *Latona's* foremost guns were still firing at her attackers. But as the fire spread through the ship, 'Y' magazine and the pom-pom magazine had to be flooded and orders were given to abandon ship. Then, as *Hero*, which had also come alongside to take off the crew, was going astern she was damaged by a near miss and her speed reduced to ten knots.

It only remained now for *Encounter* to search for survivors in the water and then put an end to *Latona* by torpedo. But at 10.30 the minelayer's after magazine blew up and she went to the bottom. Four of her officers and twenty ratings were killed and six wounded. Providentially, there were only about forty soldiers aboard her, but eight of these lost their lives.

Between them, the three destroyers were carrying close upon 1,000 Poles, and it was little short of a miracle that they came through fifteen bombing attacks, rescued half the ship's company of *Latona*, then returned to Alexandria without a single casualty. But the loss of this fast new ship was a grievous blow to Cunningham's Fleet. Night after night she had made the run to Tobruk, in defiance of the *Luftwaffe* and Rommel's long-range guns. Ironically, it was as the direct result of the sinking of *Latona* on the last night of Operation '*Cultivate*' that the Australians were not deprived of the glory of helping to hold Tobruk until victory was won.

CHAPTER TWENTY-THREE

U-Boats!

While Operations '*Treacle*', 'super-charge', and '*Cultivate*' were in progress the ordinary day-to-day business of supplying Tobruk went on. The British troops and the Poles who had replaced the Australians, had to be fed, the ack-ack gunners and the artillery still needed ammunition as well as new guns and gun-barrels, the sappers wanted mines and the armoured units wanted tanks. For even if the personnel of the garrison changed, the function of the fortress remained unaltered. It was still there to pin down Rommel's Army and to direaten his flank and rear should he attempt to launch an offensive against the frontier.

Indeed, whatever ambitious hopes Rommel might have had, by the autumn of 1941 the German High Command spoke despairingly about Tobruk's powers of resistance. Despite constant Axis air raids, they said, there was no general change in the situation at Tobruk. Their planes had not succeeded in putting an effective stop to the fortress's nightly provision by sea. In fact, according to their Air Headquarters in Africa, the anti-aircraft defences over Tobruk had become so strong that they were nearly as formidable as Malta's. The Germans complained too of the aggressiveness of the garrison's nightly sorties against their positions, which they suspected were overtures for a breakout planned to synchronize with the start of a new offensive.

Such suspicions were not far off the mark, for the ships of the Inshore Squadron were working like beavers to strengthen the fortress before Operation 'Crusader'. During September alone they had brought over 1,200-tons of stores and 750-tons of petrol to Tobruk, while the 'A' lighters landed twenty-nine tanks as well as guns and quantities of ammunition.

From their base at Mersa Matruh the 'A' lighters were kept busy that autumn, since the safe arrival of their cargoes was vital to the new offensive, they were given fighter cover during daylight on the westward run. There were also appointed to them young RNR navigating officers to ensure that they would be in the right spot at the right time to rendezvous with the Hurricanes. They were even escorted by anti-submarine trawlers, for by the end of September the U-boats were reported to have arrived in the Mediterranean.

It was the doubtful honour of the 'A' lighters to be the first to encounter a German submarine in the early hours of the morning of October 10th. Three of the craft, loaded with tanks and their crews, had sailed at dusk from Mersa Matruh. They were unescorted, since they were not due to meet up with their A/S trawler until about noon.

At four in the morning they were steaming west in what their Commanding Officers called 'bastard quarterline'. *A18* was leading with *A2* astern and slightly to starboard, followed by *A7* a little to port. When they were in the vicinity of Ashaila Rocks, off Sidi Barrani, Sub-Lt George Sinclair, RNR, acting as Navigator to the Florilla in *A18*, sighted a submarine ahead and to starboard. He could see her clearly in the moonlight, but even while he was still trying to identify her, she opened fire.

Sub-Lt Dennis Peters, DSC, RNVR, the Commanding Officer, was in his bunk and was awakened by the crash of gun-fire. As he dashed from the little cabin in the wheelhouse to the bridge, he was met by the wounded Navigator bring helped down by two sailors. Still heavy with sleep, Peters had to take in the whole scene in a matter of seconds, while all hell was let loose around him. Shells and tracer bullets were whistling overhead as he clambered to the bridge.

The first shell from the U-boat's forward gun had struck the funnel aft of the bridge and carried away the little mast and the wireless aerial, its shrapnel severely wounding Sinclair.

After months on the 'Spud Run' Peters was hardened to dive-bombing attacks and high-level bombing by Ju 88s and Savoias at night. But this sudden encounter with an enemy submarine on the surface shelling him from almost point-blank range was a new and terrifying experience.

'We opened up with our starboard pom-pom,' Peters said afterwards, 'and I held a course for the U-boat. With the pom-pom blazing away and the roar of the engines it was difficult to think coherently – if at all.'

In the confusion and noise of battle, the crew and the soldiers aboard were convinced that *A18's* Commanding Officer intended to ram the U-boat and actually began lowering the huge bow ramp for a battering-ram. Peters, however, never gave such an order. But he certainly steamed straight for the submarine and as he did so the starboard pom-pom scored several direct hits on its conning-tower.

The great lumbering landing craft charging at full speed, with the sparks belching from her squat funnel and the shells streaming from her pom-pom, must have been an awesome sight that struck terror into the Germans. Their fire became wild and the U-boat started to submerge.

But when *A18* was only a few hundred yards from her attacker the starboard pom-pom jammed and Peters was forced to turn away so as to bring his port pom-pom to bear. As he did so, the U-boat ceased firing and crash-dived.

As soon as she had disappeared Peters came down from the bridge to attend to the wounded Sinclair.

'He implored me not to go on as the safety of the three craft, depended on him. He told me he was finished, and then passed out,' Peters told me afterwards.

Athough Sinclair was the only casualty, *A18's* was in a bad way. Her degaussing cable had been cut by a shell and several armour-piercing incendiary bullets had passed within inches of her starboard petrol tank, containing thousands of gallons of 87-octane petrol.

Peters turned back for Mersa Matruh, expecting the others to follow him. But in the darkness the three craft lost touch and *A2* and *A7* continued on their way to Tobruk. The pair of them failed to rendezvous with the Hurricanes and were heavily attacked by *Stukas* before they arrived.

Having unloaded the tanks and their crews, the two landing craft sailed again for Mersa Matruh soon after sunset on October 11th. Darkness enveloped them as they passed through the boom at the harbour entrance. Neither of them was ever seen again.

During that night a faint wireless signal from dark was picked up. It said, 'Am being attacked by U-boat...' and ended abruptly.

After that there was silence. MTBs from Mersa Matruh carried out a sweep in search of the craft, but found no trace. Reconnaissance aircraft reported sighting wreckage to the eastward of Bardia. Weeks later a writing-case belonging to Bromley was washed ashore near Bug-Bug and was retrieved by a wandering Libyan.

I heard of the loss of *A2* and *A7* in Alexandria on the same day that I received a signal to the effect that the 'A' lighters were to be withdrawn from the 'Spud Run', their task having been completed.

Since July, when they had first begun to operate regularly from Mersa Matruh, ten 'A' lighters, of which five were lost, had carried 2,800 tons of stores and forty-eight heavy and seven light tanks to the fortress, as well as guns and vehicles. But ever since their first passage in April, on their way to the Aegean, they had been running up the North African coast in defiance of the *Stukas*. Of the original 1st Flotilla of eighteen, seven were sunk in Greece and Crete – one with all hands – and most of their crews killed or taken prisoner.

In May I had sailed with 'Nobby' Clark in *A2* to Crete to land the only tanks ever to reach the island. Since then I had made many trips with him to Tobruk. He was, without exception, the finest type of RNVR officer. As a signal rating early in the war in an A/S trawler he had won the DSM and for his work in Crete and on the 'Spud Run' he was awarded the Distinguished Service Cross.

At the time when he disappeared there were friends who tried to console me that clark had been taken prisoner. But although I prayed this might be so, I knew in my heart he had died fighting. His landing craft bristled with weapons and he had instilled into his crew a great deal of his own high courage. Indeed, but a few weeks before his last voyage I had tentatively proposed that it was time that he and they were relieved.

'We want to see Tobruk relieved first,' he answered for all of them.

In all, thirty-seven men, including an officer in the Royal Engineers, four Australian soldiers, and two Italian prisoners-of-war, sailed from Tobruk in *A2* and *A7*. Thirty-six lost their lives. By a miracle, one man survived. He was Petty Officer William Alfred Henley, DSM and Bar, RN. It is thanks to him that I am able to tell the story of the last hours of the two 'A' lighters.

Henley, who had joined the Navy as a boy in 1922, had served for many years in submarines, was coxswain of *A7*. When he was picked up by U-75, he had in his pockets a wallet, containing the photographs of his wife and children and a small brown notebook. He was three weeks aboard the submarine before she returned to her base at Piraeus, and during that time he recorded in this note book his memories of that fateful night.

Lieutenant Ecklemann, the U-boat's commander, allowed him to keep this diary. While a prisoner-of-war Henley was moved from one camp to another during the four years he was in Germany; from Bremen to Lansdorf, to Blechhammer, Thorn, Techscen and Sagan. He made three attempts to escape and finally took part in the 'death march' from Sagan to Frankfort-on-Main, which lasted for six weeks and on which more than half the 3,000 prisoners died by the roadside. Through all these terrible adventures, Henley managed to cling to his precious diary and to bring it back with him to England when he was repatriated at the end of the war.

It is a simple, stark document written while the fearful memories were still fresh in his mind and therefore the more poignant.

After the tanks had rumbled ashore over the ramps at Tobruk, the crews of the two landing craft had spent the rest of the day sleeping in the caves, while clark and Bromley had gone to Navy House to report their encounter with the U-boat and to find out what news, if any there was of *A18*.

'Nobby' Clark and Dennis Peters were old friends in the RNVR before the war. Having gone to HMS *King Alfred* – together as cadet ratings in 1940, they had been commissioned at about the same time and had then both volunteered for Combined Operations. That winter they had been given commands of the first two tank landing craft to be launched from Hawthorn Leslie's yard on the Tyne. Later they had sailed in the same transport for the Middle East. They were, in short what the sailors call 'oppos'.

Clark had spent an anxious day waiting for news of *A18*, for since no one had seen her turn back for Mersa Matruh, it was feared she had been sunk. However, shortly before sailing, a signal was received to the effect that Peters had arrived at his base.

That evening when the two craft sailed at dusk the weather was fine and calm. Too calm, now that there were enemy submarines to contend with as well as night bombers. However, since the moon would not rise for another two hours or so, they had little to fear from the latter. But as senior officer of the two craft, it was Clark's responsibility to lead the pair of them safely to Mersa Matruh, without escort or little likelihood of any fighter cover. Having served in an anti-submarine trawler, he was alive to the cunning of U-boats, so that night he had given orders for the look-outs to be doubled and the guns' crews to be closed-up until daylight. The decision had rested with him whether to steer a course that would take them well clear of the land before dawn or to shape straight for Mersa Matruh. He had decided upon the latter.

At a distance, travelling at speed through the darkness, the long low landing craft could themselves have been mistaken for two submarines on the surface – except for the tell-tale roar of their twin 650-horse-power engines.

It was the distant throb of high-powered motors that alerted Lieutenant Ecklemann in the conning-tower of U-75 as she lay on the surface under the shadow of the saw-edged hills of the Bardia escarpment. Pressing the alarm bell for 'action stations', he seized his night-glasses.

E-boats or enemy MTBs?

As the for'ard gun's crew raced along the deck, Ecklemann shouted at them to keep quiet and resting his heavy binoculars on the conning-tower dodger, peered into the darkness.

By the pale light of the old moon he picked up the shadowy forms of two vessels. They were surely neither E-boats nor MTBs, for in spite of the noise of their high-reving motors, they were moving at not more than eight knots.

What were they? Supply ships of some sort that the British had been running in and out of Tobruk every night for months past? If so, the chances were that they were loaded with troops.

Ecklemann dismissed such an idea as mere wishful-thinking. Ships loaded with troops did not sail unescorted, but with destroyers racing round them like sheep-dogs.

By now he could see the curiously bluff bows of the approaching vessels pushing up the white water before them. They looked like barges or even petrol-carriers and by their motion in the gentle swell, he judged their draft to be shallow.

It was then that Ecklemann recalled the signals he had picked up from

U-34 on patrol between Mersa Matruh and Sidi Barrani in the early hours of the morning. She had reported engaging strange enemy surface vessels at close range. They had opened fire with quick-firing guns, killing the for'ard gun's crew and seriously damaging the conning-tower. As U-34 had crash-dived, the leading vessel had attempted to ram her.

Remembering these signals, Ecklemann decided to keep out of range of those quick-firing guns and to be prepared to dive. But first to give the approaching ships a round or two from his for'ard gun, just in case they were petrol-carriers. U-75 was perfectly placed in the shadow of the land to shoot up both of them and with luck, set them on fire, without wasting precious magnetic torpedoes.

The first shells from U-75 appeared to crash into *A2* from nowhere and as dark's pom-poms opened up, the submarine switched her fire to *A7*.

'We had several unlucky hits in the engine-room,' Henley wrote in his diary. 'It was soon on fire. John Stuart, our Motor Mechanic, was badly wounded and his leg broken, and Day, his mate, wounded and burnt. Leading Stoker Edwards was killed outright. Stoker Pirie, although in a bad way, remained at his post fighting the fire after he had dragged his comrades clear. Those of us in the wheelhouse were OK, so we dressed their wounds as best we could and gave poor John morphia.'

At this stage, Henley was in the wheelhouse and could see little of what was taking place either on deck or on the bridge. But since neither of the craft was again hit by shell-fire, it is evident that the combined fire of the landing-crafts' pom-poms forced U-75 to submerge.

A2 although she had suffered several direct hits and some of her crew had been wounded, was still not seriously damaged. *A7* on the other hand, now lay stopped with her engine-room and mess-deck right aft both on fire. Henley and one of the crew. Ordinary Seaman Chaplain, struggled through the smoke and fumes with gas-masks and found that all the electric leads had burned out and it was impossible to start the motors. This they reported to Sub-Lieutenant Bromley on the bridge, who passed the information to Clark by dimmed Aldis lamp.

A2 then came alongside and after the wounded had been transferred, Clark asked Bromley if he could either blow up or scuttle his ship. The answer was no. So it was decided that *A7* should be taken in tow.

I got all hands on the wires and prepared to be taken in tow,' Henley
wrote. '*A2* asks for rum and I pass a new jar to her and go forward.
A terrific explosion shakes us. I see *A2* drifting away helpless.

Was it a torpedo?

Several of the crew are in the water. Where is the Captain and the
Skipper?[1] I take charge, fearing the magazine will blow up, I give
orders to throw all the ammunition overboard.

The fire has started again in the mess-deck. Some of the lads try to
put it out with buckets.

I call to *A2*, but there is no reply. Only men in the water. We throw
lifebelts to them, I hear the Captain and Skipper Peel. I pass a ladder
over the side and throw a line to them and haul them aboard. Both
are OK.

I hear someone else shout that they have not got a belt. Clapham
helps me over the side with an extra lifebelt and with a line tied round
me to haul me back. I swim to a ship-mate about twenty yards away.

While I am swimming, there is another terrific explosion. This time
it is *A7*...

I was sucked under. It was hell. But having two lifebelts helped me
to the surface. It was these that saved me from drowning and being hit
by flying débris...

When I look round I see *A7* listing and drifting away from me. The
cries of poor John and the others are awful...

I swam around for a while and then I saw the submarine. She was
passing near *A2*. Then she opened fire at the landing craft and the men
in the water. I was very terrified. I tried to swim away from her line of
fire, and as I did so, *A2* burst into flames. I swam as hard as I could.

Would her petrol explode and catch fire?

I am going further away. I hear someone crying out, and as I get near
I see it is Leading Seaman Newton, cox of *A2*, clinging to some wood.
I give him the lifebelts and strap him to some wreckage. But his arm is
broken and he is in a very bad way. We both cling together.

The submarine passes quite near to us, but we are afraid to shout
unless he machine-guns us.'

A2 burnt for about half an hour before she sank. Henley and Newton,
half-clinging, half-lying on their balk of timber, watched the long, black
shape of the U-boat steam slowly past them to pour high-explosive and

[1] 'Skipper Peel, RNR, was the First Lieutenant of *A7*.

incendiary shells into the listing hull of *A7* and then disappear into the night. By then, Henley guessed that it was about 1.30 in the morning of October 12th, for the moon was high. It seemed to him that his ship burnt for hours before she finally sank with an eerie hissing sound like a giant whale.

Then there was silence.

'We pray for the dawn. We drift around and find more wood. Poor Newton looks all in.

At last dawn breaks! There is no sign of anyone else, only floating wreckage. The sun rises and that is good for we are feeling cold. I feel about all in. The sea becomes choppy and the wind gets up. A large wave washes us apart. I try to swim back to Newton, but I cannot as I have cramp. Soon, we are far apart. I hear his faint cries... I lay back and rest...

Time rolls on, the sun rises higher. I get warm. Then, I actually see the land. How my hopes are raised. I gather strength and try to swim, but somehow it gets further and further away. I lie exhausted and wonder if there are any others alive. I think about poor Blackout, our ship's dog.

Last I saw of him was under my bunk... and the motor bike with which we were going to have such fun at Mersa, for there were plenty of them at Tobruk, and it was fun to fetch them back...

The morning passes and as I drift I think of my family and the past... my son. Jimmy, my thoughts run first to him, dear kid... my Eileen and my wife, Emme. I shout their names and call to God above to hear me...'

All through that day Henley just drifted and swam a little to keep warm. As the sun sank low on the horizon, he managed to collect several coats. These he gathered and wrapped round him. Then, just before sunset, he spotted more wreckage.

'I swim to the floating bits and join them together with bits of rope, using empty rum jars as floats. They help me to rest. I spot other wreckage and a Carley float. It is filled with the entrails and rotting guts of the men who had been machine-gunned by the submarine.

Around me there are dead bodies in a fearful state. I am shocked and horrified by them. They were once my pals. I knew them all. Two I recognize as the two Italian prisoners we were taking back to Mersa –

poor devils! Their bodies appear unmarked, so I guess that they have been killed by the concussion…

I say my prayers. Oh, God save me! I swim away from the dead men for I am afraid I will lose my nerve… Oh, my wife, my children, give me courage!

How the time drags! Will the day never end?… The sun is sinking at last, the sea becomes calm and the stars are bright… Soon darkness comes and I am so weary and tired… It is very dark as the moon will not rise until ten-thirty or eleven… I don't dare to swim any more, so I settle for the night amongst my wreckage…'

During the night, Henley said he began to become delirious and kept imagining that he heard ships approaching. The bouts of delirium were followed by spells of cold sanity, so that he wondered whether he was going mad, and struggled to keep his reason by praying and thinking of his family.

Then, in the moonlight, he thought he saw the silhouette of the submarine some distance off.

I shout and scream till I become exhausted and give up. I shout again a bit louder. God give me strength. I yell again and again. Do I hear an answer? Or is it just the echo of my own cries?

I listen straining my ears. Yes, it is the submarine all tight, but it is going in the wrong direction. Oh God, am I to suffer much longer

I just lie and wait. The moon is getting higher. Again, I shout louder still, I see the submarine quite clearly. I scream, "Help!"

They answer me. They come up quite close. I let go my wreckage and start swimming. God is good to give me strength…

A hand reaches out and I grasp it. Other hands grab at me. I am hauled aboard. I can hardly stand, but I am safe… God has answered my prayers!

The Captain asks who and what I am, and tells me he is a German and that I have been swimming for twenty-four hours. It is now twelve-thirty am on October 13th. The 13th! Who would have thought that thirteen would be my lucky number?

During the three weeks Henley was aboard U-75, he was treated with kindness. One day, Ecklemann called him to the periscope to look at the *Queen Elizabeth*, *Valiant* and other ships of Cunningham's Fleet.

Fortunately, the U-boat was unable to load her tubes in time to fire before the ships altered course.

When he landed at Piraeus, he saw U-34 and the Germans told him she had been badly damaged by the gunfire of our ships and that all her gun's crew had been killed.

Henley was questioned for many days in Athens by the German Intelligence, who were puzzled at the time by the fact that the landing craft appeared almost unsinkable. He stuck to his story that he knew nothing whatsoever about such vessels.

CHAPTER TWENTY-FOUR

Operation 'Crusader'

Auchinleck has been severely criticized, particularly by Churchill, on the grounds that by delaying the start of his desert offensive he gave Rommel time to reinforce his Army.

'Generals are often prone, if they have the chance, to choose a set-piece battle, when all is ready, at their own selected moment,' Churchill wrote apropos of Auchinleck's decision.

When it is remembered this was written after the battle of El Alamein, the most resoundingly successful set-piece of the war, such criticism cannot but strike one as unfair. But, of course, Churchill was writing for posterity and was intent on justifying his own repeated demands that the desert offensive should have been launched two months earlier.

In effect, Churchill is saying: 'If only Auchinleck had taken my advice, he would have completely defeated Rommel in the late summer of 1941. But by delaying his offensive until he could stage a set-piece so beloved by generals, he gave Rommel the heaven-sent opportunity to receive fresh troops and tanks.'

It is enlightening to consider the truth. Between August and November, 1941, the Germans shipped to North Africa the *Afrika*

Division. This was a motorized division, especially formed for service in the desert. During that same period, the Italian Army in North Africa was strengthened by the Trieste Motorized Division, while the Sabratha Division, which had been decimated in 1940, was re-formed. Some Italian artillery units were also landed.

Although about a hundred M13 tanks and some light tanks were sent to the Ariete Division, Rommel received no fresh armoured formations. German records prove that the two Panzer Divisions – the 15th and the 21st – were strengthened by some eighty tanks of all types. These were old tanks which had been damaged, recovered, and then repaired in the base workshops and *not* new ones sent across to North Africa during the lull between August and November.

Those are the facts of the case and they must be borne in mind when considering the wisdom of Auchinleck's resistance to the pressure exerted upon him by Churchill to launch Operation '*Crusader*' by the end of September at the latest. Another important point to remember is that, had Auchinleck allowed himself to be brow-beaten, he would have been forced to start his offensive without either the 22nd Armoured Brigade, which did not arrive at Suez until October 4th, or the 1st South African Division, whose vehicles did not reach Egypt until the middle of November. As it was, both these units were virtually thrown into battle with little or no training in desert warfare.

'The essential preparations were barely completed when the campaign was launched,' Auchinleck wrote in his despatch, 'and the standard of training of many of the troops engaged left much to be desired. This was due to no fault of their own, but solely to lack of time and shortage of equipment.'

The story of '*Crusader*', which began at dawn on November 18th in a downpour of rain, has been told often enough. Its pattern followed those of all battles waged in that tactician's paradise, the Western Desert, where the protagonists are the armoured units rather than the infantry battalions, and victory is won by the flow of petrol and water rather than blood of soldiers. With their swift outflanking movements by light tanks and armoured cars, their clashes of heavy armour, when, mounting an escarpment, the opposing tanks meet face-to-face, breathing fire at each other like legendary dragons and their moments of savage in-fighting between infantrymen with bayonets, rifles and hand grenades, such conflicts should be an inspiration to any writer.

Yet, because they range over the vast, featureless desert, their ebb and flow hidden in swirling dust-clouds, as the opposing armies fight for some uncharted hillock, these battles defy description and accounts of them are deadly dull.

For the first three days of '*Crusader*' everything went well for the 8th Army, although the reports coming in from the front, in the Commander-in-Chief's own words, 'grossly exaggerated enemy tank losses'. Nevertheless, Rommel was taken by surprise and forced to give ground.

Churchill, unfortunately, seized upon this initial success as an opportunity to tell Parliament that British and Empire troops were now meeting the enemy for the first time 'at least equally well armed and equipped'. Such a statement not unnaturally raised the nation's hopes so that the people were ill-prepared for what was to follow. Stimulated by the news from North Africa, the Prime Minister, like his commanders in the field, had been guilty of gross exaggeration. The 8th Army may have had superiority in quantity, but certainly not in quality. None of its tanks was a match for the German Mark IIIs and IVs armed with 50-mm and 70-mm guns. Nor did we possess an anti-tank gun comparable with the German 88-mm.

But to return to Operation '*Crusader*'. Briefly, the plan was for the two divisions of the 8th Army, under General Alan Cunningham, to advance north and east towards Tobruk. The 30th Corps, under General Norrie, which comprised the 7th Armoured Division, the 4th Armoured Brigade Group, the 22nd Guards Brigade Group and two brigades of the 1st South African Division, was to deliver the main attack. Its orders were to make a wide sweep on the desert flank, engage Rommel's main armour and, having defeated it, to strike north to Tobruk. It was for Norrie to order the garrison to make its sortie from the fortress at the crucial moment. Meanwhile, the 13th Corps, commanded by General Godwin-Austin, and composed of the 4th Indian Division, the New Zealand Division and the 1st Army Tank Brigade, was to attack and pin down the Axis frontier defences from Halfaya in the north to Sidi Omar in the south, outflank them, and press on to Tobruk. In this overall plan, the relief of Tobruk was merely incidental, for the purpose of the operation was to drive the Axis Army out of Cyrenaica and, finally, North Africa.

The 7th Armoured and the 1st South African Divisions, together

166

with the 4th Armoured Brigade Group, had started off at a gallop in spite of the heavy going. By nightfall on November 18th, they had advanced across the El Abd track running from Sidi Omar to El Gubi, where they split into four columns, which would the next day search out the enemy's armour.

In the morning, the 22nd Armoured Brigade attacked the Trieste Division near El Gubi and knocked out forty-five of its tanks, but lost twenty-five of its own. As the Italians withdrew, the South Africans advanced into El Gubi. Meanwhile, the two centre columns were heading north and west. The right-hand column, the 4th Armoured Brigade Group, advanced towards the Capuzzo track leading from Bardia to Gambut, while the 7th Armoured Brigade, finding the going ahead too soft, swung north-west towards Sidi Rezegh. This hundred-foot-high ridge overlooking the Capuzzo track about fifteen miles south-east from Tobruk became the hub of the battle for it virtually was the key to the fortress.

But at first, Rommel chose to ignore the threat to this important position and despatched a force of some sixty tanks to attack the 4th Armoured Brigade, whose main armour consisted of some 166 light American Stuart tanks. Although the attackers were outnumbered and forced to withdraw, they had tested the strength of these light tanks and discovered the weakness of their armour and fire-power. Thus, the next, morning when the 4th Armoured Brigade renewed the attack, it found itself up against a vastly superior German force. It was outgunned as well as outnumbered, but it put up a brave fight. Throughout the whole of November 20th, the battle raged and the reports reaching Cunningham's headquarters led him to believe that not only were Rommel's Panzer divisions committed in battle but had lost a considerable number of tanks.

In fairness to all concerned, these reports were not so inaccurate as they may have seemed. For the Germans did have a number of tanks knocked out. Our troops saw them hit and brought to a standstill. But they underestimated the brilliance of the enemy's recovery organization which enabled many of these tanks to return to action. Even as the battle was on, the Germans sent up their huge wheeled and tracked tank-transporters to recover their damaged tanks and drag them back out of range to the repair bases.

While this battle was being fought, the 7th Armoured Support Group had captured Sidi Rezegh and the 7th Armoured Brigade had established itself on the aerodrome there. Thus these two brigades had reached a position of great strategic importance only about fifteen miles from the Tobruk perimeter. Cunningham, therefore, allowed orders to be given for the 13th Corps to start operations and for the sorties from the fortress to begin.

For two days the garrison had been poised ready to spring. Its Commander was no longer Morshead, but General Scobie, GOC British 70th Division, for 'Ming the Merciless' had handed over the fortress on October 19th and sailed for Palestine to join the rest of the Australian Corps. Now the only Diggers in Tobruk were the 2/13th Battalion who had been left behind when *Latona* was lost. The new garrison was composed of the British 70th Division, the Polish Carpathian Brigade and the 32nd Army Tank Brigade.

Its task in Operation '*Crusader*' was to sally forth from the fortress on the morning of November 20th and drive its way through to El Duda, a point on the ridge about three miles north-west of Sidi Rezegh and approximately the same distance from Bel Hamed. Having done this, it was to hold open this corridor and cut the enemy's lines of communication along the Axis by-pass road.

All through the 19th the men of the garrison sat waiting and listening to the gunfire. But that evening when no signal came from Norrie, they resigned themselves to another bitterly cold night in their posts behind the perimeter wire. The next day, Scobie received the order to break out at dawn on November 21st. But this order was tragically premature, for by the time it reached the fortress headquarters everything had started to go wrong for the 8th Army.

Suddenly, Rommel reacted violently the capture of Sidi Rezegh and hurled the full weight of his armour against the 7th Armoured Brigade and the 4th Armoured Brigade Group.

This savage assault changed the whole situation. Now it became a question whether our armour could hold out on the high ground at Sidi Rezegh until the Tobruk garrison could reach El Duda.

The Germans and Italians crouched in strongpoint 'Tiger' facing the eastern perimeter, stiff and heavy-eyed after the long winter night's vigil, heard above the intermittent crash of gun-fire, the eerie wail of pipes. Borne to them on the chilled dawn wind, the alien sound made their flesh creep and with numbed fingers they gripped the triggers of their machine-guns and rifles.

Then, like phantom figures in the grey light, they saw their attackers, fanning out to left and right of the tanks. Company upon company, with bayonets fixed, they came charging across the desert, yelling and screaming wild, high-pitched war-cries.

But these were not the mad Australians, whom the besiegers had grown to dread, or the Indians, who attacked at night with the stealth of panthers. They were wild men from north of the Border – the Black Watch – led into battle to the skirl of their pipes. What would the Englishers think of next? The men in 'Tiger' had seen Yeomanry officers who led their men with walking-sticks and hunting horns and now, these savage Scots with their bagpipes! No wonder Rommel called them amateurs in war.

Even when their piper fell mortally wounded and the music of his pipes died with him in a last fearful screech, the men following him never faltered. On they came, howling like dervishes, their short bayonets glinting in the first light of the rising sun.

As they met the first hail of fire from 'Tiger', they leapt into the air to fall, kicking like shot rabbits and then lie still. But there was no stopping them.

By the time they had overwhelmed 'Tiger', half the 2nd Battalion of the Black Watch were casualties. But they went on to capture a second strongpoint, known to the garrison patrols as 'Butch' and by the afternoon they had taken more than a thousand prisoners, of whom the majority were German. By nightfall, the garrison troops had shortened the distance between themselves and their objective to seven miles. But the enemy's defences were deeper and stronger than had been expected. Furthermore, they were held by Rommel's crack troops brought up for his assault on the fortress. The minefields, too, were thick on the ground and these, together with the heavy guns, inflicted fearful damage on our tanks, so that it was soon apparent that there was no chance of reaching El Duda by the following day.

Although in Tobruk Scobie had only the haziest idea what was happening at Sidi Rezegh and to the east of Capuzzo, he was left in little doubt that things were not going according to plan with the relieving force. But, by the morning of November 22nd, the Garrison Commander was in a predicament. His small force of tanks had taken a terrible hammering in the sortie and were sadly in need of maintenance. Without their support, his infantry could make little impression on the enemy's strongpoints. Casualties had been high, the ground gained was thinly held and there was no telling that if Rommel discovered this, he might not launch an attack against Tobruk at any moment.

But, although Scobie could not know it, Rommel had even more ambitious plans. Flushed with his success against the British armour at Sidi Rezegh, he sent for General von Ravenstein, in command of the 21st Panzer Division, telling him somewhat melodramatically that he was to be given the chance of ending the campaign that very night.

Ravenstein's orders were to take tanks, motorized infantry, and mobile artillery and anti-tank guns, and make a dash for the frontier. He was to look neither to right nor left, but push through and beyond the frontier wire and then swing north-ward to Sollum. While Ravenstein was doing this, Rommel explained, another force from the 15th Panzer Division commanded by General Neumann-Silkow would follow up and attack General Cunningham's headquarters at Port Maddalena, while a third force would move east to capture the railhead at Bir Habata with its supply dumps.

Von Ravenstein's force dashed headlong eastwards, shooting up everything in sight. It outflanked the 7th Armoured Division, and threw the 30th Corps headquarters into a state of confusion, so that its administrative and supply trucks turned and fled for the frontier like a flock of panic-stricken sheep before a pack of wolves. By the afternoon of November 24th the rot had set in, and hundreds upon hundreds of British vehicles were streaming eastwards, and they did not stop until they reached the boundary fence. So rapid was both the advance and the retreat that there were times when the fleeing British troops and the pursuing Germans passed and repassed one another in their trucks without recognition, and von Ravenstein's tanks and armoured cars actually swept by our two huge supply dumps at Bir El Gubi and Gabr Saleh and never spotted them. When von Ravenstein was told about them, after he was taken prisoner, he was amazed and said that if he had known of their existence the Axis would have won the battle.

By this dramatic thrust to the frontier Rommel hoped to cut our lines of communication, and so force Cunningham to withdraw right back to his starting point. Once he had achieved this, Tobruk would be at his mercy. And, first and foremost, Rommel's heart was set on capturing Tobruk.

In fact, Cunningham proposed calling off the offensive. To continue it might mean the destruction of his entire tank force and the loss of Egypt. Thus, Rommel's gamble so nearly came off. But he had reckoned without Auchinleck.

CHAPTER TWENTY-FIVE

THE 'RELIEF'

Rommel's raid deep behind the 8th Army's lines had left havoc in its wake. The 5th South African Brigade had been cut to ribbons, its headquarters overrun, vehicles blown to pieces and left burning, and some 4,000 of its men were either prisoners or missing. Scattered all over the desert were units, which a few hours before had been holding part of a continuous line, now completely cut off. Little groups of guns and tanks, by-passed by the enemy, were stranded in the desert. Hospitals and field-dressing stations found themselves surrounded, their staffs taken prisoners and as quickly abandoned and left to treat British and Axis wounded alike. Their signals trucks destroyed, brigade and battalion commanders, at a loss for orders, manned the machine-guns along with their men, shooting up enemy tanks and armoured cars as they dashed by in a fog of dust. At Army Headquarters, intelligence officers buried their aching heads in their hands and gave up trying to plot the course of the battle.

Into the midst of all this utter confusion Auchinleck arrived by plane, accompanied by his Deputy Chief-of-Staff, Ritchie, and Tedder.

Faced with such chaos, a lesser man might have conceded to his Army Commander's proposal to withdraw from the battle while the going was good and while there yet remained some armoured units to be regrouped and refitted. But Auchinleck gave his categorical refusal to such a plan and issued orders to 'attack and pursue the enemy with all available forces, regain Sidi Rezegh, and join hands with the Tobruk garrison', which was to co-operate by attacking the enemy on its front.

This was undoubtedly the Commander-in-Chiefs finest hour, for by his refusal to accept even the possibility of defeat, he saved the day. Then he returned to Cairo where he immediately decided to relieve Cunningham of his command, since in his own words he had 'reluctantly come to the conclusion that he was unduly influenced by the threat of an enemy counterstroke against his communications'.

So at this crucial moment Cunningham went and Ritchie took his place. But from then on it was Auchinleck who fought the battle.

On November 25th, Scobie received a signal at the Fortress Headquarters telling him that the 2nd New Zealand Division would make a concerted effort to reach Sidi Rezegh the next day, and that by then the garrison was expected to have captured Ed Duda. With his tanks hurriedly serviced, Scobie launched an attack early on the morning of the 26th, and after fierce fighting his infantry captured the last enemy strongpoint, 'Wolf', between them and their objective. But there was still neither sight nor sound of Freyberg's New Zealanders.

At one o'clock the garrison troops saw some tanks on the horizon, and from the turret of one of them three red flares rose into the clear blue sky. There was a pause and then three more red flares burst above the tanks. As they did so, the men from Tobruk broke into wild cheers, for those six red flares were the 8th Army's recognition signal, and for the first time for seven months the troops from the beleaguered fortress were within sight of the relieving force.

From that moment the men of the Northumberland Fusiliers and Essex Regiment, supported by the tanks of the 32nd Army Tank Brigade, raced for Ed Duda. By four o'clock that afternoon, after violent hand-to-hand fighting, they had driven the last of the Axis troops from the ridge and the corridor to Tobruk was open at last.

But all through that night the weary garrison troops clung grimly to their positions on the high ground, and it was not until the early hours of the morning of November 27th that the 19th New Zealand Battalion with a squadron of British 'I' tanks battered their way through Sidi Rezegh and Bd Hamed to meet men from the Fortress at Bd Duda crest. Then it was that General Godwin-Austin made his famous signal; 'Corridor to Tobruk clear and secure, Tobruk is as relieved as I am.'

But, once again, this jubilant signal was dangerously premature. For even while it was being despatched, Rommel was regrouping his tanks for another blow at the 8th Army.

On November 25th, having gathered his strength together, he launched a major assault into the Sidi Rezegh-Bel Homed-Ed Duda area with the 15th and 21st Panzer Divisions, supported by some Italian troops. His scheme was to cut right through the corridor from east and west simultaneously.

Fortunately, through an intercepted radio signal, the 8th Army was warned of Rommel's plan, and was able to muster some tanks to send into the attack. But it was touch and go whether the corridor could be held open. On the ridge at Bel Hamed and Sidi Rezegh, Freyberg's troops, probably the finest fighters in the Western Desert, resisted all the enemy attacks. But at Ed Duda, the 1st Battalion of the Essex Regiment, finding themselves up against a strong force of German heavy tanks, were forced to give ground.

When night fell it looked as if the western wall of the corridor might cave in altogether and the garrison be forced to retire within the perimeter again. For eight of Scobie's fourteen infantry battalions were already trying to hold the corridor, thinly supported by the remainder. He then received a signal from 8th Army Headquarters, saying; 'At all cost corridor must be held.'

Scobie had only one fresh battalion in reserve – the 2/13th Australian. But it had been mutually agreed between Blamey and Auchinleck that only in an emergency were the Diggers to be committed to battle. Now, however, there was an emergency and a desperate one, and so Scobie sent for the Battalion Commander, Lt Colonel 'Bull' Burrows.

On paper, he said, the 2/13th no longer existed on the garrison's strength, but, in fact, it was still there, and now, no matter what promises had been made in high places, he was calling upon the Diggers to fight once more for Tobruk.

By six o'clock that evening Colonel Burrows had given his orders for the battalion to move out to Ed Duda immediately.

Two and a half hours later the troops were on their way to the gap in the perimeter to rendezvous with their Commanding Officer, who had gone ahead to contact the Commander of the 16th Infantry Brigade, under whose command they would be.

As they passed through the perimeter wire the oldest inhabitants of the fortress felt a strange thrill – a strange sense of unreality – at driving through the wire in their vehicles, instead of crawling through it on their bellies as they had done so often before.

At 'Tiger' strongpoint the convoy halted to await the arrival of another convoy and their escort of armoured cars. Then, at midnight, in the bitter cold, they set off across the eight miles of desert to their positions on the eastern slopes of Ed Duda, where they were to spend the night.

Their orders were to attack at 11 o'clock the following morning, through the positions held by the Essex Regiment, over some 4,000 yards of open country, and to drive the enemy from the lower slopes of Sidi Rezegh.

At first light, the Australians found they were bivouacked on a long low hill, and soon discovered that this position was within range of an enemy heavy battery. Moreover, this proved to be a German battery whose gunners plastered their positions with high and low-angle salvoes, forcing the Diggers to scratch shallow holes in the rocky ground with their bare hands to escape the shrapnel raining down on them.

That day the Australians' orders were repeatedly counter manded as the battle for the corridor ebbed and flowed, and all the time they were under heavy shell-fire from the German artillery and tanks.

By dark, when they were due to attack again. Burrows spotted two dozen German tanks ahead of him. While his men took cover, he went back to call up the garrison's tanks. Six of the latter attacked, but the Germans could not be shifted, so Burrows called for artillery support. The heavy barrage knocked out two of the enemy tanks, setting them ablaze, and as the others retired the Australians prepared to attack. As they did so, they were joined by odd troops from the Essex Regiment determined for revenge.

As the moon waned, Burrows gave his men their last orders, telling them to yell 'the Australians are coming!' as they charged, and yell they did, as they raced up the slope in the darkness, leaving the lumbering 'I' tanks behind them. Ahead they could hear the enemy chattering excitedly and recognized the words: *'Englander kommen!'*

Then, by the livid green light from a Very pistol and to a shout of 'Come on, Aussies!' they went in with hand grenades and fixed bayonets.

The odds were more than four-to-one against them, but the sheer weight of their charge overwhelmed the Germans before they had a chance to resist. Indeed, the attack was over so quickly that, except for those in the immediately vicinity, the Germans did not realize Ed Duda had been recaptured. Throughout the rest of the night the Australians and the Royal Horse gunners were shooting up Staff cars and trucks as they drove unsuspectingly up to their positions.

During the mopping-up after the attack, Private Clarrie Jones took a German captain prisoner. The latter demanded to know the name of Jones's regiment, and, when told, refused to believe it. All the Australians had left Tobruk, he declared knowingly. In the fading moonlight Jones thrust his metal shoulder-titles under his prisoner's nose, and told him to look for himself.

But the German laughed. *'Ach!'* are the English dressed as Australians to frighten us!' he insisted.

For two days the 2/13th held their position at Ed Duda before they were withdrawn and their place taken by the 4th Battalion of the Border Regiment. Later, they left in convoy for Tobruk.

> 'Never did we dream, during those weary months of siege,' Lt Colonel Colvin wrote afterwards, 'that we would ever welcome a return to the perimeter, but it was with a feeling of relief that we finally passed through the perimeter wire to take over a position from the Durham Light Infantry, astride the El Adem Road.'

Day after day the two armies fought for those ridges around Tobruk. When Ed Duda resisted, Rommel switched his armour against Bel Hamed and Sidi Rezegh, and under the weight of his attacks we were driven from both these positions. Now, although the garrison troops still clung resolutely to Ed Duda, Tobruk was once more surrounded.

Next, Rommel made a desperate bid to relieve his troops bottled up in Capuzzo and Bardia. But now Auchinleck was at Desert Headquarters, and never for one moment did he allow his armour to rest. His orders were: 'Attack everything you see, and keep on attacking.' And the 'Jock' columns, small roving tank formations that took their name from Brigadier 'Jock' Campbell, VC, one of the finest of all desert fighters, constantly harried Rommel's flank, racing into the attack and off again before the Germans realized what was happening. In this battle of thrust and counter-thrust the initiative slowly but relentlessly passed to the 8th Army.

In daylight, Rommel's armour was ceaselessly set upon by the RAF while night after night our bombers went forth to raid his supply bases.

In the first days of December the New Zealanders retook Bel Hamed, while the 4th Border Regiment repulsed no fewer than three heavy attacks on Ed Duda. On December 5th, our fighters reported shooting up huge concentrations of enemy transports all heading west past Tobruk. Two days later, the 11th Hussars from Sidi Rezegh and the South Africans moving up from Bardia joined hands again with the garrison, and it was the turn of the Axis reconnaissance planes to report huge concentrations of enemy transports moving west towards Tobruk.

On the night of December 9th-10th, the Polish Brigade captured Ras El Meduuar in the Salient, and by the next morning stood triumphantly on Hill 209.

After 242 days of siege the fortress of Tobruk had been relieved.

CHAPTER TWENTY-SIX

STRANGE INTERLUDE

After a month's respite, the 'A' lighters returned to Tobruk in November, for, by then, the garrison was about to break out, and more tanks and supplies were urgently needed.

I went to Alexandria to await the arrival of the craft from Port Said. On November 26th I received a signal telling me that they would be in that morning, so I drove to the dockyard to meet them. It was a morning I shall never forget.

Cunningham had taken the Fleet to sea, and at about ten o'clock I stood on the quay watching the ships returning slowly up the Grand Pass. Two battleships, three cruisers, and their escorting destroyers.

Two battleships?

Three days before, *Queen Elizabeth. Valiant*, and *Barham* had put to sea. Now only *'Queen Elizabeth'*, Cunningham's flagship, and *Valiant* were returning to harbour.

Where was *Barham*?

I felt a fearful sense of foreboding as I stood there watching the ships in the brilliant morning sunshine. But I had not long to wait before my worst fears were justified.

A long string of ambulances came down the jetty, and then Rear-Admiral

Creswell's car drew up, and the Flag Officer in Charge Alexandria got out to join the little party of senior officers watching a destroyer moving slowly alongside the quay.

Her decks were packed with bedraggled men. Survivors!

There was no mistaking them. Men wrapped in blankets, or clad in pathetically ludicrous oddments of clothing, their half-naked bodies stained yellow and brown with crude oil. Dazed, bewildered men. Men who looked as if they had been suddenly wakened from a deep sleep.

There is a hush amongst the gathering crowd on the quay. It breaks into huddled, speculating groups, whispering together. Above the subdued murmur of voices ring out the orders from the destroyer's bridge, the trilling of a boatswain's whistle, and the rattle of the gangways as they are run aboard.

The party of senior officers, standing a little apart, the gold braid on their caps gleaming in the sunlight, moves forward to join the destroyer's captain. They all salute as a thin man in a grey sweater and old flannel trousers descends the gangway.

Admiral Pridham-Whipple, who had flown his Flag in the *Barham!*

There is a buzz of recognition as he climbs quickly into a waiting car and drives away. To right and left officers and men salute as the car passes.

Then the mournful procession of survivors begins to file ashore. First the stretcher cases, their hideous wounds and burns hidden from the inquisitive eyes of the crowd by the dun-coloured blankets thrown over them. But, here and there, it is possible to glimpse features still distorted with pain and waxen at the edge of death. Swiftly, tenderly, the stretchers are slid into the ambulances.

There follow the 'walking wounded', limping ashore supported by their mates and the destroyer's crew. Some laughing and smoking, others silent, their eyes dull, and their faces drawn with pain.

Lastly, the survivors. A rag-tag party. One is naked except for a grimy towel knotted round his loins. Another wears only his cap 'flat back' on his greasy curls, torn underpants, and a huge pair of seaboots. Another still grasps the lifebuoy that but a few hours before had proved his most precious possession.

Slowly the motley line straggles through the crowd to the clothing store, presently to reappear carrying armfuls of new kit.

Another destroyer follows the first alongside the quay. She, too, is loaded with survivors. There are cheers and shouts as the men ashore recognize their messmates on her crowded decks.

'There's Shiner, the old bugger!'

'Blow me down if it ain't Chalky!'

'Wot 'yer, Bert! I knew they'd never drown yer!'

Again the sharp orders from the bridge, the shrill piping whistle, followed by the clatter of gangways.

Again we watch the stretchers come ashore and the stream of survivors, almost unconsciously trying to count them.

How many are there? Two hundred? Three hundred, perhaps? And with a pang of horror one remembers that, *Barham's* ship's company was well over a thousand strong.

Amongst the crowd of survivors I recognized a midshipman whom I knew. When last I had seen him he had been walking *Barham's* quarterdeck, immaculate in his whites, with his telescope under his arm. Now he was naked, except for a towel and a pair of carpet slippers. From him I heard the terrible story of *Barham's* end.

She was struck by four torpedoes and sank in as many minutes, taking with her some 700 of her crew, including her captain. The midshipman, with fifty or sixty others, had survived by a miracle.

'Somehow, I found myself struggling under the water – deep down – inside a giant air-bubble,' he told me. 'We could breathe quite freely, but it seemed to hold a milling mass of men, fighting to get free. Then, there was a terrific explosion, and the whole crowd of us were blown to the surface. Somehow or other I remembered to hold my breath. But a lot of the poor devils didn't, and their lungs burst.'

All that afternoon, as I waited for the landing craft to arrive, I was weighed down by a deep depression. With the end of the *Barham*, on whose quarterdeck I had danced many years before when she was Guard Ship at Cowes Regatta, it seemed to me at the time that the submarine menace in the Eastern Mediterranean had reached its vortex.

We left Alexandria on a wild evening of rain-squalls, when black, scudding clouds hunted each other across the pale face of the moon. Every white horse in the moonlight became the sinister track of a torpedo, so that in spite of the driving rain and the bitter cold spray I had a strong disinclination to leave the bridge. All night I was haunted by the ghastly fate of those who were below decks in the *Barham* when she sank.

Not until the morning, when a Savoia saw fit to bomb our little convoy, did I begin to feel braver. She came roaring down upon us through the low, scudding clouds, and we, rolling our sides under the heavy beam sea, let drive at her with our pom-poms. But in such weather neither side had much chance of scoring.

During those final weeks of the siege, the *Stukas* were too pre-occupied inland to trouble us much at sea. The weather was at once our worst enemy and best friend. For, while we battled with hard winds and steep seas, they protected us from the U-boats. And as often as we stood on the bridge, cold and soaked to the skin by the flying spray and spindrift hurled over us as the landing craft's great square bows crashed into the seas, we tried to count our blessings.

In those first days of December everyone in Tobruk felt the suspense and growing tension while the garrison was fighting its last grim battle for the corridor. All day we could hear the gunfire like distant thunder, and at night the jagged edge of the escarpment was silhouetted against the brilliant gun-flashes and the red glows of fires.

But when the relief happened, it came as an anti-climax. No tanks, armoured cars, or lorries came rolling into the ruined town. No marching soldiers arrived to be greeted as conquering heroes by the besieged. No flags flew; no bands played. No one even cheered. The tide of war just swept on, and almost before anyone realized it Tobruk was no longer a fortress – a bastion against which Rommel's Panzers had battered themselves senseless for months. It was a supply dump.

'All the guts have dropped out of the place!' I wrote in my diary.

The moment the siege was over Tobruk reverted to what it had always been – a hideous, smelly North African port. But, after all those months of bombing and shelling, it reminded me more than anything else of a neglected graveyard, desecrated and abandoned. I found myself loathing the place and longing to escape from it.

It was filled, too, with strangers. Sanderson had gone to set up his 'UPs' in Malta. O'Shaughnessy's place was taken by an earnest captain, fresh from home, who would refer to us as 'Desert Rats', an expression abhorrent to all who considered themselves old inhabitants. The last sunburnt, naked Digger had departed. Captain Smith remained as NOIC but was too immersed in signals and paper work to have time to play bridge or brew delicious pots of black Italian coffee. 'Bardia Bill' lay a rusting trophy in the Army Ordnance Depot, where I expressed my contempt for him in a schoolboy manner against one of his mighty wheels. The great gun, in fact, was not German at all, but French, and in close-up not nearly so impressive.

But now that the landing craft were working day and night, unloading the transports in the harbour, it seemed that I was condemned to stay in Tobruk. Then, one day shortly before Christmas, one of the 'A' lighters on passage from Mersa Matruh ran into a full gale. She was loaded to capacity, and having taken aboard a great deal of green water, she became waterlogged and unmanageable. Her Commanding Officer, convinced that she would founder, gave orders to abandon ship, and he and his crew were taken off by the escorting trawler.

When this news reached Tobruk the general opinion, shared by Smith, was that the waterlogged craft would sink. But I did not agree, for experience had taught me that so long as the buoyancy or ballast tanks were empty and undamaged, these craft would remain afloat. I told Smith this, adding that I was prepared to stake a bottle of gin on it.

The craft had been abandoned some miles to the westward of Cape Raz Azzaz, and so, taking into consideration the prevailing wind and the gentle set of the current, the chances were that she would drift ashore somewhere in the neighbourhood of Sollum or Bardia.

'If,' I said, 'it does that, the Germans holding out there might find her very useful. But even if she doesn't behave as I suggest, I'm certain she won't sink. In which case, it's possible an E-boat might take her in tow.'

Smith looked at me shrewdly. 'In other words, you want to go to look for her?'

'Yes, sir,' I admitted.

He promised he would ask the RAF reconnaissance to look out for her.

A few days later she was duly reported ashore near Bug-Bug about fifteen miles east of Sollum. Taking passage to Mersa Matruh in a Canadian corvette, I gathered up a small Naval salvage party, borrowed a 15-cwt. truck from the Army and set off westwards.

At Sidi Barrani I stopped to ask the way.

'You can't miss it,' a somewhat grumpy Town Major told me. 'You just keep on going until you come to the waterpoint on your left, and there you are. It's about thirty miles as the crow flies.'

I refrained from saying I was not a crow, but a naval officer with little sense of direction on dry land, who would not recognize a waterpoint when he saw one.

As I climbed back into the truck the Town Major came out of his office to stand on the doorstep of his shattered house.

'Don't overshoot it,' he called.

'What?' I asked.

'The waterpoint. If you go too far, you'll find yourself in the bag. The Jerries are still in Sollum,' he added ominously.

Needless to say, the speedometer did not work, and I was beginning to reflect upon the Major's warning when I saw amongst the sandhills to the right a small tent. Outside it sat a soldier. He was hatless, and wore khaki shirt and shorts. Across his bare knees lay a rifle.

Getting out of the truck, I asked him the way to Bug-Bug. He frowned sullenly, staring at me without understanding. His eyes were intensely blue and his hair was bleached almost white by the sun.

I felt the butterflies in my stomach as he fingered the trigger of his rifle. He looked so typically German. 'Bug-Bug,' I repeated, conscious of the absurdity of the name.

The four sailors had jumped from the truck and stood in a little semi-circle behind me.

'He looks like a Jerry, sir,' the motor mechanic whispered, voicing my thoughts.

I was wondering, if we rushed him, whether the four of us might possibly overpower him before he would have a chance to shoot, when he rose from his squatting position to his feet in a single effortless movement.

I saw that he was a giant, and my heart sank, for beside him we looked like pigmies.

Then he called over his shoulder to someone inside the little tent.

I am no linguist, but I was convinced the fellow spoke in German. And if I was right, and since he was obviously not alone, it looked as if we were 'in the bag'.

Blind rage overcame my fear, and I swore darkly under my breath. Through sheer damned stupidity I had driven not only myself but four helpless sailors headlong across the desert into the enemy's lines. And the war certainly wouldn't be over for at least another three or four years, I reflected angrily.

'Go back to the truck, and one of you start her up,' I ordered out of the corner of my mouth.

The man's knuckles whitened over the trigger, and just as I was about to make a dash for it at the risk of being shot in the back, another giant crawled out of the tent. He was naked to the waist, fair haired, and deeply tanned. But, at least, he was unarmed, I thought fatuously.

'What do you want, man?' he asked, grinning.

Swallowing hard I said: 'Bug-Bug. But your friend doesn't seem to understand.'

He grinned again. 'He's dumb, man! He only speaks Afrikaans. Bug-Bug's way over there. Some of the boys are there now, looking at that landing craft on the shore.'

'Tell your friend he frightened me out of my life. I thought he was a German,' I said, holding out my hand.

They were South African sappers, and their unit was camped across the track farther west, he explained. They were keeping an eye on the waterpoint, he added, kicking a pipe half hidden in the sand.

Even while we were chatting, I saw several long-legged, sun-burnt giants trotting across the sand dunes.

One of them, the man told me with a touch of pride, was Captain Smuts. 'He's a wonderful man, man!' he added, affectionately.

As I had suspected, there was little wrong with the landing craft. She had beached herself perfectly on a beautiful stretch of white sand. Her hold was filled with water and the tarpaulin covering it torn to ribbons. But by dusk the motor mechanics and the stoker had the auxiliary lighting plant running, and the next day as soon as it was light we set to work salvaging her.

Helped by the South Africans, we managed to lay the heavy anchor out astern, while the engineers were busy with the engines. By noon, most of the water had been pumped out of the hold, and it looked as if we would be afloat and on our way to Mersa Matruh by that evening.

But suddenly the wind flew round to the north-east and began to freshen, bringing with it a long swell. As the wind rose the landing craft started pounding badly in the surf, and riding further and further up the beach, since the short length of anchor wire we had been able to lay out was insufficient to hold her.

Then, just before sunset, a heavy roller lifted her stern and the anchor wire parted, and she was swept broadside on to the beach.

That night the wind increased to half-a-gale, and the seas crashing down on the tattered tarpaulin poured into the hold. In a matter of hours all our work had gone for nothing. All night the wretched craft rose and fell in the surf, driving further and further up the beach.

By dawn, almost as if in defiance of the gale. she had turned her bows proudly seawards, and her stern rested on the dry sand above high-water level.

Sadly we surveyed the havoc. The heavy pounding of her flat bottom on the hard sand had driven her propeller shafts through the hull, and the engine-room and the mess-deck were both flooded. She was beyond saving.

That afternoon, Christmas Eve, I sent the salvage party back in the truck to Mersa Matruh, where a special dinner and a free issue of beer awaited them.

I spent the night alone aboard the landing craft. The wind had died away and the sand glistened like snow as the moon rose. For a long time I sat on the bridge wrapped in an old duffelcoat. The rollers had subsided to silvery wavelets whispering over the sand and lapping gently against the ship's side.

Away towards Sollum, still in enemy hands, a star-shell burst, to hang suspended in the deep blue sky, so that tritely, perhaps, I thought of that other star seen by the Wise Men on another Christmas Eve more than nineteen hundred years ago. A star that had heralded the beginning of Christianity.

I heard the distant throb of aircraft and the dull reverberation of exploding bombs.

'Peace on earth and goodwill towards men!' I reflected.

Then I went below and brewed myself a cup of cocoa, liberally laced with rum.

I woke to find the sun shining brilliantly, and as I stood on deck, washing in a bucket of water, I felt so exactly like the ship-wrecked mariner in the story-books that I burst out laughing. The setting was so in the tradition. The wrecked craft, her tattered ensign flying, lying on her side, the endless stretch of golden sands, the rolling sand dunes, the litter of driftwood, and overhead the blue sky as unreal as a stage backcloth.

Looking along the shore I saw here and there dark shapes lying at the water's edge. The flotsam and jetsam of the storm, I thought as I dressed. But, after breakfast, when I paddled ashore, I made the macabre discovery that the shapes were corpses washed up by the gale.

One wore the torn uniform of a Naval rating. The body lay on the sands, its arms outspread, its head thrown back. The blond hair, dried by the soft wind, gleamed in the morning sunlight. He was young, and I found it hard to believe that he was not just asleep. He looked so peaceful.

The other two were the bodies of Italian soldiers, and the sodden bandages, still trailing from them, told that they had been wounded.

I set off across the sand dunes to tell the South Africans of my grim discovery, and that afternoon their Colonel came down to the shore with the Padre.

We buried the dead men in graves dug in the white sand dunes, marking their resting places with roughly made crosses of drift-wood. At the head of the young sailor's grave I planted a long ash oar whitened by the salt water. For them all I whispered a *Dei Profundis*.

That was the strangest Christmas morning of my life.

CHAPTER TWENTY-SEVEN

Hitch-Hike

Supplying the garrison in Tobruk had been a costly business for the Royal Navy. Between April 12th and December 10th. twenty-seven ships had been sunk on the 'Spud Run', and an equal number damaged; nearly 700 officers and men had been killed and wounded. Seven merchant ships had been sunk and half a dozen damaged.

In that period 34,115 men had been brought to Tobruk and 52,667 taken back to Alexandria; 33,946-tons of stores – including 108 sheep – had been landed, as well as ninety-two guns and seventy-four tanks.

Cunningham was rightly proud of the achievement of his men and their ships, and was annoyed that when Churchill addressed the House of Commons on the subject he never mentioned how the supplies reached the fortress.

'I fear the Prime Minister's speech on the supplies at Tobruk made all out here in the Service very angry,' he wrote to Dudley Pound. 'Do you think that even at this late hour the Admiralty might make a signal recognizing the work of the small ships? It would, I think, be very well received. I hear the men are a bit sore-hearted at receiving no official recognition of what has been as gallant work as has ever been done... I issued a message to the little ships myself, but it is not the same thing.'

Cunningham understated the case. There was not an officer or man in the Inshore Squadron who was not thoroughly disgusted by the lack of recognition their work received. The 'Spud Run' was, of course, just another arduous chore to the Navy. Nevertheless, we all felt that someone might have had the good grace to say 'thank you'.

Everyone in the Service was very angry and the men a bit sore-hearted, because so long as it lasted – and it lasted a long time – the siege of Tobruk was front-page news. The garrison – 'the Desert Rats' – were all heroes, and the life they led in the beleaguered fortress was a subject for a good deal of fulsome nonsense in the newspapers. Then, when the tide of battle swept past west, Tobruk was forgotten.

The truth is that a great many people, including Churchill, lost their sense of proportion over the place. In 1940 and 1941 Tobruk was both politically and militarily important. Politically, after our defeats in Greece and Crete, there was no telling what might have happened in Turkey, Syria, or Iraq, or, for that matter, even in Egypt, if Tobruk had fallen. Militarily, without Tobruk and its garrison, there is no doubt but that we should have been defeated by Rommel. Without Tobruk, he would have reached El Alamein in the spring of 1941. But for the garrison's tenacity at Ed Duda it is probable he would have beaten the 8th Army in the winter of that year. Indeed, the savage fighting in the Sidi Rezegh-Capuzzo area lasted so much longer than anyone imagined that, by the time it was over, it was difficult to say whether the 8th Army relieved Tobruk or the garrison rescued the 8th Army. One thing, however, is certain: at the end of that fierce battle both ourselves and the Germans were exhausted.

The published figures of both sides' losses in men and weapons convey as little idea of the violence of that struggle now as they did when they were first made known. To understand what those two weeks' fighting cost the 8th Army and the Axis forces it was necessary to drive across the battlefield after the dust had settled but while the ground was still warm.

When the time came to leave Bug-Bug and the kind South African sappers, who had dined and wined me lavishly on Christmas Day, I determined to return to Tobruk overland. Since I had made up my mind to see the battlefields, I avoided thumbing a lift from any of the streams of vehicles heading directly west. Instead, using discrimination, I picked a little convoy of Military Police cars and trucks bound for Ritchie's headquarters, then established some five miles north of El Adem on the Tobruk road.

As a Naval officer, albeit a very shabby one in khaki battle-dress, I was a rarity in the desert and, without actually committing myself, I managed to convey the impression that I was concerned with the recovery of damaged tanks and their shipment back to Mersa Matruh. Therefore it was important, I hinted, that I should see as much as possible of the battle area before returning to Tobruk. By the glint in his eye, it was apparent that the young officer in charge of the convoy was also an inveterate sightseer. Together we made a fairly comprehensive tour.

From Bug-Bug we headed south. Leaving the Sollum road just short of 'Hell-fire' Pass, we took to the track marked by petrol drums and petrol cans on sticks. Our progress depended upon the surface of the desert, which varied all the time. We drove over slag, rocks, stones, thorn bushes, and, of course, sand. But not just ordinary sand, but sand whose appearance was as treacherously deceptive as snowfields on a glacier. In the hollows it was blown into soft, deep drifts, and on the high ground it was baked hard by the sun or covered by a thin wind-crust, beneath which the sand had turned to glutinous mud.

As far as the eye could see the desert's surface was rutted by the tracks of countless vehicles, until it looked like a vast field ploughed by a madman without a sense of direction. Hour after hour for mile after mile we drove in low gear, jolting, rocking, and at times sinking to our axles in the sand. across the uniformly dun-coloured desert where the only vegetation consisted of apparently petrified clumps of thorn.

More than anything else this boundless desert battlefield littered with battered petrol cans sparkling like broken glass in the sunlight, the charred bones of aircraft, blackened tanks, twisted metal tracks, miles of barbed-wire, and split ammunition boxes, reminded me of some giant scrapheap. Only as I watched this hideous panorama unrolling before me did I realize the wanton extravagance of war. For, here millions of pounds had virtually gone up in smoke.

Just before sundown, at the frontier fence somewhere near Sidi Omar, our convoy halted. We climbed stiffly down from the lorries to light a fire before dark, brew tea, and boil-sausages, which we ate hungrily with great hunks of sandy bread and, as we sat listening to the *BBC* news on a portable wireless round the fire, I saw in the twilight the fires of bivouacked convoys twinkling like glowworms all over the desert. Then, as darkness fell, one by one they flickered and died out.

I slept that night under a little bivouac tent lying on the sand rolled up like a cocoon in blankets. In fact, I slept hardly at all, for in spite of the blankets, battledress, leather jacket, sweater, and several pairs of socks, I could not get warm. Nor was I the only one, for all night I heard the soldiers running about and stamping their feet, and as I listened to them I thanked God that I was in the Navy, and was not obliged to live this nomadic existence for weeks and months on end. To sleep in one's clothes beneath the stars, wash, clean one's teeth, and perhaps shave, in a billy-can of brackish water, eat bread, greasy sausages, and drink tea, all liberally mixed with sand, could be an adventure for twenty-four hours. So to exist indefinitely would be hell!

We breakfasted soon after dawn, and then headed north and west for Capuzzo. Now the wreckage of war increased with every mile we drove. It was possible without even looking at the map to tell where the two armies had fought out their fiercest encounters, for there even the barren desert somehow contrived to look seered and blasted. There, too, were the little clustered cemeteries; sad heaps of stones surmounted by rough wooden crosses bearing the names and numbers of the men who lay beneath them. Sometimes a steel helmet, pierced by a bullet or a shell splinter, dangled by its chinstrap from the cross, or a broken propeller blade marked an airman's grave. The German graves looked more regimented and tidy than ours, and above them were Gothic crosses desecrated by *Swastikas*. Time and the driving sandstorms, I thought, would obliterate these soldiers' shallow graves, and only the rusty guns and tanks with which they had killed one another would remain to bear witness to their courage.

Beyond Capuzzo we joined the track to Gambut and, just as we passed the latter, we skirted an airstrip strewn with wrecked *Stukas*, Me 109s, and Me 110s – a sight which did my heart good. Now on every side was evidence of Rommel's hurried retreat. We stopped for a meal near a huge Axis workshop and supply dump, which, although it had been looted by wandering Bedouins and, I dare say, our own troops, still showed signs of being suddenly abandoned. We helped ourselves to those wonderful German petrol containers, known as 'Jerry-cans'. which, unlike our own, never leaked a drop, and were lucky enough to find, too, some of their bitter chocolate. Had I not been present I suspected that those military policemen would have made a more thorough search. I know that I felt it my duty to uphold the honour of the Navy by seeming dis-interested in loot.

So, at length, we came to the escarpment, and there I asked my driver to stop so that I might look down on Tobruk and the harbour, deep sapphire-blue in the afternoon sunshine. Standing up in the truck, I could see all the blackened wrecks I knew so well – *San Giorgio*, *Ladybird*, *Liguria*, *Draco*, *Serena*, and the test. I could see the battered white shell of Navy House, the White Ensign fluttering over it. And as I stood there, I like to think that hereabouts Rommel must have stood cursing the men of the garrison who refused to surrender.

CHAPTER TWENTY-EIGHT

THE RAIN CAME

Auchinleck was the first general to beat the Germans in battle in the Second World War. That fact is worth remembering when reading, for instance, the memoirs of Montgomery or history as written by Churchill.

That Rommel fought and ran away, and so lived to fight another day, does not alter the fact that he was fairly and squarely beaten in Operation *'Crusader'*. His retreat to the west never became a rout as had Graziani's a year before, because the cream of Rommel's Army was German. The Panzer Divisions consisted of fine, disciplined soldiers, who, no matter how battle-weary, could be counted on to fight courageous rear-guard actions, to stand and face the advancing enemy and, if needs be, die where they stood.

From the critical moment when Auchinleck issued his order for the 8th Army to fight to the last round and the last tank, Rommel was beaten and forced to retreat right back to Agheila.

Churchill says that as the Axis Army withdrew by the desert route through Mechili, pursued by the 8th Army, it was hoped to repeat the success achieved against the Italians in 1940. Exactly who fostered such hopes he does not say. Was it Auchinleck, Ritchie, Godwin-Austin, or Messervy, now commanding the 7th Armoured Division? It is hard to believe that any of those generals thought that by a swift advance they could make a great haul of prisoners when, before it ever reached Benghazi, the 8th Army's lines of communication were stretched to the limit. Perhaps only Churchill, thousands of miles away in Washington, allowed himself such day-dreams, momentarily forgetting that he had Rommel to deal with and not Marshal Graziani.

Our advance was not only hamstrung by logistic problems, but by the elements, for day after day the rain poured down, to turn the desert into a sea of mud, and gales of wind drove huge seas through the bomb-breached breakwater at Benghazi, stopping the salvage and repair parties' work and rendering the harbour unsafe for shipping.

By the end of December, too, one disaster after another had overtaken the Navy, upon whose support the fortunes of the 8th Army were so dependent. *Ark Royal* and *Barham* had been lost. *Queen Elizabeth* and *Valiant* had been rendered useless for months to come by intrepid Italians who had fixed limpet mines to their bottoms. The very day after this calamity Force 'K' from Malta, dashing to intercept an important enemy convoy to Tripoli, ran into a minefield. *Penelope* and *Aurora* were damaged, but managed to extricate themselves. But *Neptune*, having struck three mines, was sunk with the loss of her entire crew, except for one rating. The destroyer *Kandahar* steaming into the minefield to save the cruiser's crew, was also mined. Thus was Cunningham's Mediterranean Fleet reduced to a handful of destroyers and three cruisers.

Until this tragedy the Germans regarded the situation in the desert with despondency. Efforts, their Chiefs-of-Staff said, must be made to supply the *Afrika Korps*, make good the considerable losses, and reinforce Rommel with first-rate troops. This, in their opinion, could only be achieved by air transport across the Mediterranean because the British Navy dominated that sea. But the Germans admitted that the destruction of Force 'K' altered the entire picture. Thanks to the minefield they said Tripolitania could now be held.

By January 11th Rommel had retired to his strongly defended positions round Agheila. The rain poured down. The desert was a quagmire. The arid wadis were swirling, surging red torrents. On the advanced airfields the Hurricanes' wheels sank deeper and deeper into the mire. All over the face of the desert the convoys of lorries bringing the supplies to the 8th Army slithered, skidded, their wheels spinning, and finally ground to a half, up to their axles in mud.

Battering our way through a gale, we sailed in an 'A' lighter from Tobruk for Benghazi, loaded with tanks and cased petrol. Long before we reached our destination those 'flimsy and ill-constructed containers', as Auchinleck described them, had leaked their last drop of petrol into the bilge.

At Benghazi the mountainous seas swept over the break-water. As we rolled and wallowed on a lee shore, we received a signal telling, us to go away. The harbour was lousy with magnetic mines, dropped the night before by enemy aircraft.

'Try Derna,' the signal told us. We tried, and came within an ace of being swept broadside on to the shore by the gale. So we went back to Tobruk.

I was ordered to Derna and Benghazi by road, to inspect their harbours for suitable places for the landing craft to beach. On a cold morning, when the hard north-westerly wind brought wild rain-squalls in from the sea, I set out in a 3-ton lorry driven by a sturdy young South African. He had, he told me, come to Libya by way of Abyssinia and Eritrea.

'All the way in this truck?' I questioned, as we rattled and bounded over the pot-holes.

'How did you guess, man?' he grinned.

The road from Tobruk to Derna is definitely a road, and before its surface was pitted with bomb and shell-holes and cut to pieces by the tracks of countless tanks, it must have been a fine one. For mile after mile it runs parallel with the coast, over high undulating country that grows increasingly fertile as one travels westwards. Low bushes, grass, and wild jonquils break up the drab monotony of the desert.

Our progress was slow, for all the bridges spanning the wadis had been demolished, so that we were obliged to make endless diversions over the desert until we found a crossing made and marked by the sappers. Over and over again the great truck, laden with ammunition, stuck fast in the mud and had to be manhandled back to mobility. But nothing ruffled the good temper of the lad from Capetown who, between plying me with cigarettes, entertained me by singing Afrikaans songs.

Once, as we were bowling merrily along, he suddenly wrenched the wheel to send the great truck careering off the road.

'Jump, man! Jump!' he yelled, as we skidded to a halt. 'A Jerry plane!'

Leaping from the truck, we raced across the desert and threw ourselves flat. As we grovelled in the mud, I heard the staccato rattle of cannon-fire and saw the shell-bursts sending up little feathers of dirt along the road. I felt certain the plane would turn steeply and shoot up the lorry; instead it went roaring on its way down the road.

'That was a close thing, man!' my driver said, lifting his head and staring after the disappearing plane.

'Too close!' I told him, and for a few minutes I lay where I was, for I was not sure whether my legs would bear me.

He gave me a cigarette, and I noticed with admiration that as be held out a match his hand was perfectly steady.

On the high ground above Derna we passed an airfield on which I counted the wrecks of fifty German fighters. The hangars were razed to the ground and all over the field were neat bomb dumps. On this same field, my driver told me, more than thirty planes had been captured bogged down in the mud.

From the airfield, the road wound its way down the escarpment in a series of hairpin bends to Derna, and on every corner we passed deserted pillboxes and strongpoints, beside which were neat little groups of graves.

Derna is the only place on the coast between Alexandria and Benghazi I would care to revisit. It is a lovely little town, built by the edge of the sea at the foot of the towering escarpment; green, lush, bright with bougainvillaea and shaded with palm trees. Its narrow streets and alleyways open out unexpectedly into small fountained squares surrounded by cafés and shops overgrown by vines.

Even though its houses had been looted and many of them wrecked, Derna still had charm. But, perhaps, I am prejudiced in its favour by the memory of a boiling-hot bath I enjoyed in one of its villas and the bottles of Chianti I discovered in a cupboard under the stairs.

Having inspected the little harbour and found room for two landing craft. I journeyed on to Benghazi. This time my driver, was a bun-faced boy from Wigan. Having spent over a year in the desert, he vowed to me he would never again waste a summer holiday on Blackpool sands.

At Derna we left the desert behind and followed the coast road to Cyrene, where, to the boredom of my driver, I insisted on stopping to look at the lovely amphitheatre and the broken columns of the Graeco-Roman city. Surely, he grumbled, I had seen enough ruins?

From Cyrene we dropped down into the wide plain across which the road runs to Barce. Under the Fascist regime this vast plain had been transformed into a rich dairy settlement, while the highlands encircling it had been planted with fruit trees. The plain itself is dotted with the little white farmsteads of the Italian settlers. Once, these farms had prospered, for the soil around them was rich and red and well irrigated. Now most of them were windowless and their walls pitted by bomb splinters. The tanks of four armies had crushed their fences and churned up their neat little fields, and smashed the banks of their canals. Now, because of the insatiable vanity of a dictator, declarations of whose greatness yet besmirched their façades, these farms had been laid waste. Their ploughs rusted in the fields over which a few lean beasts still roamed. At some of their gaping doorways bedraggled women and pale-faced children stared after us without interest as we drove by.

At sundown we reached Barce, where an overworked but patient Town Major in the Buffs found parking space for the lorry and quarters for the driver, before leading me to the officers' mess. This was in the main hotel of the town, and I was amazed to find a bar well stocked with whisky, gin, sherry, and beer. That night at dinner I was waited upon by soft-footed Indian servants, for the hotel had been taken over as the headquarters of the 4th Indian Division. Later, as I lay in a comfortable bed with clean sheets, I found it hard to believe that the Germans were only a few miles away.

Barce, the market town to which the Fascist collective farmers had once brought their produce, was packed with troops, day and night the supply lorries rumbled into the town. But never enough lorries with never enough supplies, the soldiers told me, and when in answer to their questions I told them that I was on my way to Benghazi, to find suitable berths for my landing craft, they looked hopeful and said; 'The sooner you get there the better.' For those bottles in the officers' mess were misleading, and I soon discovered that in truth the Army was short of everything; not only petrol and ammunition, but food. Everything was running out, and the units further forward were living on biscuits, bully beef, and precious little else.

'We've almost reached the end of our tether,' the soldiers told me as I climbed into a lorry and set out for Benghazi.

All the way along the road that ran as straight as an arrow I thought about what the soldiers had said, with a growing feeling of apprehension. The desert war was a war of logistics in which the lines of communication, like strips of elastic, could be stretched so far and no further. The longer an army's supply line became, the weaker that army grew. It had happened to Graziani, Wavell, and Rommel. Would it happen to Auchinleck also? I had an uncomfortable feeling that it would, and my first sight of Benghazi and its harbour did nothing to mitigate that feeling.

Given time, and a spell of reasonably fine weather, the demolition parties might clear the quays and prepare berths for the supply ships and mooring space for the tankers. Given time, the sweepers might clear the harbour of mines. But, with Rommel retreating towards his bases and the *Luftwaffe* just across the way in Sicily, I did not think such time would be granted to us.

All that day as I wandered about Benghazi I carried with me a heavy sense of depression.

The town itself reminded me of a film set run by the late Cecil B de Mille for one of his spectacular productions, and then abandoned. In its heyday it must have been tawdry, gimcrack, and pretentious. It had been constructed so obviously to awe the stranger with the grandeur of the Fascist Empire and with an eye to triumphant marches and processions; its buildings were granthose, its squares spacious, and its avenues, lined with palms, wide and imposing. But, like the regime under which it was built, its foundations were flimsy, and beneath the weight of war they had cracked and collapsed.

I felt as I walked about Benghazi, through the broad streets and across squares once adorned with fountains and ugly formal flower-gardens, that even if it had never been bombed, it was destined to fall into decay. But since it had been bombed as well as shelled by ourselves and the Germans scores of times its shoddiness was laid bare.

I hated the place. The pack of lean, starving dogs dozing miserably in the pale sunlight on the steps of the cathedral made my heart ache. The Duke of Aosta's palace, looted and ransacked, its marble floors strewn with shattered Sèvres, the priceless tapestries on its walls ripped to ribbons, its brocade curtains hanging in shreds, disgusted me. The convent of the *Sacré Cœur*, its chapel stinking, and foully desecrated, its sunlit courtyard overgrown with weeds, made me feel sick. I shuddered as I passed shops across whose shuttered windows the single word 'Jew!' was scrawled over and over again. And as I made my way through the narrower streets there followed in my wake not only starving dogs but starving children begging for pennies and cigarettes. Once, I remember, a door opened, and a blowzy Italian slut croaked at me to come inside. Somehow, the fact that life yet went on in this ruined city made it seem the more repulsive.

I slept for two nights in Benghazi on a camp-bed in the marble hall of a bank, glared at by a bronze bust of Il Duce. On the last night, when the building rocked to the crash of the Nazi bombs, I got out of bed in a rage and hurled the bust to the floor. It was not bronze but plaster, and when it disintegrated into a myriad pieces I was seized with the giggles.

In Benghazi I found plenty of likely spots where my landing craft could beach. But I returned to Tobruk convinced they would never have the chance to use them.

I got bade to Tobruk to hear that the Germans holding out in Sollum and Halfaya and Bardia had surrendered. We had taken 14,000 prisoners and a great quantity of stores, and liberated over a thousand of our own men at the same time. With all Cyrenaica in our hands. I wondered whether I was wrong about our holding Benghazi.

Then, on January 21st, Rommel launched his reconnaissance attack.

CHAPTER TWENTY-NINE

THE ROT SETS IN

Not only lowering rain-clouds darkened the horizon at El Agheila as the 8th Army looked westward. Cunningham's Fleet virtually no longer existed. The Air Officer Commanding's squadrons in Malta had been practically demolished by the *Luftwaffe*. At the moment, the Mediterranean was very much Il Duce's *mare nostrum,* and across it flowed the supplies of tanks, guns, and men Rommel needed to set the *Afrika Korps* on its feet again. Making the most of their opportunity, the enemy landed these weapons and men not only at Tripoli but on the beaches near the front line at El Agheila.

Rommel started by making a series of reconnaissance raids to discover the strength of our defences and to force our armour to race about the desert wasting precious petrol and ammunition. But the information gained from these raids, as well as the reports from his aircraft, encouraged Rommel to bolder action. On January 21st he set out personally with three columns comprised of the 21st Panzer, the Ariete. and the 90th Light Divisions to break through our weak defences, play hell with our lines of communication, and if possible drive us out of Benghazi before we could firmly establish ourselves there. For no one knew better than Rommel the value of that port to the 8th Army as a supply base in any further advance westward.

Auchinleck was in Haifa when Rommel's attack was launched. Ritchie believed this sudden advance to be little more than a reconnaissance in strength. Indeed, it might well have been. But Rommel was ever the opportunist, and the moment he was convinced of our weakness he exploited it, and his raid rapidly developed into an offensive.

As always in these desert battles, the information reaching Army HQ was both sketchy and misleading. But on this occasion our communications were poorer than usual, due possibly to the fact that the 1st Armoured Division, which had just relieved the battle-weary 7th, was new in the field. Disturbed by the news, Auchinleck flew to Ritchie's headquarters at Tmimi, taking Tedder with him. He found the situation at the front alarming. Once again Rommel's mobile columns had penetrated deeply through our defences, had then fanned out, splitting our armour into isolated groups, which were overwhelmed one after another. The 1st Armoured Division, commanded by Messervy, came up against the 21st Panzers in the Agedabia area and was badly mauled. In Benghazi, Tuker, commanding the 4th Indian Division, convinced that Rommel was set upon attacking the port, warned his local commanders to be ready to evacuate and destroy their supply dumps.

By January 27th Rommel had reached Msus with his main force, and there his columns divided. One advanced on Benghazi, while the other headed north-west, apparently intent on reaching Mechili.

Quite wrongly, as it turned out, 8th Army Intelligence decided that Rommel's main objective was Mechili and that the column advancing upon Benghazi was composed of the Ariete Division. Tuker was therefore ordered to hold out and to leave a battalion to defend the port. As the result of this, one Indian brigade only extricated itself in the nick of time. During a downpour of rain and under cover of darkness, the majority managed to escape.

It was not until the 8th Army had retreated right back to Gazala that order was restored.

This setback to our fortunes was serious and, courageously, Auchinleck shouldered the full responsibility for it. 'I am reluctantly compelled to the conclusion,' he telegraphed to Churchill, 'that to meet German armoured forces with any reasonable hope of decisive success our armoured forces as at present equipped, organized, and led must have at least two to one superiority.'

Churchill dogmatically disagreed with this conclusion. He claimed that the 1st Armoured Division was one of the finest we had and consisted of men who had 'more than two years' training'. Nevertheless, they had hardly heard a gun fired in anger until they faced the *Afrika Korps*. And then they discovered that the German guns could knock holes in their tanks long before they could get within range to answer back.

There is nothing more demoralizing, especially to troops committed to battle for the first time, than the realization that their weapons are inferior to those of the enemy, and this repeatedly happened to our soldiers in the desert.

That, as Churchill claims, they abandoned their tanks in running order is positive proof of the effect that this inferiority in arms had upon the morale of our troops. This technical inferiority of our tanks was not the only reason for this, and many other, reverses in the desert, but it was undoubtedly a major one. Those whose misfortune it was to witness the awful end of a British tank set ablaze by the German heavy guns, and whose painful duty it was to evacuate their mutilated survivors to Alexandria, can never forget at what a cost we won the war with these technically inferior weapons.

By the time Gazala was reached both sides were exhausted, and neither was capable of striking at the other for many months to come.

It is possible to find a score of reasons for this dismal end to what had looked like being a complete victory over the Axis forces in North Africa. But in the final analysis out advance ended in retreat because the Axis Army was superior to the British Army from every point of view and until, as Auchinleck had so frankly pointed out, we could amass enough guns and tanks to give us a two to one advantage over the enemy, we would not win a decisive victory.

When '*Crusader*' was launched in November we had 455 tanks to Rommel's 412. But we had not a single tank to match the German Mark IIIs and IVs. Nor did we have a solitary anti-tank gun.

Before El Alamein, Alexander and Montgomery had 1,114 tanks against Rommel's 600. Moreover, 495 of our tanks at El Alamein were brand-new Shermans and Grants mounting 75-mm guns. With such a superiority in November, 1941, Auchinleck could have driven Rommel into the sea just as Alexander did many months later.

As the 8th Army sat behind its defences at Gazala, Churchill and his Chiefs-of-Staff became fretful about Auchinleck's apparent desire to stage a second 'set-piece' battle. They were concerned for the fate of Malta. So, for that matter, was Auchinleck, who appreciated the importance of being far enough forward in the desert to possess airfields for our fighters to reach the island.

Supplies were reaching the 8th Army. New anti-tank guns – Roberts 6-pounders mounted on fast trucks. New American tanks – Grants, with 75-mm guns. But in the holds of the ships arriving at Suez and in the Canal there were only a few of these new weapons. Most of the supplies unloaded were the same as before and Auchinleck was determined to have a preponderance of weapons – old and new – before he started another offensive against Rommel. To accumulate what he needed would take time, particularly now that the war against Japan was straining our resources to their limits. Two Australian divisions had already been despatched to the Far East, as well as tanks and aircraft.

After a respite, in February, the telegrams started arriving again from Downing Street:

> '…I must ask what are your intentions. According to our figure you have substantial superiority in the air, in armour, and in other forces over the enemy. There seems to be a danger that he may gain reinforcements as fast as or even faster than you. The supply of Malta is causing us increased anxiety, and anyone can see the magnitude of our disasters in the Far East…'

Auchinleck made his intentions perfectly clear. They were to build up the armoured striking force of the 8th Army as rapidly as possible, to strengthen his forward positions and push the railway forward towards El Adem; to build up in the forward area reserves of supplies for the renewal of the offensive; to regain the first chance of staging a limited offensive to regain landing-grounds in the Derna-Mechili area, provided this could be done without prejudicing chances of launching a major offensive to recapture Cyrenaica or the safety of Tobruk.

Auchinleck stated that in his opinion he would have sufficient strength to launch his new offensive by June 1st.

Churchill agreed with none of this and invited Auchinleck to come to London for consultation. Remembering what had happened when he had accepted such an invitation shortly after assuming command in the Middle East, Auchinleck declined. He could not, he said, leave Cairo. Shrewdly Churchill remarked that his Commander-in-Chief conceived himself stronger in resisting from his headquarters to requests which he knew would be made to him.

Since, however, it was not the moment for the Mountain to come to Mahomet, Churchill decided that Stafford Cripps, who was on his way to India, and General Nye, should call upon Auchinleck in Cairo.

The result of this meeting, attended by Tedder and Admiral Cunningham's representative, was not at all what Churchill had expected. Cripps declared himself to have no doubts about the Commander-in-Chief's offensive spirit. Cripps said that he believed that Auchinleck's Scottish caution and desire not to mislead by optimism caused him to overstress in statement the difficulties and uncertainties of the situation. But the fact of the matter was that Auchinleck, like his fellow Commanders in-Chief in the Middle East, had learnt from experience the dangers of optimism. Given an inch, the exuberant Churchill would always take a mile.

While the telegrams were speeding between London and Cairo, Admiral Raeder, flushed with the successful passage of his battle-cruisers through the Channel, was trying to talk his Führer into attacking Malta. There was, he said, no time like the present, for never again might the situation in the Mediterranean so favour the Axis. First capture Malta and then launch an all-out offensive against Suez, was Raeder's plan. But, after what had happened in their Invasion of Crete, Hitler and his generals did not take kindly to any further plans for 'seaborne landings on islands in the Mediterranean. Better by far, they countered, to bomb Malta until its garrison surrendered.

Rommel, too, talked of the capture of Malta. His Panzer Army was, he said, to attack as soon as possible after the capture of the island. However, he took the precaution of adding that if Malta was still resisting after June 1st it might be necessary for him to proceed with his plans.

In April, Churchill again diverted Cripps to Cairo on his way back from India, instructing him to explain to Auchinleck how deeply the War Cabinet was concerned by the inactivity of the 8th Army. But, the Prime Minister warned the Lord Privy Seal, there was no use pressing a general beyond his better judgement.

Yet, but a few weeks later, Churchill did more than that. He told his Commander-in-Chief that he would be right to attack the enemy and fight a major battle, if possible during May, and the sooner the better. Either Auchinleck obeyed these orders or he would be relieved.

Even Churchill felt obliged to confess that this was a most unusual attitude to adopt towards a high military commander.

CHAPTER THIRTY

ROMMEL STRIKES

If Raeder was unable to talk Hitler into a direct attack on Malta, he at least managed to convince his Führer that North Africa was something more important than just the Italian theatre of war. The time was ripe, Raeder said, to prepare the Grand Plan – the conquest of all Egypt and Persia and the linking up with the Japanese in the Indian Ocean. Victory in North Africa, the Admiral argued, was all an essential part of that Plan, and in order to make possible that victory, Rommel's Army must be reinforced. There was no better moment than the present to send the necessary convoys across to Tripoli. Hitler listened and agreed, and so while Malta was attacked on an average six times a day, and nearly 7,000-tons of bombs were dropped in one month on the island, fuel, tanks, guns, ammunition, and fresh troops were delivered to Rommel.

Supplies came to Auchinleck too, but only after a 12,000-mile journey round the Cape of Good Hope to Suez, where the congestion of shipping was not the least of our problems. For, once the supplies were off-loaded, they still had to travel 500-miles across the desert by road and rail. The convoys of lorries stretched from the Delta to Tobruk and beyond. Day and night the South Africans and the Indians laid the railway westward, advancing at the rate of a mile a day, and halting only when the blast of the whistle warned them of the approach of the dive-bombers. Other engineers and pioneers laid the pipe-line that carried fresh water from Egypt to El Adem. And on all this feverish preparation the desert sun blazed relentlessly down.

At sea the transports still made their way along the coast, still hunted by U-boats and bombers, and the crews of their few escorting destroyers were hard put to it to keep from falling asleep at their guns.

At Gambut, thirty miles east of Tobruk amongst the sand dunes, in a cluster of camouflaged tents and trucks, Ritchie had his headquarters. Just across the Via Balbia, conveniently close at hand, was out main fighter base.

Under Ritchie were his two Corps Commanders, Gott and Norrie and when the three of them were not conferring with Auchinleck in Cairo they were shut up together in Ritchie's caravan, veiled by its camouflage netting from the prying eyes of Rommel's reconnaissance planes.

Away to the west was the Gazala line. It was not, in fact, a line at all in the military sense of the word, but a series of forts or 'boxes' strung out behind a dense minefield stretching for about thirty-five miles inland from the coast.

These 'boxes' were islands about a mile square, completely surrounded by minefields and barbed-wire and were defended by guns pointing to the north, south, east, and west. Each one was a self-contained unit with its supply of ammunition, water and food. But they were all linked together by lanes through the minefields so that supplies and reinforcements could reach them.

The Gazala box was manned by South Africans and the one just to the south of it by British North Country Territorials from the Tees and Tyne. In the centre was the Knightsbridge box, held by the Guards Brigade. On the extreme right, at Bir Hacheim, the box was defended by the Free French, under General Koenig. A little to the east was the El Adem box, manned by the Indians. Then there was the Tobruk box, the largest of all, guarded by the 2nd South African Division and the 9th Indian Brigade. It was commanded by General Klopper. His senior officer was Major-General Dan Pienaar, a grey-headed veteran of the First World War, who commanded the 1st South African Division from his headquarters at the extreme north, at a point known as the 'Bastion'.

Tobruk was not, however, really a box. It was not, to start with, surrounded by guns sticking out in all directions. For in the five months since relief it had become the principal base and administration area of the

8th Army. It was a vast supply dump and its wire now served to keep out light-fingered looters rather than an enemy.

Defending these boxes from the outside as well as the in, were the 1st and 7th Armoured Divisions, commanded respectively by Lumsden and Messervy. But the disposition of this armour depended upon Ritchie's appreciation of Rommel's intentions.

That then, briefly, was the situation of the 8th Army in and around Gazala in May, 1942.

On the other side of the deep minefields and the barbed-wire was the Axis Army. Along the front from the sea southwards were the Italian Infantry and behind them, astride the Trig Enver Bei, waited the Axis armour – the 21st, 15th, and 90th Light Panzer Divisions and the Ariete Division.

Auchicleck, in his long despatch covering the period of his Middle East Command, says that in May the 8th Army had numerical superiority over the Axis in tanks, as well as a larger reserve upon which to draw. The operative word was, of course, 'numerical'. For alas the British armour, even when bolstered up by American lease-lend tanks, was still not as good as the German. The American Grants mounted a 75-mm gun, but that gun was situated too low in the hull and had too little traverse. We had the Roberts anti-tank guns, but far too few of them.

However, so long as there are two generals living who remember the Second World War, they will argue to their last breath as to whether or not the basic reason for our many defeats was the lack of a really good tank. Deep in their leather armchairs in Pall Mall and Piccadilly these ageing soldiers will harangue each other about our anti-tank guns.

'Why the devil didn't we use our 3.7s against the Hun tanks?' one will demand.

'We should have made better use of the 25-pounder, for there was a good gun if ever there was one,' the other will insist.

And so on, for ever and ever.

In the air the Desert Air Force could muster some 600 planes of all types as against the Axis' 550. We had 384 fighter; the Axis 351, But of the latter, 120 were Me 109s, which were faster and better aircraft than our Hurricanes and Kittyhawks. The Germans had too, the great advantage of being able to call up reserve squadrons from Sicily, Crete, Greece, and the Dodecanese as and when they required. Moreover, there was far closer cooperation between the *Luftwaffe* and the *Afrika Korps* than there ever was between the 8th Army and the RAF.

Finally there were the opposing navies. With his Fleet reduced to a few cruisers and destroyers and many of his submarines despatched to the Far East, with the best will in the world there was little Cunningham could do to help Auchinleck. But beyond dealing with the enemy convoys, the Navy had never been counted upon to play such a role as it had done in the previous operations. Indeed, as far back as January, when the three Chiefs-of-Staff had met in Cairo, Cunningham had said that in the unhappy event of Tobruk ever becoming a beleaguered fortress again the Navy could not guarantee to supply the garrisons. This decision was accepted and fully understood by Auchinleck.

Those, then were the forces facing each other at Gazala in May.

From the disposition of his forces it will be realized that Auchinleck's plan was a defensive one. At the same time it must be remembered that this plan was virtually forced upon him by pressure from Whitehall. Since he had been told to get on with the battle or get out he was obliged to do the best he could with the troops and weapons at his disposal.

Many will regret, however, that having given in to Churchill on this major issue, Auchinleck did not also concede to Churchill's request to take over the command of the 8th Army in the field. He refused because he was weighed down by the great and widespread responsibilities of his position as Commander-in-Chief Middle East. But Auchinleck was above all a great fighting soldier, especially in a moment of crisis, as he had proved the previous winter and had he been at the front from the very beginning the result of the summer battle at Gazala might have been altogether different. As it was he left it to Ritchie. But even before the battle began he gave the latter some particularly sound advice. He told him to concentrate both his armoured divisions across the Trig Capuzzo.

'It does look from the map,' he said, 'as if this would be too far north to meet the main attack should it come round the southern flank.' Then he issued Ritchie a stern warning: 'I consider it to be of the highest importance that you should not break up the organization of either of the armoured divisions,' he told him. 'They have been trained to fight as divisions, I hope, and fight as divisions they should. Norrie must handle them as a Corps Commander and thus be able to take advantage of the flexibility which the fact of having two formations gives him.'

Unfortunatley this warning had not been heeded when Rommel struck.

Day after day, as the temperature soared and the atmosphere grew more and more oppressive, the tension increased and the nerves of the waiting troops became more strained.' Day after day the activity over and around the front at Gazala increased. More fighters were in the sky. More shots rang out from the boxes. More armoured cars raced over the bone-dry desert to disappear in feathers of dust into the quivering heat haze. More *Stukas* came singing down to release the bombs in their claws on the endless lines of lorries strung out for mile upon mile eastwards to Mersa Matruh and beyond. Hardly a night passed when the bombers, British and German, did not go droning through the starry sky or when the ack-ack guns were not in action.

Yet in spite of the heat the men at the front were given little rest. There was not much time. Every day our reconnaissance planes returned to report rapidly growing concentrations of enemy vehicles west of Gazala. No one doubted now that Rommel was, about to strike. Mines had to be laid and miles of wire strung round the forward positions. The boxes had to be made ready, time was running out. The Guards, together with the 2nd Regiment of the Royal Horse Artillery and an anti-tank battery of the Northumberland Hussars, moved up to the Knightsbridge box on May 17th. It was on a perfectly flat piece of desert and covered an area of some two square miles astride the Trig Capuzzo. Immediately behind the wire and the minefields were four companies of riflemen. In the centre the gunners and the anti-tank guns sited in depth throughout the box defended the position against enemy armoured attacks. By May 26th the box was ready to give battle.

It was the same all along the Gazala Line from the sea to Retma in the extreme south. The men and their guns stood ready behind their wire fences. All these desert forts were sealed – all, that is, except Tobruk, which was not a fort at all any more. The wire outside the Red Line had rusted in the winter rains. Searing desert winds had filled the anti-tank ditch with sand. As for the protecting minefields, nobody really knew where they were. In the south-east, large gaps had been made in them when the garrison had broken out to fight at Ed Duda. The sappers had removed hundreds more to be relaid around Gazala. To the west, in the famous Salient, there was an uncharted 'sea' of mines, Italian, British, Australian, German, and Polish, avoided by fools and wise men alike.

By the middle of May they began taking the heavy ack-ack guns away from Tobruk. The 'A' lighters carried them back to Mersa Matruh together with their crews.

'Towards the end of May, 1942,' Lieutenant Charles Curtis, of the South African Navy, writes, 'I was staying in Navy House at Mersa Matruh on my way to Tobruk and I met the Commanding Officer of an 'A' lighter which lay at the end of the concrete landing ramp. His name was De Kok and he came from Uitenhage in the Cape. He asked me where I was bound and I told him to Tobruk to mess about with boats, for I too, was in Combined Operations.

He said: "Sub, you won't get there in time – Tobruk will fall, and soon."

I asked him why he made this bald statement, and he then explained that he had been employed on the 'Spud Run' from Alexandria to Tobruk for some months. Towards the enemy his ship carried a cargo of ammunition, victuals and naval stores. In the other direction, he brought wrecked motor transport for cannibalization in the RASC dump near Mersa.

The last two return voyages had been different. His cargo had been 3.7 AA guns, the heavy anti-aircraft defence of the 'Home Town'.

'If,' asked De Kok, 'the Army is going to hold Tobruk, why is the flotilla being used to evacuate these guns and their crews?'

De Kok, who asked this pertinent question, was one of the outstanding officers of the Western Desert Lighter Flotilla. A tough South African, of Dutch descent, he was decorated over and over again for gallantry and was killed off Sicily shortly before the invasion of that island. Like many others of us, who had known Tobruk during the peak of the siege, he had watched the fortress being allowed to fall into decay with mixed feelings. To paraphrase the words of the famous 'Song of Tobruk', composed by Dennis Peters, 'we sighed for the port as it once used to be; where the sands of the desert sweep down to the sea'.

Nevertheless, during those last days of May, there were still those who talked glibly about holding Tobruk.

Rommel's armour began to move forward on May 26th. A red-hot khamsin sent dust-storms whirling across the desert like mad dervishes and the visibility was reduced almost to nil. In such weather it was impossible for our aircraft to see what was happening and even our armoured cars shadowing the enemy could not send back accurate reports.

Under cover of the storm, Rommel led his 10,000 vehicles forward at such a pace that his tanks were hard put to it to keep up. Blinded by the stinging, driving sand, their faces masked with handkerchiefs, the troops of the great Axis host advanced all that day. When night fell and the wind and the dust-devils died and as the *Afrika Korps* rolled towards its enemy by the light of the full moon, its official diarist recorded that the morale was superb and every man was tense in anticipation of the first encounters with the English. Optimistically, he claimed that by midnight the English had failed to detect the army sweeping upon them. He was wrong. Our armoured reconnaissance had been watching every move and had passed back to their brigade headquarters precise information of what was afoot.

Incredibly, however, the 7th Armoured Division were unprepared for what happened soon after dawn on May 27th. Its brigades were dispersed over the desert to the east of Bir Hacheim and were caught unawares. The two Panzer Divisions and the 90th Light Division swept right over the 7th Motor Brigade and the 4th Armoured Brigade like a tidal wave, leaving behind shattered and burning tanks and armoured cars.

Divisional Headquarters were overrun and Messervy captured in his pyjamas. Thus witthout his badges of rank, he managed to hookwink his captors that he was his batman.

When one of the Germans eyed him suspiciously and remarked that he looked somewhat elderly to be still a private Messervy agreed, grumbling that he was a reservist and 'they didn't ought' to have called him up. In the mêlée of battle Messervy escaped and by the same evening was again commanding his division.

By half past six on the morning of May 27th, the Commanding Officer of the 3rd Indian Motor Brigade Brigadier Filose, reported that the 'whole bloody *Afrika Korps*' was in front of him, in fact from the Retma box, he faced the Ariete and a part of the 21st Panzer Divisions.

The box was held by the 2nd Royal Lancers, the 18th Cavalry, the 11th Prince Albert Victor's Own Cavalry and two troops of the 2nd Indian Field Regiment. In its centre were the gunners with twenty-four field-guns and a British troop with six anti-aircraft Bofors. Two squadrons of tanks which should have been in support failed to arrive before the attack began.

The enemy set upon the box with fearful savagery, but although short of anti-tank guns the garrison drove off the first wave of armour of the Ariete Division. The courage of the Indian gunners was tremendous and they literally went on firing until they dropped dead beside their guns. Before they died they took a heavy toll of the German tanks. But there were too many German tanks and it was the same pathetic story of not having enough guns capable of destroying them. The Panzers rolled into the box, either killing or wounding every man in sight. Then, suddenly, into the midst of the battle appeared some carriers of the 18th Cavalry in a gallant but vain endeavour to save the day.

The Germans rubbed their eyes in astonishment, for there in the middle of their tanks stood a lone Naval officer, blazing away at them with his revolver. He was small and decidedly old. But when they called upon him to surrender he just went on firing at them until his revolver was empty. Then the Germans gathered him up and dragged him bodily into captivity. Their astonishment gave place to bewilderment when they discovered that the ferocious little man was none other than Admiral Sir Walter Cowan, Bart, KCB, DSO, MVO.

What on earth, they wondered, could this distinguished officer of seventy-two be doing in the middle of the Western Desert, dressed in khaki and wearing the three gold rings of a Commander RN on his shoulders? Surely the 18th Army was not *that* short of officers, the German Intelligence asked humorously.

They could not guess that 'Titch' Cowan, as he was lovingly known, had volunteered for the Commandos and had come to the Middle East with 'Layforce', commanded by then, Colonel 'Bob' Laycock. Even when they were told, the Germans never really believed it. Nevertheless, they made great propaganda out of their capture of the 'little Admiral'.

CHAPTER THIRTY-ONE

ROMMEL REPULSED

Rommel had reckoned on capturing Tobruk within five days of the start of his offensive. But his Intelligence was hopelessly misinformed as to the strength and dispositions of the 8th Army. Thus he attacked without realizing the strength of Bir Hacheim or even the existence of the Guards Brigade at Knightsbridge. Strangely enough, too, Rommel expressed surprise when he first ran into the Grant tanks for the Intelligence appreciation attached to his Operational Order of May 20th included an accurate description of these tanks and their armament.

So, on the face of it, by eleven o'clock on May 27th, everything seemed to be going well. His Panzers had overrun Messervy's headquarters. The 90th Light Division had pulled off a splendid bluff. Accompanied by vehicles fitted with propellers, to raise a dust-cloud and so fool the enemy that they were tanks, it had dashed on as far as the El Adem crossroads, frightening General Norrie into the El Adem box with all his Staff. A great many tanks and anti-tank guns had been knocked out and a number of supply dumps had been destroyed, including one containing the entire stock of whisky for the 8th Army.

Small wonder, then, that Rommel personally congratulated his Corps Commander, urging him to continue in vigorous pursuit of the enemy. It really did look as if he had the 8th Army on the run. Then at high noon, in the full heat of the summer's day, the 2nd Armoured Brigade, whose existence was unknown to Rommel, suddenly appeared out of the shimmering haze. They rolled over the horizon from all points of the compass. A black mass of tanks. It was an awe-inspiring sight, but the Germans knew how British tanks behaved, and were confident that they only had to wait until they came within range and then blow them off the face of the desert with their 75-mm and 88-mm guns. But this great force of tanks behaved strangely. Instead of dashing into battle, they divided into three groups; one on each flank and one in the middle.

Then from hull-down positions they opened fire. Their shells whistled and screamed and burst all round the Germans. But, this time, they were 75-mm armour-piercing shells instead of little 2-pounders. The anti-tank guns were hurling 6-pounder shells from nearly 2,000 yards away.

To make the situation even more perilous, the Panzers were caught without their famous batteries of 88-mm anti-tank guns in support, and soon the air was filled with desperate messages calling upon their artillery for help. But before that help arrived the British armour had penetrated through the assault columns to sever the Panzers' lines of communication.

Rommel himself was caught in this madstrom of fire, as he dashed from El Adem to reach his Panzers and came within an ace of being killed. From that moment everything went wrong for him. The Guards Brigade in their Knightsbridge box, which was the hub of the whole battle, repulsed one attack after another. All along the line from Retma to the sea the British resisted doggedly.

Rommel called up his *Stukas*. Again and again he threw his tanks and infantry against the boxes. But still they resisted. Then he gave up, forced to admit that he had gravely under-estimated the strength of the British armoured divisions. He was, he confessed, very worried indeed and well he might be, for his entire *Afrika Korps* was stranded in the minefields. encircled by the enemy, with their supplies running out and without hope of replenishing them except by the perilous journey south of Bir Hacheim.

In spite of this precarious position and dangerous shortage of supplies, Rommel stuck tenaciously to his plan. All through the next day – May 29th – he personally led his troops against the enemy in the face of a raging, seering sandstorm. But by the end of that dreadful day, with his ammunition practically exhausted, he was forced to admit defeat. Abandoning his plan, he withdrew his forces into a triangular area between the Sidra and Aslag Ridges. At their backs was the main minefield of Gazala and on their right flank another of our minefields running north from Bir Hacheim. In this area, which came to be known to the British as the Cauldron, the whole Axis striking force halted, ringed by what remained of its armour, while the German and Italian engineers worked like beavers to clear gaps in the minefields to open up a short cut to their supply base.

On May 30th Rommel went off through one of these gaps to confer with Kesselring and von Below, Hitler's personal ADC. He returned with a new plan: to establish a direct line of communication westwards; to annihilate the garrison at Bir Hacheim; and to split and overrun each one of those boxes strung out across his path to Tobruk. But the success of this plan depended upon a box, the existence of which Rommel did not discover until he retreated into the Cauldron. This was situated near Sidi Muftah and was held by the 150th Brigade and the 44th Royal Tank Regiment. Its guns dominated the gaps in the minefields through which flowed the lifeblood of the Axis Army. 'It all turned on the 150th Brigade box,' General Fritz Bayerlein said and back in Cairo, Auchinleck was of the same opinion. He knew that if that bridgehead through the minefields was denied to him, Rommel's troops would die of thirst even before they starved to death.

On this little square mile of desert surrounded by its wire and mines, and defended by the men from the Tees and the Tyne, the whole battle hinged, Auchinleck ordered Ritchie to cling to it at all costs.

Both sides fought to the death for it. On May 30th the Germans brought every gun they could to bear on it, but still it held. The next day, having called upon its garrison to surrender, they attacked in even greater strength. The Brigade fought for every inch of ground. But by June 1st their ammunition was running low and the enemy secured a foothold within the fortress. Rommel himself actually took command of the leading infantry platoon at the height of the battle, when each separate point was fought for and each individual bunker taken only after bloody hand-to-hand fighting.

General Cruwell, Commander of the *Afrika Korps*, was shot down and had to make a forced landing in the box, where he was taken prisoner. General Gause, Rommel's then Chief-of-Staff, and Lt Colonel Westphal were both wounded before the battle for the box ended.

Too late, Ritchie tried to send help to the exhausted garrison, for by the time the order was given the gallant 150th Brigade had ceased to exist.

Three thousand had been taken prisoner, while 101 of their tanks and armoured cars and 124 guns had been captured.

Rommel's bridgehead was established, and through the widening gaps in the minefields in the Gazala Line came the stream of trucks bringing the Axis Army the water, the food, the fuel, the guns, the tanks and the men – in fact, everything that Rommel needed for the fulfilment of his plan.

CHAPTER THIRTY-TWO

THE BEGINNING OF THE END

Why was not the supreme effort made to destroy Rommel's bridgehead?

The question is inevitable. Yet it is difficult to answer. It cannot be done simply by saying that Ritchie was short of tanks and guns. At so crucial a moment he would have been justified in risking all his armour to sever the lifeline of the Axis Army.

It could be said that Ritchie did not understand the importance of the box at Sidi Muftah or the serious consequences of its loss. Yet Auchinleck had stressed both these points to him.

Even after the destruction of the 150th Brigade, Ritchie considered the 'situation still favourable and improving daily'. Indeed, he said so in a signal to Auchinleck. The latter replied that while he was glad his commander thought this, he viewed the 'destruction of the 150th Brigade and the consolidation by the enemy of a broad and deep wedge in the middle of (Ritchie's) position with some misgiving'. The Commander-in-Chief added: 'I am sure, however, there are factors known to you which I do not know.'

In that final remark lies the key to the whole tragedy of the defeat of the 8th Army in the summer of 1942.

Auchinleck did not know all the facts. Hundreds of miles from the front, in his headquarters in Cairo, he was dependent upon the signals he received from his commanders in the odd for vital information. These commanders were not above taking the optimistic view to please their master.

Such a position was utterly invidious. Yet Auchinleck was forced into it by the very nature of his command. As Commander-in-Chief Middle East, his responsibilities were too great and the area under his command too vast Both had been reduced since Wavell's day, but not nearly enough. Fortunately for the future of the war, by the time Alexander took over, Syria and Palestine had been made a separate command, and so he was able to devote his entire attention to the Western Desert. But that did not happen until after the summer campaign had been lost.

Unlike his adversary, Rommel, Auchinleck could not be with his troops in the front line all the time, directing the battle from a jeep or an armoured car or a tank. When, at moments of crisis, he did fly up to the front from Cairo, he often arrived only in time to pull the badly burnt chestnuts out of the fire. Not because he had left it too late, but because, in a war of movement such as was being waged in the desert, the whole character of a battle can change in less time than it takes an aeroplane to fly three or four hundred miles.

Auchinleck has been accused of 'looking over his shoulder' at Syria, Palestine and even Turkey, when his whole attention should have been concentrated on Libya. If, in fact, this was the case, then the onus lies with Churchill and his. They had urged Auchinleck to take personal command of the 8th Army. But they took no steps to relieve him of those responsibilities that in his opinion prohibited him from doing so.

There can be no doubt but that he was needed at the front. For this was Rommel's offensive and in order to anticipate and counter its every move it was vital to be on the spot.

It is waste of breath to argue what might have happened if Auchinleck had commanded the 8th Army in the field. By doing so once before he had beaten Rommel. Incidentally it is, interesting to note how much Rommel had learnt from that beating and to do so it is only necessary to compare his out-flanking movement in May with that of Operation '*Crusader*' in November. If Rommel's Intelligence had been as good as was Auchinleck's six months before, he would have out-manoeuvred the 8th Army and captured Tobruk according to his original plan.

Auchinleck chose to leave the conduct of the battle to his lieutenants in the field. None of them was a match for Rommel. They lacked decision. While they were still discussing the merits of some particular move, Rommel acted. His actions were not inspired by genius. They were orthodox in their conception. But by being always in the forward area he was able to execute his moves while his immediate opponents were still brooding over them. Rommel did that repeatedly. He did it, for instance, at Bir Hacheim. While that fortress was putting up its magnificent and epic fight, Ritchie, Gott, Messervy, and Briggs, who commanded the 5th Indian Division, were still arguing whether to drive south of the fortress to cut Rommel's supply line, or to 'crush the enemy' in the Cauldron. In the end, while they failed to do either, Rommel went on to take the Knightsbridge box.

These generals reached their nadir of vacillation over Tobruk.

When, after bitter fighting and great heroism, the garrisons were driven one after another from their boxes, the fate of the Gazala Line was sealed. A withdrawal had to be made to some strategic point where the 8th Army could stand firmly to resist and break the tide of Rommel's advance.

Where was the best place?

This was the question that exercised the minds of all concerned with our fortunes in the desert; not least amongst whom was Churchill.

The answer, of course, was that after the fall of Bir Hacheim the 8th Army should have fallen back on the frontier defences. But at this moment of crisis, as Churchill wrote, 'Tobruk glared upon us and, as in the previous year, we had no doubt that it should be held.'

It seems inconceivable that Churchill had not heard of the decision taken by his Commanders-in-Chief never again to hold Tobruk. Perhaps, weighed down by his vast responsibilities, he had forgotten about it. Yet, if he was informed of this decision at the time when it was taken, why did he not stamp on it?

He says categorically that he was unaware of the conditions at Tobruk in 1942, and that to him it was unthinkable that its well-proved fortifications had not been maintained and also strengthened. In his opinion, since Auchinleck was fighting a defensive battle, Tobruk was a valuable factor in the plan.

Such a view was correct only if Tobruk had been considered as an intrinsic part of that plan from its inception, and only if the fortress could have been prepared to withstand a siege without the support of the Navy. Those were two big 'ifs'.

However, the decision had been taken not to hold Tobruk. And that should have been that. But, alas, it was not.

At the eleventh hour, under pressure from Churchill and after the exchange of many telegrams, Auchinleck agreed that Tobruk might be allowed to become 'temporarily isolated by the enemy'. Ritchie, he informed Churchill, was putting an adequate force into the fortress with that end in view.

He then gave Ritchie quite definite orders:

'...Tobruk must be held and the enemy must not be allowed to invest it. This means that 8th Army must hold a line Acroma-El Adem and southwards and resist all enemy attempts to pass it. Having reduced your front by evacuating Gazala and reorganized your forces, this should be feasible and I order you to do it.'

This signal was sent from Cairo at 11.30 a.m. on June 14th. But by the time it reached Ritchie the enemy were heavily attacking in the environs of Acroma. However, Ritchie replied that he did not consider the latter place vital once the troops had been withdrawn from the bastion. He intended to give all he could to strengthen the 7th Armoured Division in guns and anti-tank guns. by collecting under them all the available motorized units and armour for employment on the southern flank. He added, with less optimism than usual, that he could not guarantee that Rommel would grant him the time to do this.

In the event of his forces being overrun, Ritchie said that he would be faced with the decision to allow Tobruk to be invested or order the garrison to fight its way out. The garrison could fight its way out, but it would undoubtedly lose a considerable amount of equipment and transport, and arrive at the frontier in a disorganized condition.

Ritchie ended his signal with the following words:

'Having regard to the resources of ammunition, food, and water now in Tobruk, and in ships in Tobruk, I feel confident that it could hold out for two months on its own resources.'

On this same day, June 14th, Churchill telegraphed to Auchinleck that he presumed there was no question of giving up Tobruk, for as long as it was held no serious enemy advance into Egypt was possible. He added that he had been through all this before in April, 1941.

The following day Auchinleck replied that, although he did not intend the 8th Army should be besieged in Tobruk, he had no intention of giving it up. He then repeated what his orders to Ritchie had been.

The same day, Churchill answered, to say that he was glad of Auchinleck's determination to hold Tobruk, and that the War Cabinet interpreted his orders to mean that, if the need arose, Ritchie would leave as many troops in Tobruk as would be necessary to hold it.

Auchinleck assured Churchill that the War Cabinet's interpretation was correct, and repeated that Ritchie was putting into Tobruk what he (Ritchie) considered an adequate force to hold it, even should it be temporarily isolated. Auchinleck then went on to say that the basis of the garrison was four brigade groups with sufficient stocks of ammunition, fuel, food, and water. The 8th Army, he said, would hold the El Adem fortified area as a pivot of manoeuvre and would use all available forces to prevent the enemy establishing himself east of El Adem or Tobruk. 'Very definite orders to this effect have been issued to General Ritchie,' he added, 'and I trust he will be able to give effect to them.'

From all these telegrams it is perfectly obvious that Churchill and his advisers would not tolerate any retreat to the frontier.

It is somewhat obscure, however, whether or not they knew the state of the Tobruk defences. Certainly Auchinleck must have done.

Gott, whose responsibility Tobruk had been for some time past, knew, since he had been to look at them. When walking round these defences with Klopper, Gott is reported to have expressed the view that Tobruk was 'a nice tidy show' compared with what it had been when Morshead had taken over at the beginning of the first siege. Gott is further reported to have said that in his belief Tobruk would hold out, even without the Navy, and suggested to Ritchie that he himself should take over command of the fortress.

However, Gott is dead. But if he did say such things, then 'Straffer' Gott, who was one of our finest and most experienced desert generals, must have believed the defences as good as, if not better than, when the Australians had arrived into the fortress in retreat from Benghazi. And if he did, he undoubtedly told his Commander-in-Chief so.

Perhaps they were not really so inadequate as legend has made them out to be? Obviously they were not as good as they had been in December. But were they any worse than they had been in April, 1941? In those days, the fortress was not bristling with heavy anti-aircraft or anti-tank guns; the perimeter was not thickly sown with mines or entangled with barbed-wire.

In those days, the Blue Line hardly existed and the anti-tank ditch was filled with sand. In those days the garrison scarcely had a tank.

In fact, any of the old original men of the garrison, wandering into the Red Line in June, 1942, might well have remarked with a nostalgic smile: 'Brother, this is where we came in!'

CHAPTER THIRTY-THREE

THE NEW GARRISON?

It had happened in April, 1941, and now it was happening all over again, fourteen months later. The scene was almost exactly the same. The same hopeless congestion of trucks, carriers, and guns and their quads jamming the road and straggling over the desert. The same dusty, red-eyed soldiers plodding through the sand or rocking and swaying together like puppets in their lorries as they bumped over the pot-holed road.

An army retreating in the same direction to the same place – Tobruk.

The scene was almost exactly the same – but not quite. South African soldiers in little pith helmets had taken the place of the Diggers in their slouch hats. There were more guns about; a few of them the new 6-pounders. And even a few tanks. Before, there had been none. But to the observer, fascinated by the similarity, it would have been easy to overlook such small differences, as he watched this great mass of men and machinery moving slowly through the grey dawn into the fortress.

As the last stragglers passed into the perimeter, the roads were cratered, the bridges blown, the gaps in the minefields closed and wired – just as they had been before.

But once inside the crumbling fortress the similarity ended with startling abruptness. For now there was no 'Ming the Merdless' to tell the weary, bewildered troops that there would be no surrender or no retreat. In his stead was a Major-General of but one month's seniority, who was none too sure of himself or his position, when it came to dealing with some of the campaign-hardened Brigadiers under him. Naturally, he did not talk about Dunkirk or the Navy for, strangely enough, everyone seemed to know that this time there would be no destroyers or 'A' lighters running supplies into Tobruk. Moreover, no one minded very much, for in Klopper's headquarters in the Pilastrino Caves, for all to see, was an Operational Order headed 'Freeborn' which provided for the evacuation of the fortress in case of any danger. It was signed by Ritchie, and so far as anyone knew it had never been countermanded.

It has been said that the new garrison arrived in Tobruk as tenants into a strange house that had fallen somewhat into disrepair and, as such, they have been excused for what happened to them. But that is, of course, rubbish. The house was strange and certainly it was dilapidated. And so, indeed, it had been when the Australians had taken up residence there before. It would be nearer the truth to say that the new garrison arrived as lodgers to stay a little while and then move on. Since they had no intention of staying for any length of time, it was not worthwhile expending a great deal of energy putting the place into repair.

The lodgers were not despondent or without hope. According to Klopper, their 'spirits were very high', and he did not think their morale could have been better. Indeed, on June 16th, he wrote to his friend Major-General Theron in Cairo that in Tobruk 'there is a general feeling of optimism, and I think there is every reason for it, although we expect to put up a strong hard fight'. The South Africans were, he said, all looking forward to a good stand, and were supported by the very best British troops.

At least the last part of that statement was true. For in the fortress were units of the Coldstream Guards, the Cameron Highlanders, the Sherwood Foresters, as well as the 11th Indian Brigade, which was composed of veteran desert fighters.

Briefly the garrison was disposed as follows: the north coast and the western and southern perimeter from the sea to the El Adem road were held by the South Africans. Eastward from that point were the 2nd Camerons, the 2/5th Mahrattas and the 2/7th Gurkhas. The 201st Brigade Headquarters, the 3rd Coldstream, and the Sherwood Foresters were in the centre of the old Blue Line near the Pilastrino Ridge.

The artillery situation, although not good by any means, was better than it had been at the beginning of the siege in April, 1941. There were two regiments of medium artillery left in the fortress, neither up to full strength – the 67th and the 68th Medium Regiments RA. In field artillery the garrison was definitely strong, although there were many complaints that far too much of the ammunition was still in the dumps and not beside the guns.

The anti-tank gun state was poor, since there was no Anti-Tank regiment. The garrison, however, could muster some sixty-nine anti-tank guns, including eighteen of the new 6-pounders. As for anti-aircraft guns, they numbered about the same as in April, 1941; eighteen 3.7s still remained together with a number of Bofors.

The 4th and 7th Royal Tank Regiments, under Brigadier Willison, had about fifty-four tanks between them.

In all, there were about 35,000 men within the perimeter, of whom some 10,000 were base and area troops under the command of Brigadier Thompson.

Still sitting in Navy House was Captain Smith, with his staff of officers and ratings, and Captain Walter, DSO, RN, who had relieved Captain Poland as Senior Naval Officer Inshore Squadron. Still there, too, were the 'UPs'.

Nowhere better than around the harbour could one sense that all was not well with Tobruk during those sweltering June days. For after all, the harbour was the heart of the fortress, pumping its life-blood through the arteries that radiated from it to the perimeter. It was also the central exchange for the 'bush' telephone service functioning with high efficiency throughout the fortress. All the best of the news – and the worst – spread outwards from the harbour. And at the beginning of June most of that news was disturbing, if not downright bad.

It was said down at the harbour, for instance, that the supply ships were taking away more stuff than they brought in. From the harbour, too, had started that rumour about the Navy washing its hands of Tobruk. Old 'Cuts' Cunningham, as the ratings called him, had gone from 'Alex', fed up, they said, at having no 'battle-wagon' in which to put to sea. Harwood, who had sunk the *Graf Spee* off the River Plate, was now the boss of what was left of the 'Med' Fleet.

A lot of the base wallahs were packing up too, and some of them, believe it or not, had their baggage addressed to Haifa, Port Suez, and even

Durban!

That sort of talk was common enough around the harbour, and it 'bred an uncomfortable feeling of insecurity and impermanence that was foreign to the old fortress. What was more, it gave a certain credence to those other stories which were in circulation. Stories like the one about those South African field-gunners supporting the Indians upon the western perimeter, who had never heard a shot fired in anger. And those tit-bits of gossip about Hopper not hitting it off with Willison or old Thompson from 88th Sub-Area HQ, or Brigadier Anderson, the tough, one-time ranker commanding the 11th Indian Brigade. Perhaps it was true that these old soldiers knew more about defending a fortress than Klopper. After all, Thompson had been CRA in the last siege, and should know what he was talking about.

All these rumours and the gossip were insidious and subversive, and they drifted about the fortress like a ghostly Fifth Column, unseen by Klopper and his Staff, whose outlook was scarcely less rosy than the walls of the 'Pink Palace' at Pilastrino in which they lived.

The impression must not be gained from what has been written that the fighting men of the garrison all came streaming into the perimeter at the last minute. A great many did do that, just as they had done in April, 1941. But the foundations of the garrison had been laid for some time. The 2nd South African Division, comprising the 4th and 5th Infantry Brigades, had arrived there in March by way of Bardia, Sollum, and Halfaya.

While in all fairness it must be said that they did not have as long to prepare and repair the defences as their predecessors, they should have made a better job of it than they did. But there can be no doubt that far more time was spent swimming and sunbathing than laying minefields and digging the sand from the anti-tank ditch. Klopper cannot be held altogether responsible for such dilatoriness, for he had not yet taken over from Major-General Villiers. At the same time more than a month before he had told his officers at a Staff conference that Tobruk would be held as a pivot for the manoeuvre of our armoured forces. Thus, it should not have been necessary for Gott, as late as June 14th, to be obliged to keep practically the entire garrison employed on the defences when they should have been engaged in the desperate fighting beyond the perimeter.

It is necessary to remember these facts, however defamatory they may seem to be to the honour and character of those concerned, if one is to understand the débâcle to come. Comparisons, however odious, must be made between the first days of the first siege and those of the second. Many who have written about that second siege, either through ignorance or prejudice, preferred to compare Tobruk as it was in December, when the siege was raised, with the fortress as they found it in June. How, such writers have asked, could any troops be expected to hold such a place? Not even the old 'Desert Rats' could have done it! Rommel would have taken the place in a matter of days!

But the facts must be faced. Morshead and his men *did* hold just such a place. Rommel *did* attack it not once but many times. Within thirty-six hours of the last man withdrawing into the fortress in April, the Germans were sniffing at the wire. But they never took Tobruk.

CHAPTER THIRTY-FOUR

TOBRUK SURROUNDED

The Tobruk-Bardia road goes winding up the escarpment. Some six miles south-east of the town it is joined, almost at right angles, by the road from El Adem. From the air this junction is like a capital Y. It was known to the garrison as King's Cross. The arms of the Y are wide and the area between them was held by the 11th Indian Brigade, commanded by Anderson, the former Cameron Highlander. It was a large area to be held by a brigade, and Anderson had not wasted any time in drawing Klopper's attention to this fact. He had also complained that large portions of the minefield had been removed and that the anti-tank ditch in front of his troops 'wouldn't have interfered with the progress of a garden roller'.

Willison, too, had gone to Klopper and insisted that his tanks should be situated roughly at the tail of the Y. In the first siege, he said, the Australians had dug him tank pits there-abouts, and he would like to occupy them again. Klopper agreed to this. Nevertheless, his mind was preoccupied with the western defences, since none other than Ritchie had warned him that it was from that direction Rommel's attack would probably come.

Now that, on the face of it, was an extraordinary thing for the Commander of the 8th Army to have said. For, even before Rommel's attack, it was not difficult to anticipate its direction. The popular way into

Tobruk – and out, for that matter – had always been in the south-east. Wavell's troops had come in that way in January, 1941, to capture Tobruk. Rommel had tried to break through at that sector at Easter and in May of that year, and he had planned to use that same approach route in November. When the garrison had fought its way out to join the 8th Army it was from this same sector that it made its sortie.

Auchinleck in his famous despatch wrote:

> 'It was only to be expected that the enemy when he invested the fortress would turn again to his original and elaborate plan of the previous November for attacking it from the southeast.'

Yet when Ritchie flew into Tobruk on June 16th, to confer with Gott and Klopper for the last time, he warned the latter to pay special attention to the western sector of the perimeter. It is difficult not to feel sorry for Klopper. For, the day before, Willison had lectured him like the proverbial Dutch uncle about the disposition of his troops. The Brigadier had prefaced his remarks by saying that he hoped he was not speaking out of turn, and had then gone on to say exactly what he thought. He said that he had been in Tobruk when it was besieged before, and now the whole of the dispositions seemed to him far from satisfactory. Previously, all the infantry brigades had held the perimeter, and not two, with the third looking out to sea. Willison said, too, that formerly he had commanded all the armour in the fortress, and that now there were twice as many armoured cars in Tobruk as there had been before. He then asked that these should be placed under his command.

Klopper was not unlike the manager of an hotel, in which all the guests were complaining at once. But his particular guests were not grumbling about the food, or the plumbing, or the beds, or the lack of hot water, but about the shortage of ammunition, the lack of minefields, the rusting barbed-wire, bad communications, and the absence of definite orders. It was almost impossible even at that stage to draw a round of ammunition from the Ordnance Depot without signing for it in triplicate!

To say that confusion reigned beyond the perimeter and inside it during those last hectic days would be no exaggeration. It is a fact, for instance, that Klopper did not know that either of the boxes at El Adem or Bel Hamed had fallen until he was told about it by the 11th Indian Brigade Liaison Officer. This officer had set out for El Adem only to discover that it was occupied by the enemy. He was captured, but managed to escape back to Tobruk, where he related his experience to the Fortress Commander.

It is reasonable to speculate whether Ritchie even knew that these two key positions had gone – El Adem on June 16th, and Bel Hamed by the night of June 17th-18th. He certainly never warned Klopper even of such a possibility during his flying visit to Tobruk. But, when it was too late, he sent details of Rommel's plan to attack in the south-east sector by wireless to Klopper's headquarters.

To be wise after the event is often fatuous. Nevertheless, it is permissible to say that, had there been a more senior and seasoned Garrison Commander in Tobruk, he would have been able to control the situation and have acted on his own judgement and initiative. Indeed, incredible as it may seem, an attempt was actually made to fly Morshead into Tobruk when the situation was past saving.

On June 18th, Klopper held a conference at his headquarters, and announced to his brigade and battalion commanders that the fortress was surrounded and the gates closed for the last time. It was an acrimonious meeting at which Willison, not without justification, once again had a good deal to say. Since the distribution of the troops had not been changed, and no defence scheme had been drawn up, he asked if fresh preparations were to be made now that Tobruk was in a state of siege. Willison also drew attention to the fact, once more, that great areas were crammed with transport of all sorts without any attempt being made to camouflage them. Klopper still promised Willison that the armoured cars, some fifty in number, would be placed under his command, and said that he would send the CRA, Colonel Richards, up to Willison's sector since he was worried about his artillery support.

While this bickering was going on in the Pilastrino Caves, out on the perimeter the troops were still without orders. The Guards Brigade, whose first task it would be to counterattack, was given no opportunity of making a reconnaissance, and received no orders of any sort until June 19th. Yet the Brigade's duty was to defend the inner perimeter, or Blue Line, around Pilastrino fort. Three days were spent digging positions, with the Coldstreams in the centre, the Foresters on the left, and the Worcesters on the tight. The Brigade had fortified these positions as best they could, with sandbags and old ammunition boxes, utilizing the original flea-infested Italian dug-outs just as their predecessors had done.

For the next three or four days, still without orders, the Brigade waited, sending out one column to shoot up the enemy. But as they waited they noticed, according to the Coldstream official historians, 'one or two unusual, perhaps disquieting, occurrences – Naafi supplies, for example, were being handed out at the dumps with lavish generosity – but no one supposed that Tobruk could not once more be defended as successfully as before'.

So far as the Brigade knew, Rommel had surrounded Tobruk by then, and, having captured the airfields at El Adem and Gambut, his tanks were driving onto the frontier. In common with many others, the Guards believed that the Germans were heading for Alexandria, and with the rest of the garrison were resigned to the prospect of a long and weary siege.

Further to the east the 11th Indian Brigade, thanks to the efforts of Willison and Anderson, had at last been given the support of two batteries of the 25th Field Regiment, as well as one South African battery of 25-pounders and two medium guns. But the Brigade was still short of anti-tank guns when, on the morning of June 18th, armoured cars out on patrol in this sector reported a formidable enemy column moving east.

However, the 25th Field Regiment engaged the advanced vehicles of this column so heavily that they were driven off.

To the south-west and outside the perimeter the South Africans were busy strengthening the defences of the Acroma Keep. This was the only outpost of the fortress under South African command, and was built at the end of April, 1942. It was situated on the Axis by-pass road some seventeen, miles from Tobruk. When Rommel began his offensive it was hurriedly occupied by its garrison, consisting of 'B' Company of the 2nd Transvaal Scottish, supported by battalion mortars and a machine-gun platoon from the Die Middellandse Regiment. Its artillery was very much of 'bush' variety, beloved by the Diggers, and consisted of a German 88-mm and four Italian 47-mms, none with sights.

In the neighbourhood of Acroma Keep on June 15th was, Private X, of the 2nd Transvaal Scottish. He was with Stopcol, a formation comprised of a company of his regiment, the 6th South African Field Battery, and the 6th South African Anti-Tank Battery, which, with some engineers and signallers, were attached to the bulk of the 8th Royal Tank Regiment. It was, in fact, one of several mobile armoured columns, consisting of a squadron of Valentine tanks, a battery of Bofors, and two companies of infantry.

With Stopcol, Private X moved up to Point 208, known as the 'Pimple', a slight unfortified hump west of Acroma.

'There was no hope of digging slit trenches in the solid rock,' he wrote, describing his meeting with the enemy, 'but we managed to dig some flimsy sangars. Each man was given a sticky-bomb and told to wait for the enemy, tanks. At first light the next morning we saw the skyline black with approaching tanks and vehicles, all marked with black crosses. The game was on!

Our Valentines went out to meet them, but within a few minutes had lost half their number. The remainder then turned and came tearing back to our positions.

By this time the enemy tanks were within range of our Bofors, which opened fire, and we saw their hot shells bouncing off the turrets of the German Mark IVs. The enemy fire was falling thick amongst us and we took what cover we could.

Back came our Valentines. The Squadron Commander jumped out of his tank and shouted: "All infantry get the hell out of here!"

We promptly got!

No sooner had we started than we received a direct hit from a shell on the back wheel of our truck. Fortunately, we were able to jump on another, taking with us our one casualty who had his leg taken off. Within two hours we were back in Tobruk.

I don't know what happened to our Valentines. But on the way back we passed a battery of 25-pounders which were firing at the Jerries over open sights. We counted fourteen tanks they had knocked out.'

The defenders of Acroma Keep had the enormous satisfaction in their first engagement with the enemy of destroying two tanks at point-blank range with the 88-mm gun. For three days they fought courageously, and on one occasion the South Africans actually had Rommel pinned down in the minefield under a mortar barrage. But even while the latter was ordering the Italians to take Acroma at all costs, and while the fort was still intact and its garrison full of fight. Klopper ordered it to be abandoned.

Reluctantly the South Africans retreated behind the perimeter wire, having suffered one casualty since they had moved into the fort on May 24th.

CHAPTER THIRTY-FIVE

THE LAST HOURS OF TORBRUK

Torbruk was surrounded. Encircled by Rommel's mighty Army.

Unknown to its Garrison Commander or his Staff in their underground caves at Pilastrino, or to his men sitting in their sangars and slit trenches behind the wire and the minefields of the perimeter, the Panzer Divisions had suddenly swung west and north from their advance towards Egypt to attack Tobruk.

The Axis troops were in fine fettle. Their tanks, armoured cars, and lorries had refuelled from the dumps abandoned by the 8th Army, and their artillery had been replenished with ammunition from other dumps that they themselves had left behind in November, and which the British had never bothered to demolish.

Rommel himself was now in command of the operation. He had arrived near Gambut especially to see that the disengagement of the *Afrika Korps* from its positions in that area went according to plan. There had been some confusion over the interpretation of his orders. But he had soon cleared that up and now he was with his waiting troops. They had all seen him standing up in his car, the old scarf round his throat, dust-goggles pushed above the peak of his cap. This was his finest hour and it was good to be with him at such a time.

Zero hour was 0520. June 20th.

As the veil of mist rose and the first rays of the sun turned the desert from grey to pink, the Mahrattas saw silhouetted against the pale green sky a black host of tanks, trucks, and infantry advancing towards them. To the west of the El Adem road the South Africans, too, saw lines of troops and guns arrayed along the escarpment.

One by one, as their observers reported back to them these enemy concentrations, the Tobruk batteries opened fire, and the Axis batteries replied until the ground shook beneath the weight of exploding shells.

Then, as the sun climbed the horizon, the noise of the guns was almost drowned by the roar of aircraft, *Stukas* and Ju 88s, heading like darts for the famous entrance to Tobruk held by the 11th Indian Brigade.

Rommel's orders to his dive-bombers were to blast a gap 600 yards wide in the minefields through which his Panzers would pass and his orders were carried out to the letter. Under the rain of bombs the Indians and the Highlanders were helpless, the gunners behind the infantry could see nothing through the mountain of dust and black smoke thrown heavenwards by the bombs.

The *Stukas* kept up a shuttle service between the perimeter and El Adem airfield, but ten miles away, in the lulls in the gunfire and the bombing our forward troops could hear the shrill whine of the enemy planes taking off.

Under cover of the barrage, and half-hidden by the smoke and dust, the German and Italian sappers dashed forward to lift the mines, and the infantry poured through the gaps to overwhelm two companies of the Mahrattas. The timing was perfect, as well it might have been, for the plan had been laid many months before and, since then, rehearsed down to the last detail. As tanks, lorried infantry, and anti-tank guns moved into the gap they lit purple, green, and red flares, and the diving *Stukas* dropped their bombs precisely ahead of this gaily coloured smoke-screen. Meanwhile other *Stukas* and heavy artillery were busy plastering the rear areas with bombs and shells. By early morning of June 20th the first enemy salvoes were crashing into the harbour area.

The previous night Tobruk had had its usual prolonged air raid, but when dawn came all was quiet, and Lt Commander Harris, DSC, of the South African Navy, who was 'Number One' at Navy House, got out of bed early. Taking his shotgun, he went on to the roof of the famous bomb-battered building to see if he could bag a pigeon or two for the pot.

'I hadn't been up there more than ten minutes when the band started,' he wrote in his description of the last hours of Tobruk. 'A battery of 180-mm guns fired on the town, and the first shells landed in daylight in the harbour area since December 6th, 1941.

The 180-mm shell is 7.6-in. and must weigh 150-pounds – quite a sizeable bang when it goes off. Shells landed here, there and everywhere, and after one had crumped near us and another rumbled overhead so close that I felt the wind of it, I decided to go below.

At 8.00 I fell in my ratings and endeavoured to proceed with the day's work as if things were perfectly normal. A somewhat difficult business when a shell might land anywhere near at any moment. However, we got busy on various jobs, though the Maltese cooks and stewards took quite a bit of tongue-lashing before they would take things normally and get on with the breakfast.

Up to this time the battle had raged round the town, and we knew we had been surrounded for three days. But so far as the Navy in Tobruk was concerned no one expected a frontal attack so soon. This momentous day was merely regarded as another of the old siege days, and if anthing most of us felt quite elated at being in the centre of things again, though somewhat resigned to know we were in for hard times. I visualized months of it, and felt depressed at the thought of even another two months in Tobruk.'

Harris says that at that time of the day – about 8.30 am to 9 am – there was little information coming through to Navy House from Army HQ, and the position was 'obscure'.

In fact it was also 'obscure' in the Pilastrino Caves. It was, 'obscure' everywhere in Tobruk. It would be nearer the truth to say that the entire fortress was in a state of utter confusion. At eleven o'clock that morning Klopper himself complained that he was 'completely in the dark' and declared his intention of going to King's Cross to find out what was happening. However, his Chief-of-Staff, Lt Colonel Kriek, persuaded him against it.

When Lt Colonel Alexander, the Commander of the 17th Field Ambulance, came to the 'Pink Palace' at one o'clock, he was impressed by the cheerfulness of Klopper and his Staff as they came out from lunch. Their high spirits might have been damped somewhat if Klopper had had the courage of his own opinion and had gone to King's Cross. For in that area our troops and our tanks were being cut to pieces by bombs, 88-mm shells, and heavy machine-gun fire. By noon, at about the time that the Garrison Commander and his Staff were sitting down to their cheerful lunch, our tank force at King's Cross, driven back behind the old Blue Line, was being smashed. One after the other the wretched Valentines were going up in flames or being pounded into scrap by the enemy's heavy anti-tank guns. The situation was desperate. Out of four squadrons of tanks only six were left. The Guards Brigade and their supporting units were in a bad way. Their anti-tank guns were knocked out one by one almost before they had time to fire three rounds. One gun was fought single-handed by Lieutenant St Clair Erskine, after all its crew had been killed around him, and until the portee was shattered beneath his feet by a direct hit.

By two o'clock the 11th Brigade HQ near King's Cross had been surrounded, and an hour later Anderson arrived at the 'Pink Palace', still hoping that he might be able to reach his Camerons fighting near the El Adem road.

Meanwhile, down at the harbour, still without definite news, Harris was methiodically trying to get on with the day's work. He had gone down to the quay and on his way had stopped to examine the result of a shell which had scored a direct hit on the old derelict Post Office building. As he walked out of the latter, another shell came sailing through the window and exploded close behind him.

After that he calmly spent the morning organizing the unloading of ammunition from two 'A' lighters.

> 'I decided,' he wrote. 'to make a start with my motor-boat crew, mainly for the good of morale, as they had taken to the shelters – a fatal proceeding, as once anyone gets shelter-conscious he is just about useless thereafter.
>
> Shells burst every few minutes, some behind us in the town, others on the dockside and in the bay. The prospect of working on top of and with, 150-tons of shells wasn't alluring, but the stuff had to be got ashore.'

With three other officers from Navy House, a few volunteers, and the crews of the two landing craft. Harris humped the ammunition ashore.

> 'Occasionally a near-miss would startle my party, and then I'd have the unenviable job of digging the lads out of the deep shelter, the dockside

entrance to which was very near the landing craft we were unloading. It was hot, dry work, and about 11.00 I accepted an invitation from the captain of the craft to a cup of tea on the quarterdeck,' Harris relates, 'where we were sitting quietly drinking when a heavy shell burst twenty-five yards from us, showering the ship with 'dirty water.'

By the early afternoon news from the front was still vague. But air attacks were more or less continual. The red flag was hauled up over Navy House, and stayed up. But, finally, Harris had it hauled down and stowed. No one, as he said, needed to be told there was an air raid on. He could hear it and see it everywhere he looked.

Everywhere one looked, too, there were signs in plenty that Tobruk as a fortress was falling apart. On the flat Salaro Plain, where were the two little airfields, the Naafi was burning furiously, and the German tanks wandered about unhindered shooting up the mass of trucks – 700 of them. In spite of Willison's warning, they had never been dispersed or camouflaged, and now the German tank commanders were having a high time making a glorious bonfire of them. Other enemy tanks and armoured cars were calmly refuelling at our petrol dumps, before moving on at leisure to knock out the few remaining batteries of Bofors.

But the Germans, as they admitted afterwards, did not have it all their own way. They never knew, they said, when these little isolated pockets of men and guns would not decide to resist to the last round of ammunition. For example, there were those 5.7s near the junction of the Derna-Pilastrino road. Their crews did not receive the warning that the German tanks were upon them until it was too late to remove the blast-walls around the emplacements to enable them to depress their guns. So they just blew away those emplacements. Their crews were magnificent. They kept on blazing away at the tanks until every man of them was either killed or wounded, destroying four tanks and putting several others out of action.

This heroic battle was spotted by some South African armoured cars from across the road, but when they tried to interfere the Germans just blew them to bits. Then they gathered up their wounded and carried them off to the nearest dressing-station.

By the time the Panzers had swept across the Derna road, and sent their advanced columns on towards the coast, Tobruk was finished. But, astonishingly, Klopper still did not know it. For in their forward surge the Panzers had passed right by the Pilastrino Caves. Other units were still fighting it out with the Guards Brigade on the ridge above the Fortress Headquarters.

There had been a moment at four o'clock in the afternoon when it had looked as if the Germans were determined upon taking the Headquarters. The 'Pink Palace' and the Caves were under shell-fire from about twenty tanks as well as heavy artillery from the King's Cross area.

Everyone on the Staff remembered the time, as June 20th was the birthday of one of the officers, and when the shelling started they were all just sitting down to celebrate the occasion with a nice cup of tea!

Down the road came a great stream of armoured cars and guns. Less than a thousand yards from the entrance of the caves tanks were seen refuelling from a petrol point.

There seemed no possibility of escape. Klopper gave the order for the immediate destruction of all signals and codes. He then told his Staff to make a run for it. It was every man for himself, and the rendezvous, if anyone ever reached it, was Sollum.

In a matter of minutes, black smoke belched from the Fortress Headquarters, and the grey ash of secret signals and code-books rose into the sky, to drift northwards to join the huge black cloud of smoke hanging over the town.

But the Germans never attacked the Caves. The tanks and the armoured cars that had come careering down the road, halting so impudently to fill up with fuel, belonged to the 21st Panzer Division, and they were in a hurry because no less a person than Rommel himself was shouting at them to get on with it!

Disconsolately, for now their code-books had gone and their telephone exchange and wireless sets were wrecked, Klopper and his Staff watched the Panzers sweep past.

They were not to know that Rommel was more interested in capturing the great petrol tanks in the harbour area than a mere Major-General and his Staff. They could always be rounded up later. But Rommel was getting anxious – and angry – about that ominous black pall of smoke hanging like a thunder-cloud over the harbour.

Earlier that afternoon Harris, standing on the terrace outside Navy House, had been looking through the telescope at the escarpment, when he saw one of the 3.7 guns depress and blast a German tank out of existence at point-blank range. It was a cheering sight. But when, a few seconds later, he saw the gun itself knocked out, he was left in little doubt but that the Germans were well inside the perimeter. In spite of the fact that very little information was reaching Navy House, he had suspected for some hours that the Germans were not far away. Now those suspicions were confirmed.

Harris then turned his telescope on to the small assault landing craft that was carrying Lt Commander Pearson, RN, across the harbour. It was the latter's duty to place the demolition charges in the various lighters moored out in the bay. As he watched, Harris saw a German armoured car appear over the top of the escarpment and open up at the assault craft with its 20-mm, but the demolition party proceeded on its way unharmed.

Soon a series of explosions in the harbour brought Captain Smith from his office to enquire what was going on.

Pearson, Harris told NOIC, was blowing up the lighters.

'NOIC was furious, and danced with rage, for Pearson had mistaken his orders, and instead of merely laying the demolition charges he was firing them. So one lighter and then another went up. But I don't think it was long before Smith decided that it was better that way after all,' Harris commented afterwards.

By five o'clock that evening, Smith brought all ships to the first state of readiness to evacuate Tobruk, while Harris continued to study the panorama of the harbour and the escarpment through his glass.

'It was about 5.30 when the first dozen trucks drove down to the south edge of the harbour,' he wrote, 'and their drivers set fire to them; an action which we considered at the time pretty cowardly, little realizing how the battle was going.

Squadrons of about twenty Ju 88s flew over and did mass bombing attacks, and although the effectiveness of some of their raids was just about nil, I don't think there was a single 3.7 AA gun left by six o'clock.'

No one thought of supper that evening at Navy House, and Harris was soon back on the terrace with his telescope.

'I saw a British tank come down the escarpment, and watched German lorries drawn up on the hill and unlimber their little 28/20 anti-tank guns and open fire. I could watch both the gun-flash and the hit together. After about ten hits the tank swerved off the road and down a bank into the bay. Although I watched for ten minutes, I saw no one come out of it.'

At the Pilastrino Caves, Klopper's only means of communication with the outside world were his signals vans, dangerously exposed in the open. However, at six-thirty-five that evening, having decided to evacuate the Caves, he signalled to Ritchie that his HQ had been overrun. And, as dusk was falling, the Fortress Commander and his Staff set out for the 6th South African Infantry Brigade's headquarters on the coast well to the west of the town.

At about this same time Brigadier Johnson, who had arrived in Tobruk but a few days before, to relieve Brigadier Marriot in command of the Guards Brigade, was being marched off into captivity. He was accompanied by his Staff and the Commanding Officer of the Coldstreams, Lt Colonel Forbes. The Germans had arrived while these officers still awaited their orders.

As the sun set Major Sainthill, perforce in command of the Battalion, took stock of his situation. It was grim. But he took a quick decision, and before the enemy was aware of what was going on the remainder of the four companies of Guardsmen had clambered into their trucks and disappeared into the smoke of battle.

While the Fortress Commander and his Staff were heading west through the gathering dusk, Ritchie and Gott were making desperate efforts to get in touch with him without success. Gott, ironically, had signalled: 'Hold on, am coming.' But, while some of the garrison signallers appear to have picked up this message, Klopper knew nothing of it. Not that he – or anyone else – could have done anything.

It was almost dark when the little party reached the 6th Brigade's HQ, whose Staff were both pleased and surprised to see Klopper. They had been out of touch with him since mid-afternoon, and there were rumours rife that he had been taken prisoner.

Now the first thing to do was to contact Ritchie and the 8th Army through one of the signals vans. But without code-books endless difficulties arose. Reception, too could scarcely have been worse. After what seemed an eternity Klopper got a message through to the effect that he was still holding out; for how long he could not say.

Alone with his signallers in the van Klopper tried over and over again to speak with Ritchie personally, but the 8th Army Commander was out.

It goes without saying that no copies of any of the signals sent out from Tobruk have survived, other than those that reached their destination. But still to be seen on the files is a signal from Ritchie to the Fortress Commander Tobruk urgendy asking:

'First. Whether in your opinion the situation is in hand. Second. If not, how long do you estimate you can hold out?'

To this Klopper replied:

'Situation not in hand. Counter-attack with Inf. Batt. tonight. All my tanks gone. Do you think it advisable I battle through? If you can counter-attack let me know.'

Klopper's next instructions were:

'Come out tomorrow night preferably if not tonight. Centre Line Madauuer-Kntghtsbridge-Maddalena. I will keep open gap Hamel-El Adem. Inform me time selected and route. Tomorrow night preferred. Destruction petrol vital.'

Back in the concrete dug-out Klopper showed this signal to the officers present. Brigadier Hayton, commanding the 4th Brigade, looked at it and announced that his men could walk out on 'their flat feet', and his battalion commanders agreed.

But even at so crucial a moment Klopper's subordinates could find time to argue. Some proposed making a stand. Others suggested issuing an order to break out forthwith. One, on the verge of tears, called for an immediate surrender.

'Only by surrendering can you preserve the cream of the manhood of South Africa!' he sobbed.

Hayton proposed forming a western box. His troops and the 6th Brigade had seen little fighting. They were game. All the remaining ammunition, guns, rifles, and men should be gathered into the box, there to fight to the death.

One man had nothing to say. Anderson. He just sat there with his Staff Officer and waited for a definite decision to be taken so that he could get back to his Camerons and act upon it. And when Klopper brought the argument to an end – for it could never have been called a conference – by telling them to go and fight on the lines proposed by Hayton, Anderson was one of the first to leave the dug-out.

But the plan, like everything else in Tobruk, went up in smoke. The battalion commanders talked about 'useless slaughter', and many of them began making excuses about the impossibility of passing signals when the 'situation was in a state of flux'. Some, however, gave orders for the western box to be prepared, and set to work with picks and shovels.

But Tobruk was split in two. Half of it was in Rommel's hands. And from that half streamed the 'refugees'. Thousands of them. A seething herd, undisciplined and without arms. They gravitated towards Klopper's headquarters. Amongst them were hundreds of coloured and native transport drivers, dazed not only from the dive-bombing but with rum, and whisky, and gin.

A Staff Officer, watching these half-crazed natives, shuddered and went back into the dug-out.

Tobruk could so easily become a shambles.

Up at Navy House everything was calm and orderly. Captain Smith had sent for Harris and told him in his quiet voice to organize his men to meet the enemy. This meant that every man was to be armed with a rifle, ammunition, and hand grenades.

For the evacuation of the port – if it should become necessary – Smith gave his First Lieutenant the position of the various ships in the harbour and the approximate number of men to be put aboard each of them.

Harris paraded his men in the compound behind Navy House. The sailors fell in, in two ranks, with the chief petty-officers and petty-officers on the right.

'Number!'

The order is half-drowned by the crash of a shell exploding on the shattered roof of the building.

'Number!'

One sailor winces and is silent as another shell wrecks the wall on the far side of the compound.

'Number!'

This time the order is completed, and Harris separates the ratings into parties, each in charge of a petty-officer.

> 'The drill for the evacuation was very thorough,' Harris wrote, 'every man being questioned as to what ship he was to go to and where she was lying. There was one twin-screwed minesweeper, HMS *Abedaire*, four TLCs, two Harbour Defence Motor Launches, and four or five MTBs. For these last no passengers were detailed as they were to remain until the very end to pick up demolition parties, the NOIC, SNOIS, and their staffs.'

His duty for the moment done, Harris returned to his favourite pastime of watching the scene through the telescope. Through it he saw a number of German tanks coming down the escarpment, and hastened to report this to Captain Smith. The latter gave orders for a stand to be made.

'My lads took up their positions in the slit trenches and waited for the Hun to make his appearance,' Harris wrote. 'I was in one with a Lewis gun, a rifle, some sticky bombs, and a few grenades. We waited a few minutes, which seemed like hours, when a runner came to me from Captain Smith. I dashed to him and was given orders to evacuate the town and port. No orders were more joyfully carried out...'

When asked by the sailors whether they might risk the short run back to their quarters, I refused emphatically.

They naturally looked gloomy at the prospect of abandoning their possessions. So I felt obliged to implement my refusal with the statement that I would personally drop any man who disobeyed me. As I had organized and shot in a number of competitions they respected my shooting well enough, so no one tried it.

The lads rushed off, some by truck, but mostly on foot.

One lad, Steward Pope, went off on a motorbike, conjured from goodness knows where. And in about twenty seconds Navy House was cleared of nearly 300 men. All had gone except NOICs immediate staff of some three signalmen, a couple of wireless ratings, and a telephone operator. The job of these men was to send the last signals and start the fuses for the demolition of the exchange and WT cabins. I have since heard that their destruction was complete.'

Harris's job was to leave Navy House by the front entrance and walk along the bay to the ammunition caves to see that the fuses were started. He had then to proceed to the main petrol and oil tanks and attend to them. As Smith watched him leave he told his First Lieutenant not to rush the job.

'There's no hurry,' he said, 'the MTBs are waiting for us.'

But as Harris left he saw with apprehension the first of these craft streaking out of the harbour followed by the others. One of them had laid a smoke-screen which made it difficult for the other craft to see the entrance.

By then the German tanks were all round the harbour and were pouring their shells into the little fleet of departing ships.

Two 'A' lighters got clear. Another, having been hit, was burning furiously, and her passengers and crew were jumping overboard. Yet another was steaming erratically, with her rudder damaged, but replying vigorously to the enemy's fire with her pom-poms.

Harris watched the South African minesweepers with particular interest. Shells were falling all round them, and there was no telling how many times they were hit. There were men swimming everywhere. All he could do was pray for them as he hurried on his way.

> 'I found the ammunition caves,' Harris wrote, 'and broke the time-delay pencils which were set to cause explosion in one and a half hours. The caves each contained a vast quantity of Naval ammunition, 6-in. and 4-in. shells, in addition to small arms stuff, usually issued to destroyers and other Naval craft. I had put depth-charges amongst all this stuff, so it couldn't have been much use after the bang!
> On the way there I bust up three trucks with hand grenades.'

Then he went on to the main petrol tank at Tobruk – Rommel's most coveted possession. Harris describes it as 'a great affair sunk into a brick-lined coffer dam, with only the top or lid sticking up above the ground, and somewhat devated upon a rise above the bay.'

> 'I walked gaily up this rise,' he writes, 'and slap into a German tank, with the Jerry commander standing in the hatch of the turret. He waved his right hand in salutation, so I did the same. Then I turned round and with a curious feeling in the small of my back walked away down the hill.
>
> I had got right to the bottom before I realized that I hadn't seen to the fuses. So I had to go all the way back again. The last bit I did on my hands and knees. But I managed to get up to the demolitions, saw that the pencils were broken, and then returned to NOIC and SNOIS to report that all possible Naval demolition bad been carried out.'

No MTB had waited for the party. It was decided to risk escape in a 'Z' lighter. There was no other choice. She was the only remaining vessel afloat in Tobruk harbour.

CHAPTER THIRTY-SIX

THE DEATH

Before dawn on June 21st, Hayton informed the Fortress HQ that the Umvoti Mounted Rifles near Ras El Meduuar had seen a very large concentration of German tanks in the neighbourhood of the famous Hill 209. There were about 150 of them and, according to report, an attack was expected at first light.

This was the gravest news, and Klopper realized that it could only mean that the western box would be caught between the devil and the deep. From west and east German armour would pour a decimating fire into the box on to the 'cream of the manhood of South Africa'.

But, like so much of the news circulating through the fortress, this story was not true, and it was shortly denied.

Over and over again in Tobruk there appeared strange will-o'-the-wisps in the fog of chaos and confusion. Sudden telephone messages out of the blue to announce; 'We are pulling out!' or ordering all guns to be spiked. Reports such as this from Meduuar, giving facts and figures, and sounding so feasible. Yet without substance. Where did they come from? Who made them? A Fifth Column? German Intelligence? Or the cowardly few, who, having seen the red light, wished to save their own skins, but not Tobruk?

It is unlikely the answers will ever be known. It is certain, however, that these mysterious happenings played an insidious part in the final débâcle. Particularly that last report about the tanks massing for a dawn attack near Hill 209 because, unaccountably, Klopper was never informed that it was not true.

When he spoke to Ritchie for the last time over the wireless, and talked of 'the situation being a shambles' and of 'terrible casualties' resulting from attempting a last-ditch stand, Klopper had that report in mind.

The last time he saw Anderson, who had come to HQ to confirm the surrender order, which he had heard but refused to believe, Klopper spoke of those 150 tanks. Because of them, he said, no breakout at dawn was possible. The situation was hopeless, and to save useless bloodshed he had decided to surrender. He had given orders that all units were to destroy their equipment. Any wishing to escape were at liberty to try. Trucks could be kept for that end.

Typically, even that final, irrevocable order from the Fortress HQ led to utter confusion.

Some never received it.

On Pilastrino Ridge, where Major Sainthill had gathered the remnants of his battalion, the Guards knew nothing about it.

The only rumour that had reached them was that a relief column was on its way. That very morning, exhausted though they were, the Guards had driven off a German tank attack.

From their position on the high ground, the Coldstreams could see in the half-light the fires spreading in the town and round the harbour. They could hear the roar of the petrol and ammunition dumps going up, and the smoke from them veiled the sunrise.

Then, as the day grew lighter, the Coldstreams were startled by a shattering explosion close at hand, and decided that the guns of a nearby South African field battery had opened up. But the guns were not firing at the enemy. They were being destroyed.

The Coldstreams would not believe it. Sainthill made further hurried inquiries. It was true. All guns and, vehicles were to be destroyed and all troops were ordered to stand fast pending the arrival of the enemy.

'None of us could believe such a thing possible,' Sainthill said afterwards, 'and from everyone I sensed a silent yet unanimous refusal to accept surrender.'

Looking at the drawn faces of his officers and men, he made up his mind. The 3rd Coldstrcam would not surrender. They would escape and join up with the 8th Army.

Some received the signal and were gripped with fear.

Private X and his mobile force were somewhere on the southern perimeter when the news reached his company.

> 'The runner from Company HQ,' he writes, 'said that there was room for one more man from each section on the last vehicles which was making an escape dash from HQ in five minutes' time. We immediately played 'matches' to see who would be the winner, and the lot fell to my friend, Bill. Corporal R, the only Jew in our section, immediately pleaded with Bill to give him a chance. He said the Germans would torture him to death if he were taken to Germany. For one moment I thought Bill was going to hit him. Then he turned away and just said: "Go!"

Some received the signal but refused to believe it.

The South Africans in the western sector of the perimeter had seen little fighting since the fortress was surrounded. But, a few hours before that last signal reached them, they had been told that Klopper's orders were that they were to fight to the last man. They had steeled themselves for this purpose, knowing full well what it meant. They had spent the whole night digging and strengthening their positions. Now all that had been wasted time. Now, there was no chance even to escape, for they had destroyed their trucks in preparation for that last stand.

A sergeant went up to one youngster who was digging furiously and said: 'You can stop that, son. We've surrendered.'

'Surrendered?' the youth asked incredulously. 'We can't have done! We haven't started fighting yet!'

Some received the signal and disobeyed it.

Lt Colonel Colin Duncan heard the order from the South Africans on his right and viewed it with grave suspicion. When some Italian tanks approached, from behind his positions, Duncan told his men to hold their fire until the tanks were right on top of them. All the tanks were knocked out and their crews killed. More tanks came rolling up to the Highlanders' positions, and each in turn was destroyed. In all, the Camerons accounted for seven tanks. When a German truck filled with infantry appeared it was received with a hail of machine-gun fire, and went up in flames. When the *Stukas* screamed down to bomb the slit-trenches the Scots shot down one of them. That night the Camerons were still fighting.

Some died before they received the signal.

Captain Smith and Captain Walter, together with Harris, went aboard the 'Z' lighter lying alongside the Jetty. She was a thoroughly unseaworthy contraption, 150-feet long, with low sides and a great flat deck. Someone had discovered her in Alexandria dockyard and, realizing her value as a lighter for unloading, had despatched her to Tobruk. How she had ever survived the voyage no one could imagine. She was powered by two petrol engines and could make about eight knots in fine – very fine – weather. Now she was manned by soldiers from the Docks Group.

'We set off into the middle of the harbour,' Harris writes, 'and everyone knew we were going to catch it. Smith and Walter were on the little bridge with an Army officer and the helmsman. It wasn't long before the first shell hit us. After that, it just rained tank shells, anti-tank and machine-gun bullets. One went right through the engine-room and set the petrol alight. But for some reason the fire only burnt for a few seconds, though the engine-room party came out terribly burnt and were a most pitiful sight.

We then drifted helplessly with both engines knocked out. The Huns plastered us, and practically everyone on board was wounded. An 88-mm kept firing from the top end of the bay, using high explosive, but his shooting was bad and his shells kept exploding just astern all the time.

The suspense was awful as one felt that the next time he simply had to hit us.

Finally he put one right into the bridge, wounding both, Captains Smith and Walter. The former came down with his left arm practically severed. We helped him down the ladder, and while two men applied first aid, I went to see how Captain Walter was. I found him walking about with his left arm held up. I asked him if he was wounded, and he told me that he was. I made him sit down while I found a shell dressing. It was then dark, so the Hun stopped shelling and left us to drift about.

I saw no sign of either the Army officer or the soldier, so I don't know what became of them.'

Later that night Captain Smith died of his wounds on the deck of the drifting lighter.

He never heard that Tobruk had surrendered. He was spared that. The news would have broken his heart.

In the early hours of June 21st, Klopper gave his compass and his car to seven young South Africans of the 6th Brigade who were determined to escape. He wished them luck and said with a wry smile: 'I wish I was coming with you!' Then he turned and went back to his dug-out to make the final arrangements for the surrender.

From the 6th Brigade's HQ a little party of officers went off in a truck, above which fluttered a white flag, to parley with the enemy. Soon after their return another and much larger white flag was hoisted above Klopper's Headquarters. This tragic ceremony was performed by South African native drivers.

The huge flag fluttered feebly in the still air, starkly white against the black pall of smoke that shrouded the burning fortress, clearly visible for all to see. All that is, who could bear to look at it.

CHAPTER THIRTY-SEVEN

Post Mortem

The tumult and the fighting died slowly. In the town and the harbour area thousands of troops milled about without purpose; British, South Africans, Poles, Indians, Czechs, Palestinians, Maltese, and Cypriots.

Private X, on his way to the prisoner-of-war cage, noted that hundreds of them were South African natives, most of whom were 'jibbering with fright, or else so stupidly drunk that they did not know what they were doing. And many were shot by the Germans for refusing to march to the cage. These natives, when they heard the news of Tobruk's surrender the previous evening, had breached the stores of Army-issue brandy at Divisional HQ and proceeded to get paralytic drunk.'

Many were past caring about what happened. Others cursed Klopper for not giving them the chance to escape and for ordering them to destroy their transport. Private X was amongst those who were filled with a sense of deep resentment.

'No matter how small the chance was to escape,' he wrote to me from his home in South Africa, 'we should have been given that chance instead of being ordered to burn our transport and destroy our weapons. They should have been used to fight our way out. No doubt we would have suffered very heavy casualties, but we were all in good heart, and prepared and willing to take a chance. Had we received the order to break out at any time between midnight on June 20th and an hour before dawn on June 21st, many thousands of the garrison could have been saved to fight another day. As it was the first news we received of the surrender was at dawn on June 21st. Then, there was no hope of escape, and no wonder we felt we had been betrayed.'

That a breakout was possible was proved by Major Sainthill and his Coldstream Guards. In broad daylight, he led seventeen officers and 185 guardsmen, together with six 6-pounder guns, in a convoy of trucks and armoured cars right through the Axis lines back to the frontier. On their way his column was joined by units of the Worcesters, the Sherwoods, and a number of South Africans. The convoy started more than sixty strong, but soon after it passed through the wire in the neighbourhood of Meduuar it was heavily shelled. Even so, although there were some casualties, the cloud of dust thrown up by the shells and the vehicles acted like a smoke-screen under cover of which the convoy escaped.

Scores of others attempted to break out after the surrender order had been given. But, by then, it was too late, and only a few got away. Some suffered fearful hardships and were in the desert for days without food or water before they reached the frontier wire at Beira.

Incredibly, the Cameron Highlanders and some of the Indians continued fighting on the south-eastern perimeter, until late in the evening of June 21st, hours after Klopper himself had surrendered. Indeed, the Germans tried to make the Fortress Commander issue an order to the Camerons to surrender. This he refused to do and late that evening a German officer accompanied by a South African came to warn Colin Duncan that, unless his men laid down their arms, they would be blasted out of this world by the concentrated fire of the whole Axis artillery force on the perimeter. Only then did Duncan give his parole.

The next morning a gunner officer, looking through the barbed-wire of the prisoner-of-war cage, watched the arrival of the battalion in Tobruk.

'We heard, although we could scarcely believe it, the skirl of pipes. There, in the brilliant sunshine, marching down the centre of the road from the escarpment, came a long column of men. The Jerry traffic was brought to a standstill or forced on to the verges. A strange awed murmur went up from the cage; 'The Camerons!'

'In columns of threes they marched with a swing to the tune of their pipers – 'The March of the Cameron Men' – each company led by its company commander, just as though they were on parade. It was a supremely moving sight, although some of us could only see it hazily through our tears.

'Even the Jerry sentries sprang to attention as the battalion neared the gates. There, the Camerons halted. Their Colonel reported to the Brigadier, saluted, and dismissed his men, who had held out for twenty-four hours after the surrender order had been issued.'

To the very end Tobruk was rife with wild rumours. Private X, for example, was told that when Klopper and his entire Staff surrendered personally to Rommel, at the 6th South African Divisional HQ, they were 'all blind drunk'. This story, of course, was without substance.

Private X claims that he actually saw Klopper driving with Rommel and four other German officers through the town. 'Rommel,' he said, 'was shouting and appeared to be in a towering rage.'

Even this statement is questionable. For although Rommel actually entered Tobruk at five o'clock on the morning of June 21st, according to report, he did not meet the Fortress Commander until nine-forty that morning, some six kilometres outside Tobruk. Curiously enough, it is true that when they met Rommel was in a towering rage because the vast supplies of petrol he had hoped to capture had been destroyed. For a moment he had lost all dignity and self-control, and, cursing the English, shouted: 'For this you shall walk – walk – all the way to Tripoli.'

It is likely, however, such stories will persist. For the surrender of Tobruk with its garrison of 30,000 after twenty-four hours' fighting will probably remain obscured in secrecy. if not for ever, at least until all those concerned with it are dead. A Court of Enquiry was convened in Cairo by Auchinleck in August. 1942, to investigate certain operations in the Middle East between May 27th and July 1st.

In order to dispel the cloud of conflicting evidence that has hung over the surrender of the fortress for the past sixty-two years, I sought permission to read the report of the proceedings of the Court and to publish such parts as were relevant to this story. This request met with a courteous refusal. I was told, however, by an authority that: 'The Court sat in Cairo, but no member had any knowledge of the operations under discussion, and so no one knew what questions to put to the witnesses called. No records were available for consultation, and in consequence some rather wild statements were made. At least two vital witnesses were still engaged in the fighting and so were unable to attend. In the end the whole thing rather petered out with no findings recorded.'

While that may be a just evaluation of the proceedings, it is not entirely accurate. For, according to the Royal Air Force Official History of the operations in the Middle East at the time, the final findings of the Court were recorded as follows:

'The fact that Tobruk fell must undoubtedly be attributed to the eleventh hour reversal of policy leading to the decision to hold the fortress, regardless of the fact that the Eighth Army was then in full retreat in the face of an enemy which had been uniformly successful, and whose morale must in consequence have been high. It was impossible in the time available to make adequate preparations for the completely new role imposed upon the garrison, which up to then had only been concerned with the prevention of raids by air, land, and sea.'

Obviously, the surrender of such a huge garrison, many of whom were never given the opportunity to resist, cannot be thus summarily dismissed.

In *Crisis in the Desert*, prepared by the Union War Histories Section of the Office of the Prime Minister of the Union of South Africa, the authors were given access to Smuts' personal copy of the findings of this Court of Enquiry. This book, written by South Africans about, South Africans for South Africans, lays the onus of what happened at Tobruk upon Ritchie and Gott, and so, indirectly, upon Auchinleck. At the same time, somewhat curiously, it makes only a passing reference to the Enquiry.

It strikes me, therefore, as more important than ever that the findings of the latter should be made public in fairness to those who, like Gott, are no longer alive to defend themselves.

To this day opinions differ as to the number of prisoners and the quantity of stores which fell into Rommel's hands at Tobruk. Churchill gives the figures as 30,000 men and 10,000 cubic metres of petrol, quoting as his authority General Westphal, 'Rommel's Chief-of-Staff'. In fact, Westphal did not hold that appointment until October 20th, 1942, and far from being at Tobruk when it surrendered, he was in hospital in Germany.

The number of prisoners taken was nearer 35,000. As for the petrol, it is clear from the evidence of Brigadier Thompson, Captain Walter, RN, and Lt Commander Harris. SAN, that the bulk of it was destroyed. The truth was that the Germans found not huge supplies of petrol in the fortress, as they had expected, but captured important dumps in the environs of Bel Hamed and Capuzzo.

Apart from that disappointment, Rommel's triumph was complete, and on June 22nd he signalled to the High Command in Berlin: 'The first objective of the Panzer Army in Africa, that of defeating the enemy in the field and capturing Tobruk, has been achieved... and so opened the way into the interior of Egypt.'

He therefore requested that Mussolini be prevailed upon to remove the restriction on the movements of his troops and that he might be allowed to continue his offensive.

As the direct result of this Hitler took the vital decision to continue the campaign in North Africa and gave Rommel a free hand, and at the same time postponed the invasion of Malta until the beginning of September.

Thus, contrary to what Churchill and his Chiefs-of-Staff had argued with such force, it was the final collapse of the garrison in Tobruk and not its resistance that saved Malta. Carried away by the ride of his own success. Rommel swept on towards Egypt, the Nile, and Suez. But, at El Alamein, Auchinleck's 8th Army stood firm, and against its resistance the Axis forces spent their strength. Contrary to what has been written since, the 8th Army was never defeated. For four months it continued to attack and withstand attack, until such time as an overwhelming superiority in weapons and men enabled it to drive the Axis Army out of North Africa and into the sea.

BIBLIOGRAPHY

Bayonets Abroad. A History of the 2/13th Battalion AIF in the Second World War. Edited by Lieutenant G H Fearnside. Waite & Bull, Sydney.

To Benghazi. By Gavin Long. Canberra Australian War Memorial.

A Year in Battle. By Alan Moorehead. Hamish Hamilton.

Eastern Epic, Vol. I. By Compton Mackenzie. Chatto & Windus.

Crisis in the Desert. By J A I Agar-Hamilton and L C F Turner. Oxford University Press.

Ciano's Diary. William Heinemann.

A Sailer's Odyssey. By Admiral of the Fleet Viscount Cunningham of Hyndhope. Hutchinson & Co.

Tobruk. By Chester Wilmot. Angus & Robertson, Sydney.

Rommel By Desmond Young, Collins.

The Second World War. By Sir Winston Churchill Cassell.

History of the Coldsream Guards, By Michael Howard and John Sparrow. Oxford University Press.

The Mediterranean and Middle East, *Vol. II*. By Major-General L S O Playfair. H M Stationery Office.

Down Ramps! By Lambton Burn. Carroll & Nicholson.

Operation Victory. By Major-General Sir Frands de Guingand. Hodder & Stoughton.

Despatch. By Field-Marshal Sir Claude Auchinleck. H M Stationery Office.